LAW & MENTAL HEALTH PROFESSIONALS

TEXAS

LAW & MENTAL HEALTH PROFESSIONALS SERIES

Bruce D. Sales and Michael O. Miller, Series Editors

Miller and Sales: *ARIZONA*
Shuman: *TEXAS*

LAW & MENTAL HEALTH PROFESSIONALS

TEXAS

Daniel W. Shuman
Professor of Law
School of Law
Southern Methodist University
Dallas, Texas

Library of Congress Cataloging-in-Publication Data

Shuman, Daniel W.
Law & mental health professionals. Texas/Daniel W. Shuman.
p. cm.
Kept up to date by supplements.
Includes bibliographical references.
ISBN 1-55798-072-1
1. Mental health personnel—Legal status, laws, etc.—Texas.
2. Forensic psychiatry—Texas. 3. Psychology, Forensic.
I. Title. II. Title: Law and mental health professionals. Texas.
[DNLM: 1. Criminal Psychology—Texas—legislation. 2. Forensic Psychiatry—Texas—legislation. 3. Psychiatry—Texas—legislation. 4. Psychology—Texas—legislation. WM 33 AT4 S5L]
KFT1526.5.P73S58 1989
344.73'044—dc20
[347.30444]
DNLM/DLC
for Library of Congress 89-1807
CIP

Copies may be ordered from:
Order Department, P.O. Box 2710
Hyattsville, MD 20784

Published by the American Psychological Association, Inc.
1200 Seventeenth Street, N.W., Washington, DC 20036.

Text and cover design by Rubin Krassner, Silver Spring, Maryland
Composition by Tapsco, Inc., Akron, Pennsylvania
Printing by The Semline Book Group, St. Charles, Illinois

Printed in the United States of America

Contents

Acknowledgments

The completion of this work would not have been possible without the unflagging effort and good humor of my research assistant, Cheryl Coon. A special note of thanks is due for her contribution. Numerous individuals gave of their time and expertise to review drafts of the manuscript: Kevin Karlson, Joseph McKnight, Cynthia Morris, Joseph Norton, Valli Rowley, Ellen Solender, Katherine Stayman, and Walter Steele. Their efforts are sincerely appreciated.

Editors' Preface

The Need to Know the Law

For years, providers of mental health services (hereinafter mental health professionals or MHPs) have been directly affected by the law. At one end of the continuum, their practice has been controlled by laws covering such matters as licensure and certification, third-party reimbursement, and professional incorporation. At the other end, they have been courted by the legal system to aid in its administration, providing such services as evaluating the mental status of litigants, providing expert testimony in court, and engaging in therapy with court-referred juveniles and adults. Even when not directly affected, MHPs find themselves indirectly affected by the law since their clients sometimes become involved in legal entanglements that involve mental status issues (e.g., divorce proceedings or termination of parental rights hearings).

Despite this pervasive influence, most professionals do not know about, much less understand, most of the laws that affect their practice, the services they render, and the clients they serve. This state of affairs is particularly troubling for several reasons. First, not knowing about the laws that affect one's practice typically results in the MHP's not gaining the benefits that the law may provide. Consider the law relating to the incorporation of professionals. It confers significant benefit, but only if it is known about and applied. The fact that it has been enacted by the state legislature does not help the MHP, any more than an MHP will be of help to a distressed person who refuses to contact the MHP.

Second, not knowing about the laws that affect the services they render can result in incompetent performance of, and liability for, the MHP either through the civil law (e.g., malpractice law) or through criminal sanctions. A brief example may help underscore this point. When an MHP is asked to evaluate a party to a lawsuit and testify in court, the court (the law's term for the judge) is asking the professional to assess and testify about whether that litigant meets some legal standard. The court is often not concerned with the defendant's mental health per se, although this may be relevant to the MHP's evaluation of the person. Rather, the court wants to know if the person meets the legal standard as it is set down by the law. Not knowing the legal standard means that the MHP is most likely evaluating the person for the wrong goal and providing the court with irrelevant information, at least from the court's point of view. Regretfully, we personally know of too many cases in which this has occurred.

Third, not knowing the law that affects the clients that MHPs serve may significantly diminish their capability for handling their clients' distress. For example, a client who is undergoing a divorce and child custody dispute may have distorted beliefs about what may happen during the legal proceedings. A basic understanding of the controlling law in this area will allow the therapist to be more sensitive in rendering therapy.

The Problem in Accessing Legal Information

Given the need for this information, why have MHPs not systematically sought it out? Part of the reason lies in the concern over their ability to understand legal doctrines. Indeed, this is a legitimate worry, especially if they had to read original legal materials that were not collected, organized, and described with an MHP audience in mind. This is of particular concern since laws are written in terms and phrases of "art" that do not always share the common lay definition or usage, while some terms and phrases are left ambiguous and undefined or are used differently for different legal topics. Another part of the reason is that the law affecting MHPs and their clients is not readily available—even to lawyers. There are no compendiums that identify the topics that these laws cover or present an analysis of each topic for easy reference.

To compound the difficulty, the law does not treat the different mental health professional disciplines uniformly or always specify the particular disciplines as being covered by it. Nor does the law emanate from a single legal forum. Each state enacts its own rules and regulations, often resulting in wide variations in the way a topic is handled across the United States. Multiply this confusion by the one hundred or so topics that relate to mental health practice. In addition, the law within a state does not come from one legal source. Rather, there are five primary ones: the state constitution; state legislative enactments (statutes); state agency administrative rules and regulations; rules of court promulgated by the state supreme court; and state and federal court cases that apply, interpret, and construe this existing state law. To know about one of these sources without knowing how its pronouncements on a given topic have been modified by these other sources can result in one's making erroneous conclusions about the operation of the law. Finally, mental health practice also comes under the purview of federal law (constitutional and statutory law, administrative rules and regulations, and case law). Federal law authorizes direct payments to MHPs for their services to some clients, sets standards for delivery of services in federal facilities (e.g., Veterans Administration Hospitals), and articulates the law that guides cases that are tried in federal courts under federal law.

Purposes of This Series

What is needed, therefore, is a book for each state, the District of Columbia, and the federal jurisdictions that comprehensively and accurately reviews and integrates all of the laws that affect MHPs in that jurisdiction (hereinafter state). To ensure currency, regular supplements to these books will be drafted. These materials will be written so that they are completely understandable to MHPs, as well as to lawyers. In order to accomplish these goals, we have tried to identify every legal topic which affects mental health practice, making each one the subject of a chapter. Each chapter, in turn, will describe the legal standards that the MHP will be operating under and the relevant legal process that the MHP will be operating within. If a state does not have relevant law on this issue, then a brief explanation of how this law works in other states will be presented while noting the lack of regulation in this area within the state under consideration.

This type of coverage facilitates other purposes of the series. Although each chapter will be written in order to state exactly what is the present state of the law and not argue for or against any particular approach, we hope that the comprehensiveness of the coverage will encourage MHPs to question the desirability of their states' approach to each topic. Such information and concern should provide the impetus for initiating legislation and litigation on the part of state mental health associations to ensure that the law reflects the scientific knowledge and professional values to the extent possible.

In some measure, states will initially be hampered in this proactivity since they will not know what legal alternatives are available and how desirable each alternative actually is. When a significant number of books in this series is available, however, it will allow for nationally oriented policy studies to identify the variety of legal approaches that are currently in use and to assess the validity of the behavioral assumptions underlying each variant, and ultimately lead to a conclusion as to the relative desirability of alternate approaches.[1] Thus, two other purposes of this book are to foster comprehensive analyses of the laws affecting MHPs across all states and the validity of the behavioral assumptions underlying these laws, and to promote political, legislative, and

---

1. Sales, B. D. (1983). The legal regulation of psychology: Professional and scientific interactions. In C. J. Scheirer & B. L. Hammonds (Eds.), *The master lecture series: Vol. 2: Psychology and law* (pp. 5–36). Washington, DC: American Psychological Association.

legal action to change laws which are inappropriate and impede the effective delivery of services. Legal change may be required because of gaps in legal regulation, overregulation, and regulation based on invalid behavioral and social assumptions. We hope this process will increase the rationality of future laws in this area and improve the effectiveness and quality of mental health service delivery nationally.

There are three remaining purposes for this series. First, although it will *not* replace the need for legal counsel, this series will make the MHP an intelligent consumer of legal services. This ability is gaining importance in an era of increasing professionalization and litigiousness. Second, it will ensure that MHPs are aware of the law's mandates when providing expert services (e.g., evaluation and testimony) within the legal system. Although chapters will not address how to clinically assess for the legal standard, provider competency will increase since providers now will be sure of the goals of their service (e.g., the legal standard that they are to assess for) as well as their roles and responsibilities within the legal system as to the particular topic at issue. Third and finally, each book will make clear that the legal standards that MHPs are asked to assess for by the law have typically not been translated into behavioral correlates. Nor are there discussions of tests, scales, and procedures for MHPs to use in assessing for the behavioral correlates of the legal standards in most cases. This series will provide the impetus for such research and writing.

Content and Organization of Volumes

Each book in this series is organized into six sections. Section 1 addresses the legal credentialing of MHPs. Section 2 deals with the different business forms for conducting one's practice. Section 3 addresses insurance reimbursement and tax deductions that clients can receive for utilizing mental health services. With the business matters covered, the book then turns to the law directly affecting service delivery. Section 4 starts by covering the law that affects the maintenance and privacy of professional information. Section 5 considers each area of law which may require the services of MHPs. It is subdivided into five parts: families and juveniles, other civil matters, topics that apply similarly in both civil and criminal cases, criminal matters, and voluntary and involuntary receipt of state services by the clients of mental health services. The last section of the book, Section 6, discusses the law that limits service delivery and sets liability for unethical and illegal behavior as a service provider.

Collectively, the chapters in these sections represent all topics pertaining to the law as it affects MHPs in their practices. Two caveats are in order, however. First, the law changes slowly over time. Thus, a supplement service will update all chapters on a regular basis. Second, as MHPs become more involved in the legal system, new opportunities for involvement are likely to arise. To be responsive to these developments, the supplements also will contain additional chapters reflecting these new roles and responsibilities.

Some final points about the content of the books are in order. The exact terms that the law chooses are used even if they are a poor choice from an MHP's point of view. And where terms are defined by the law, that information is presented. The reader may be frustrated, however, because as has already been noted, the law does not always define terms or provide detailed guidance. This does not mean that legal words and phrases can be taken lightly. The law sets the rules that MHPs and their clients must operate by; thus, chapters must be read carefully. This should not be too arduous a task since most chapters are relatively short. On the other hand, such brevity will leave some readers frustrated because chapters appear not to go far enough in answering their questions. Note that all the law in a state is covered in the relevant volume. If there is no law, however, there is no coverage. If a question is not answered in the text, it is because law in that state has not addressed the issue. Relatedly, if an obligation or benefit is created by a professional regulation (i.e., a rule of a professional organization) but is not directly recognized by the law, it is not covered. Thus, for example, professional credentials are not addressed in these volumes.

Finally, we want to point out that in some instances, the pronoun "he" is used generically to refer to both sexes. Most notably, the pronoun is used when quoting directly from the law. Legal language is generally consistent in its preference for using the masculine form of the pronoun; it is not always feasible to attempt a rewording.

Bruce D. Sales
Michael O. Miller
Series Editors

Author's Preface

This book is principally a treatment of state law applicable to MHPs. A comprehensive treatment of federal law, which is also relevant to the actions of MHPs, is beyond the scope of this work as it would expand it by volumes or require a more limited treatment of each subject. The sources of state law treated in this work include the state constitution, state statutes, state administrative rules, state judicial decisions, and state judicial rules.

The Texas Constitution establishes the framework for state government and describes various individual rights that occupy a high degree of importance in Texas. Citations to the Texas Constitution appear in the following form: Tex. Const. art. I, 11 (Vernon 1984). This reference indicates that this citation is to a section of the Texas Constitution that can be found in the black bound volumes of Texas statutes and constitutional provisions published by Vernon in 1984, in the volume marked *Constitution* containing section 11 of article I.

Citations to state statutes, which result from legislation passed by the Texas House of Representatives and Senate and signed into law by the Governor, appear in the following form: Tex. Rev. Civ. Stat. Ann. art. 5547-300 § 3 (Vernon Supp. 1988). This particular citation is a reference to the black bound volumes of statutes published by Vernon labeled *Texas Revised Civil Statutes Annotated.* "Supp. 1988" indicates that this statute is not contained in the main bound volume, but rather in the pocket supplement published in 1988 compiling the legislative activity since the publication of the bound volume. The specific number refers to section 3 of article 5547-300 in those volumes. The state statutes are organized into different codes and acts, depending upon the subject of the legislation. Thus, for example, some of the references will be to the penal code addressing the criminal law [Tex. Penal Code Ann. § 8.04 (Vernon 1974)], the family code addressing family law [Tex. Fam. Code Ann. § 35.02 (Vernon 1986)], or the insurance code addressing insurance law [Tex. Ins. Code Ann. § 3.72 (Vernon Supp. 1987)].

These compilations of statutes contain additional useful material. The compilers attempt to include a citation and a one-sentence summary of any reported cases that have discussed the statute or constitutional provision in question. Thus a researcher may use these case references, called "annotations," to begin research on how the statute or constitutional provision has been interpreted by the courts. The compilations also contain references to prior statutes that have been repealed. A review of these repealed statutes may be necessary to understand an earlier judicial opinion interpreting them or to resolve an ambiguity in the intent of the legislature in changing the statute.

State administrative rules are created by state agencies operating under the authority delegated to them by the legislature to carry out specific agency functions. For example, the legislation creating the Texas Board of Examiners of Psychologists does not create a code of ethics for psychologists, but rather gives the board the authority to make administrative rules creating a code of ethics for psychologists. These rules do not appear in the black volumes of statutes but instead are kept in a three-ring-notebook series entitled *Texas Administrative Code*. References to the administrative code appear in the following form: Tex. Admin. Code tit. 28, § 3.3006 (1987). The administrative rule referred to by this citation can be found in the volume of the three-ring series containing section 3.3006 of title 28. It is contained in the 1987 update of the code.

State judicial decisions are the product of judge-made law. Reported decisions typically are those of appellate courts. They consist of decisions of the Texas Courts of Appeal, the Texas Court of Criminal Appeals, and the Texas Supreme Court. Citations to these decisions appear in the following form: Romero v. State, 493 S.W.2d 206 (Tex. Crim. App. 1973). This particular citation refers to a 1973 decision of the Texas Court of Criminal Appeals. A reference to a Supreme Court decision would contain "Tex." and the date in the parenthetical. A reference to a Texas Court of Appeals decision would contain in the parenthetical "Tex. Civ. App." followed by the court's regional jurisdiction (i.e., Ft. Worth) and the date of the decision. This decision appears in a reporter of cases in this geographic region entitled *Southwestern Reporter*, in this case the second series of that compilation. The number 493 represents the volume in which this case appears, and 206 is the page of this volume upon which the report begins. The parties to the case are Romero and the State of Texas.

State judicial rules, as contrasted with judicial decisions, are the product of judges acting in a legislative rather than a judicial capacity. In this role judges make rules of general application in the courts, not in the context of deciding cases. The rules of evidence applicable in civil proceedings (Tex. R. Civ. Evid. 603), the rules of evidence applicable in criminal proceedings (Tex. R. Crim. Evid. 603), and the rules of procedure applicable in civil proceedings (Tex. R. Civ. Proc. 173) are judicially created rules noted in this book.

Although the focus of this work is on state rather than federal law applicable to MHPs in Texas, occasional reference is of necessity made to federal decisions interpreting or limiting state law. The citations to these decisions are from the United States District Court (F. Supp.), the United States Court of Appeals (F. or F.2d) and the United States Supreme Court (U.S., S. Ct., or L.Ed.). As is the case with the reports of state decisions, the number preceding the reporter is the volume number and the number following is the page. References to federal legislation appear in the form 26 U.S.C. § 213(a) (1987). This particular citation to the United States Code, the repository of federal legislation, is from title 26, section 213(a) thereof, current as of 1987. In addition, there are citations to treatises and law review articles. These references may provide a fuller background of an issue of interest to MHPs.

Finally, although some chapters were updated until the manuscript went to press, the reader should consider the entire volume current as of December 1988.

Daniel W. Shuman

Section 1

Legal Credentialing

1.1

Licensure and Regulation of Psychiatrists

The Texas State Board of Medical Examiners regulates the licensure and practice of physicians in Texas.[1] Psychiatrists are regulated by the Board only as physicians; medical specialties are not separately regulated by the Board. The Board establishes the qualifications and procedures for licensure, regulates the conduct of physicians, conducts investigations, and establishes the criteria and administers the examination for qualification for licensure. The Board also regulates the suspension, renewal, and cancellation of licenses.

Texas State Board of Medical Examiners

The Medical Practice Act[2] creates the Texas State Board of Medical Examiners (Board), an independent agency of the executive branch of Texas government.[3] The Board is composed of 15 members, serving for staggered terms of 6 years, who are appointed by the governor and approved by the Senate.[4] The 15 members consist of 9 licensed physicians with a doctor of medicine degree (M.D.) and 5 years' experience; 3 licensed physicians with a doctor of osteopathic medicine degree (D.O.) and 5 years' experience; and 3 members of the public who are not involved with the practice of medicine either financially or by employment.[5]

1. Tex. Rev. Civ. Stat. Ann. art. 4495b §§ 1.01-5.10 (Vernon Supp. 1987).
2. Tex. Rev. Civ. Stat. Ann. art. 4495b §§ 1.01-5.01 (Vernon Supp. 1987).
3. Tex. Rev. Civ. Stat. Ann. art. 4495b § 1.02(5) (Vernon Supp. 1987).
4. Tex. Rev. Civ. Stat. Ann. art. 4495b §§ 2.02-2.03 (Vernon Supp. 1987).
5. Tex. Rev. Civ. Stat. Ann. art. 4495b § 2.05 (Vernon Supp. 1987).

The Board has the following duties and powers:[6]

1. regulation of the practice of medicine and enforcement of the Medical Practice Act;
2. maintenance of records of its proceedings that are open to the public; records of each physician licensed by the Board, including the name, age, residence, time spent in medical study, and the year and school from which the physician graduated; and records showing whether a license application was denied or accepted;
3. receipt of criminal records and reports from law enforcement agencies, including the power to conduct fingerprint checks;[7]
4. conduction of investigations, including the power to (a) issue subpoenas to compel the attendance of witnesses and the production of records, (b) administer oaths, and (c) take testimony; and
5. establishment of rules concerning fees and qualifications for licensure examination, including the power to examine the academic and professional credentials of applicants.

The Board also has the power to approve of medical schools and medical training, both foreign and domestic, and to issue consumer information regarding the Board and its procedures.[8]

Licensure

The Board may license an applicant to practice medicine in Texas who:[9]

1. is at least 21 years of age,
2. is of good professional character,
3. has completed 60 college semester hours other than in medical school (the courses should be acceptable at the time of completion by the University of Texas as credit toward a bachelor of arts or science degree),
4. is a graduate of a Board-approved medical school,

6. Tex. Rev. Civ. Stat. Ann. art. 4495b § 2.09 (Vernon Supp. 1987).
7. Tex. Rev. Civ. Stat. Ann. art. 4495b § 2.09(h) (Vernon Supp. 1987). The criminal records and reports are privileged and thus not subject to public release without a court order.
8. Tex. Rev. Stat. Ann. art. 4495b § 2.09(q) (Vernon Supp. 1987).
9. Tex. Rev. Stat. Ann. art. 4495b § 3.04(a)-(b) (Vernon Supp. 1987). Special permits for visiting professors and distinguished professors are available, provided the psychiatrist notifies the Board and has a valid license. Tex. Admin. Code tit. 22, §§ 163.6, 171.4 (1987).

5. has successfully completed a 1-year program of graduate medical training approved by the Board, and
6. has successfully passed the medical examination.[10]

Special rules apply to foreign medical school graduates and applicants already licensed in another state or country. Foreign medical graduates may be required to complete additional graduate medical training in the United States.[11]

The Board may license physicians already licensed in other states or Canadian provinces if the state's or province's registration and licensure requirements are substantially similar to Texas' requirements or if the physician is qualified to practice under a commission in the United States uniformed services.[12] The Board may deny the applicant a license if the Board concludes that the applicant does not have the necessary qualifications to provide the standard of medical care normally provided by licensed physicians in Texas.[13]

Additionally, all applicants from other states, countries, or the uniformed services must pass the medical jurisprudence examination for Texas.[14]

Temporary License

The Board may issue a temporary license to an applicant who holds a valid license in another state or a Canadian province, passes the medical jurisprudence examination for Texas, completes an application for a permanent license, and meets all other requirements for licensure. A temporary license is nonrenewable.[15]

Registration

In addition to the licensure requirements, a physician who qualifies to practice medicine in Texas is required to register annually with the Board.[16] The physician is required to register on or before January 1 of each year and to pay the annual registration fee. Physicians who are not otherwise licensed but participate in graduate medical education training programs must obtain institu-

10. Tex. Rev. Civ. Stat. Ann. art. 4495b § 3.05(c) (Vernon Supp. 1987). This requirement pertains only to those who are not already licensed to practice medicine in any state.
11. Tex. Rev. Civ. Stat. Ann. art. 4495b § 3.04(a)(5) (Vernon Supp. 1987). The foreign medical graduate also must meet additional requirements, such as passing the Educational Council for Foreign Medical Graduates' examination.
12. Tex. Rev. Civ. Stat. Ann. art. 4495b § 3.03(a) (Vernon Supp. 1987).
13. Tex. Rev. Civ. Stat. Ann. art. 4495b § 3.03(f) (Vernon Supp. 1987).
14. Tex. Admin. Code tit. 22, § 163.3(b)(2),(3) (1986).
15. Tex. Admin. Code tit. 22, § 163.6(a) (1986).
16. Tex. Rev. Civ. Stat. Ann. art. 4495b § 3.01(a) (Vernon Supp. 1987).

tional permits. The permit does not authorize the practice of medicine except as performed as part of the graduate program and under the supervision of a licensed physician.[17]

Failure to pay the registration fee automatically results in cancellation of a license.[18] The physician may renew the license for up to 1 year after the failure to pay by paying the fee plus a penalty, and after 1 year by meeting additional requirements established by the Board.[19] The registration fee applies to all persons licensed by the Board, whether or not they are practicing within the borders of Texas, except retired physicians.[20] Moreover, a practicing physician who fails to pay the fee or to register annually with the Board is considered to be practicing without a license and is thus subject to criminal penalties.[21]

Examination

The Board is required to prepare and grade the licensure examination.[22] The examination covers the subjects normally taught by medical schools and is administered anonymously. The examination must also cover medical jurisprudence and must be written in English. After successful completion of the examination, the applicant is entitled to a license provided the applicant meets all other qualifications.[23] Applicants may take the examination again if they fail and may obtain a written analysis of their performance from the Board. Examination questions that may be used in the future, past examinations, and the deliberations and records relating to the professional character and fitness of applicants are not open to public inspection. Applicants may obtain their records, however, by written request to the Board.[24]

Exemptions

The licensure requirements do not apply to[25] dentists, optometrists, chiropractors, registered nurses and licensed vocational nurses, podiatrists, physical therapists, commissioned surgeons of the uniformed services not engaged in private practice, medical assistance given in an emergency or disaster if no charge is made for the aid, students in training at medical schools provided their

---

17. Tex. Rev. Civ. Stat. Ann. art. 4495b § 3.01(b) (Vernon Supp. 1987).
18. Tex. Rev. Civ. Stat. Ann. art. 4495b § 3.01(c) (Vernon Supp. 1987).
19. Tex. Rev. Civ. Stat. Ann. art. 4495b § 3.01(b) (Vernon Supp. 1987).
20. Tex. Rev. Civ. Stat. Ann. art. 4495b § 3.01(g) (Vernon Supp. 1987).
21. Tex. Rev. Civ. Stat. Ann. art. 4495b § 3.01(d) (Vernon Supp. 1987).
22. Tex. Rev. Civ. Stat. Ann. art. 4495b § 3.05(a)-(f) (Vernon Supp. 1987).
23. Tex. Rev. Civ. Stat. Ann. art. 4495b § 3.05(a) (Vernon Supp. 1987).
24. Tex. Rev. Civ. Stat. Ann. art. 4495b § 3.05(d) (Vernon Supp. 1987). Parties may not obtain the portions of their records that were submitted to the Board on a condition of confidentiality.
25. Tex. Rev. Civ. Stat. Ann. art. 4495b § 3.06(b)(1)-(12) (Vernon Supp. 1987).

duties are performed under the supervision of a licensed physician,[26] or physicians licensed outside of Texas called in for consultation who do not have an office in Texas.

Miscellaneous Powers and Duties

The Medical Practice Act recognizes a physician's authority to delegate any act to a qualified and properly trained person under the physician's supervision, if the delegation is reasonable and within sound medical judgment.[27] The physician is required to supervise the person and retain final responsibility for the acts. The person who performs the delegated duty will not be guilty of practicing medicine without a license unless he acts with knowledge that the delegation or act was a violation of the law.[28]

The Board also regulates the activities of physician assistants, determining the extent to which a physician may delegate duties to the physician assistant.[29] A physician assistant advisory council, composed of 6 physicians, advises the Board in this area.

The Board also certifies nonprofit health organizations if the organization is formed solely by licensed physicians certified by the Board and is limited to certain purposes such as carrying out medical research, granting scholarships, or instructing the public about public health or medicine.[30]

Regulation

Unlawful and Prohibited Practices

The Board may revoke, suspend, or cancel the license of a physician, or impose other disciplinary measures the Board concludes are necessary, if a physician violates the Medical Practice Act.[31] The grounds for disciplinary action include:[32]

1. submission of a false or misleading statement or document to the Board in an application for examination or licensure;
2. conviction of a felony or crime of lesser degree that involves moral turpitude;

---

26. Tex. Rev. Civ. Stat. Ann. art. 4495b § 3.06(b)(10) (Vernon Supp. 1987). Medical residents, interns, and fellows are required to register with the Board and may be subject to other regulations.
27. Tex. Civ. Stat. Ann. art. 4495b § 3.06(d)(1) (Vernon Supp. 1987).
28. Tex. Rev. Civ. Stat. Ann. art. 4495b § 3.07(i) (Vernon Supp. 1987).
29. Tex. Rev. Civ. Stat. Ann. art. 4495b § 5.02(a)-(b) (Vernon Supp. 1987). The standards are individualized, taking into consideration factors such as the skill of the physician assistant and the nature of the responsibility delegated.
30. Tex. Rev. Civ. Stat. Ann. art. 4495b § 5.01(a)-(b) (Vernon Supp. 1987).
31. Tex. Rev. Civ. Stat. Ann. art. 4495b § 4.01 (Vernon Supp. 1987).
32. Tex. Rev. Civ. Stat. Ann. art. 4495b § 3.08(1)-(21) (Vernon Supp. 1987).

3. intemperance in the use of alcohol or drugs which in the opinion of the Board could endanger patients;
4. unprofessional or dishonorable conduct that is likely to deceive the public, including:
   a. committing acts in violation of Texas law pertaining to the practice of medicine,
   b. failing to maintain complete records of the purchase and disposal of drugs listed as controlled substances,
   c. writing prescriptions or dispensing drugs to a person whom the physician knows or should know is a habitual user of drugs,
   d. writing false or fictitious prescriptions for dangerous drugs,
   e. prescribing or administering drugs or treatments that are nontherapeutic in the nature or manner administered,
   f. prescribing or administering dangerous drugs in a manner inconsistent with public health and welfare,
   g. persistently and flagrantly overcharging or overtreating patients,
   h. failing to supervise the activities of persons acting under his supervision, or
   i. delegating professional responsibility to a person whom the physician knows or has reason to know is not qualified to perform the responsibility;
5. violation of any rule under the Medical Practice Act;
6. use of false, misleading, or deceptive advertising;
7. advertisement of professional superiority if the advertisement cannot be readily verified;
8. alteration of any medical license, certificate, diploma, or transcript;
9. use of any license, certificate, diploma, or transcript that has been fraudulently purchased, counterfeited, or materially altered;
10. impersonation of another person during the medical examination or engagement in any conduct intended to subvert the examination;
11. impersonation of a licensed physician or permittance of the use of a certificate or license by another;
12. employment of a person whose license has been suspended or who has been convicted of the unlawful practice of medicine in Texas or elsewhere;

13. performance or procurement of a criminal abortion;
14. assistance in the practice of medicine by any person or business not licensed to practice medicine by the Board;
15. inability to practice medicine with reasonable skill and safety due to illness, drunkenness, excessive use of drugs, or physical or mental condition;[33]
16. determination by a court that the person is of unsound mind;
17. failure to practice medicine in a professional manner consistent with public health and welfare;
18. removal, suspension, or disciplinary action by the physician's peers in any professional medical association, if the Board concludes that the action was in response to unprofessional conduct or incompetence likely to harm the public;
19. subjection to repeated or recurring meritorious health care liability claims that in the opinion of the Board are evidence of incompetence; and
20. suspension, revocation, or restriction of the physician's license by another state or the armed forces.

Method of Discipline

The Board, upon finding that a person committed a violation, may enter any of the following orders:[34]

1. deny the person's application for a license;
2. administer a public or private reprimand;
3. suspend, limit, or restrict the person's license by:
   a. revoking the license;
   b. requiring the person to submit to care, counseling, or treatment by a Board-approved physician;
   c. requiring the person to participate in an educational or counseling program;
   d. requiring the person to practice under the direction of a Board-designated physician for a period of time; or
   e. requiring the person to perform public service.

---

33. Tex. Rev. Civ. Stat. Ann. art. 4495b § 3.08(4)(A) (Vernon Supp. 1987). A complaint, indictment, or conviction is not necessary if sufficient evidence supports the conclusion that the physician committed the act.
34. Tex. Rev. Civ. Stat. Ann. art. 4495b § 3.08(16) (Vernon Supp. 1987). Upon a finding of probable cause, the Board has the power to order a mental or physical examination by a Board-designated physician.

Offenses

A physician commits a criminal offense, punishable as a Class A misdemeanor, if the physician:[35]

1. makes a false statement in the application for examination or licensure or makes a false statement under oath to obtain a license or registration;[36]
2. employs or pays any person or business to solicit patients;
3. fails or refuses to apply for and pay the annual registration fee;
4. uses any letters, words, or terms as an affix on stationery or advertisements indicating the person is entitled to practice medicine when in fact the person is not licensed;
5. purchases, sells, or barters for the use of a medical degree, diploma, certificate, or transcript in an application to the Board;
6. alters any medical license, certificate, diploma, or transcript;
7. uses any medical license, certificate, diploma, or transcript that has been fraudulently purchased, issued, counterfeited, or materially altered;
8. impersonates another person during the medical examination or engages in any conduct subverting the examination;
9. impersonates a licensed physician or permits another person who is not licensed to use a license or certificate to practice medicine in Texas;
10. employs any person whose license has been suspended or who has been convicted of the unlawful practice of medicine in Texas or elsewhere; or
11. assists any person or business to practice medicine in Texas who is not duly licensed.

If a physician has been convicted of any of these offenses previously, a subsequent conviction will be a third degree felony. After conviction, the physician forfeits all rights and privileges conferred by the license to practice medicine.[37]

---

35. Tex. Rev. Civ. Stat. Ann. art. 4495b § 4.12(1)-(8) (Vernon Supp. 1987). Certain violations are considered criminal offenses and are discussed under "Offenses" later in this chapter.
36. Tex. Rev. Civ. Stat. Ann. art. 4495b § 3.07(a)-(i) (Vernon Supp. 1987). A Class A misdemeanor is punishable by a fine of not greater than $2,000 and/or confinement for not greater than 1 year. *See* Tex. Penal Code Ann. § 12.21 (Vernon 1974).
37. These acts are classified as perjury and/or tampering with a government record. Tex. Rev. Civ. Stat. Ann. art. 4495b § 3.07(b). Perjury is a Class A misdemeanor; however, tampering with a government record may be either a Class A misdemeanor or a third degree felony depending upon the actor's intent. *See* Tex. Penal Code Ann. §§ 37.02 (perjury); 37.10 (tampering with a government record) (Vernon 1974).

Disciplinary Procedures

The Board has the discretion to revoke, suspend, or cancel a license for a violation of the Medical Practice Act.[38] If the physician is charged with a felony, however, the Board is required to suspend the license during the trial and revoke the license upon final judgment of conviction by the court. Additionally, the Board is required to report all disciplinary actions to the party, appropriate health care facilities, hospitals, professional societies, and the entities responsible for the administration of Medicare and Medicaid in Texas.[39]

Any person, or the Board itself, may bring charges against a physician. Charges must be written in a sworn affidavit and must detail the nature of the event in question.[40] The Board is required to set a time and place for a hearing and notify the physician of the hearing and charges by personal service of process or certified mail.[41] A physician has a right to counsel and a right to call witnesses at the hearing. The Board conducts the investigation and has extensive powers to subpoena, take testimony, and receive law enforcement reports.[42] The complaints, reports, and investigation files related to disciplinary proceedings are privileged, but the Board is required to maintain a permanent file.

A physician whose license is canceled, revoked, or suspended may appeal the decision to a district court in Travis County, Texas, within 30 days after the final judgment.[43] During the appeal, the license remains suspended unless the physician obtains a stay from the court.[44] A court may not grant a stay if a danger to the public exists and a stay may not exceed 120 days. The physician may also petition for reinstatement, but several restrictions apply.[45] If the license was revoked, the person is required to wait for 1 year before petitioning for reinstatement.

The Board may, by majority vote, probate any disciplinary order.[46] Probation is not available, however, for revocations due to a felony conviction for controlled substances except on a showing that the probation will serve the best interests of the public and the

---

38. *See* Tex. Penal Code Ann. § 12.34 (Vernon 1974). A third degree felony is punishable by imprisonment of not less than 2 years but not exceeding 10 years and a fine of not more than $5,000.
39. Tex. Rev. Civ. Stat. Ann. art. 4495b § 4.01 (Vernon Supp. 1987).
40. Tex. Rev. Civ. Stat. Ann. art. 4495b § 4.13 (Vernon Supp. 1987).
41. Tex. Rev. Civ. Stat. Ann. art. 4495b § 4.02 (Vernon Supp. 1987).
42. Tex. Rev. Civ. Stat. Ann. art. 4495b § 4.03 (Vernon Supp. 1987). A person must receive the notice at least 10 days before the hearing date. *Id.* § 4.30(a).
43. Tex. Rev. Civ. Stat. Ann. art. 4495b §§ 4.04, 4.05 (Vernon Supp. 1987). The powers relating to reviewing law enforcement reports are governed by section 2.09(h).
44. Tex. Rev. Civ. Stat. Ann. art. 4495b § 4.09 (Vernon Supp. 1987).
45. Tex. Rev. Civ. Stat. Ann. art. 4495b § 4.08 (Vernon Supp. 1987).
46. Tex. Rev. Civ. Stat. Ann. art. 4495b § 4.10 (Vernon Supp. 1987).

physician. Moreover, the Board may at any time, by majority vote, rescind the probation and enforce the original order.[47] Probation revocation hearings are held in the same manner as disciplinary proceedings.

The Board also has the power to suspend temporarily a person's license without notice or prior hearing if the Board concludes that an immediate danger to the public exists.[48] If the Board uses this procedure, it must simultaneously initiate proceedings for a hearing and hold the hearing as soon as possible.

Reports From Insurers, Medical Peer Review Committees, and Courts

Any insurer of a physician providing medical liability coverage in Texas is required to submit to the Board within 90 days information regarding any lawsuits filed against the insured that relate to a physician's professional conduct.[49] If the physician is not insured, the physician has a duty to report this information to the Board. Texas courts are required to submit to the Board within 90 days information on judgments, settlements, or dismissals of all suits that relate to a physician's professional conduct. Additionally, any medical peer review committee in Texas, physicians, and professional societies pertaining to drug and alcohol abuse may report to the Board any information that raises doubts about a physician's competence.[50]

Finally, Texas courts are required to submit to the Board within 30 days information concerning a felony conviction of a person known to be a physician or applying for a license to practice medicine.[51]

---

47. Tex. Rev. Civ. Stat. Ann. art. 4495b § 4.11(a) (Vernon Supp. 1987).
48. Tex. Rev. Civ. Stat. Ann. art. 4495b § 4.11(b) (Vernon Supp. 1987).
49. Tex. Rev. Civ. Stat. Ann. art. 4495b § 4.13 (Vernon Supp. 1987).
50. Tex. Rev. Civ. Stat. Ann. art. 4495b § 5.05(a)-(c) (Vernon Supp. 1987)
51. Tex. Rev. Civ. Stat. Ann. art. 4495b § 5.06(a)-(b), 5.07 (Vernon Supp. 1987).

1.2

Licensure and Regulation of Psychiatric Nurses

In Texas, there is not a separate scheme for the regulation of psychiatric nurses apart from the Board of Nurse Examiners, which regulates the practice of nursing. The Board establishes rules for professional conduct, regulates the practice of nursing, and enforces both its regulations and the laws of Texas pertaining to nursing.[1] The Board also controls the revocation, suspension, and renewal of licenses.[2]

Board of Nurse Examiners

The Board of Nurse Examiners (Board) is composed of nine members who are appointed by the governor with the advice and consent of the Senate.[3] Board members serve staggered 6-year terms. Six of the members must be registered nurses, three of whom are engaged in professional nurse education with a representative from each of the three established degree programs in Texas.[4] Three members must be members of the general public who are not involved with health care.

The Board approves nursing school programs and establishes

1. Tex. Rev. Civ. Stat. Ann. art. 4513-4514 (Vernon Supp. 1987). The Board also has the power to regulate advanced nurse practitioners. *See* Tex. Admin. Code tit. 22, § 221.1 (1986).
2. Tex. Rev. Civ. Stat. Ann. arts. 4525, 4526 (Vernon Supp. 1987).
3. Tex. Rev. Civ. Stat. Ann. art. 4513 § 1 (Vernon Supp. 1987).
4. Tex. Rev. Civ. Stat. Ann. art 4513 § 1 (Vernon Supp. 1987). The three programs are the Baccalaureate degree program, the Associate degree program, and the Diploma degree program.

the requirements for the three degree programs in Texas.[5] The Board has the following powers and duties:[6]

1. establishment of standards of professional conduct for all licensed registered nurses;
2. regulation of the professional nursing practice, including the power to investigate claims against registered nurses;
3. issuance of disciplinary sanctions;
4. establishment of a voluntary continuing education program;[7] and,
5. submission of recommendations to the Texas State Board of Medical Examiners regarding a physician's delegation of medical acts to registered nurses.[8]

Licensure

Every licensure applicant is required to provide the Board with proof of successful completion of an accredited program in professional nursing.[9] Applicants are also required to pay all licensure and examination fees and to obtain a passing score on the Board's licensure examination. If an applicant meets these requirements, the Board certifies the applicant to work as a registered nurse.[10]

Texas law also states that "only persons registered or licensed properly in Texas may use the title 'R.N.' and all registered nurses must wear an insignia identifying themselves as registered nurses while on duty."[11]

Temporary License

The Board may issue temporary permits in two situations.[12] Any applicant who has graduated from an accredited nursing school, holds a valid registration certificate from another state or territory of the United States, and is actually engaged in nursing is permitted to practice under a temporary permit pending final approval of a permanent license. Also, any applicant who has graduated from

---

5. Tex. Rev. Civ. Stat. Ann. art. 4518 (Vernon Supp. 1987).
6. Tex. Rev. Civ. Stat. Ann. art. 4514 (Vernon Supp. 1987).
7. Tex. Rev. Civ. Stat. Ann. art. 4518 § 7 (Vernon Supp. 1987).
8. Tex. Rev. Civ. Stat. Ann. art. 4514 § 6 (Vernon Supp. 1987).
9. Tex. Rev. Civ. Stat. Ann. art. 4518 § 3 (Vernon Supp. 1987).
10. Tex. Rev. Civ. Stat. Ann. art. 4518 §§ 3, 5 (Vernon Supp. 1987). Nursing is broadly defined as the evaluation, rehabilitation, counseling, or care of the ill; working with programs to maintain or prevent illness; administration of medications or treatments; supervision or teaching of nursing; or administration, supervision, or evaluation of nursing policies and procedures.
11. Tex. Rev. Civ. Stat. Ann. art. 4521 (Vernon Supp. 1987).
12. Tex. Rev. Civ. Stat. Ann. art. 4523(a)-(b) (Vernon Supp. 1987).

an accredited nursing program may obtain a temporary permit pending the results of the licensing examination, as long as the applicant practices under the direct supervision of a registered nurse.[13]

Registration

Registered nurses must renew their licenses every 2 years.[14] The registration fee is payable on or before March 31. Late fees are charged and the Board may impose additional requirements before permitting renewal of a license if the renewal is more than 90 days late. Any registered nurse who continues to practice without a validly renewed license is considered an illegal practitioner and is subject to license revocation or suspension.

Registered nurses may request that the Board place their license on inactive status.[15] The nurse may not practice professional nursing while the license is on the inactive list. When the nurse desires to reenter active practice, the nurse must notify the Board and meet any requirements that the Board considers necessary.

Examination

Every applicant not already licensed in another state or United States territory is required to pass the Board's nursing examination.[16] Applicants who fail the examination the first time may retake the examination and obtain an analysis of their performance by written request to the Board.

Certification From Another State

The Board may license any applicant who holds a valid registration from another state, territory, or possession of the United States or from a foreign country to practice nursing in Texas by endorsing the applicant's certificate.[17] The applicant is not required to take the Texas licensing examination. The Board must, however, examine the certification requirements of the applicant's program and determine that the program's requirements are similar to Texas' requirements. The Board must also conclude that the applicant will have the same general degree of fitness to practice nursing as applicants qualifying in Texas.

---

13. Tex. Rev. Civ. Stat. Ann. art. 4523(b) (Vernon Supp. 1987). This permit automatically expires upon receipt of the permanent license or notice of examination failure. The Board may not issue a temporary permit to any applicant who has previously failed the examination.
14. Tex. Rev. Civ. Stat. Ann. art. 4526 (Vernon Supp. 1987).
15. Tex. Rev. Civ. Stat. Ann. art. 4526b (Vernon Supp. 1987).
16. Tex. Rev. Civ. Stat. Ann. art. 4519 (Vernon Supp. 1987).
17. Tex. Rev. Civ. Stat. Ann. art. 4521 (Vernon Supp. 1987).

Exemptions

The licensing law does not apply to gratuitous nursing of the sick by friends or family, treatment solely by spiritual means or prayer, acts done under the control or supervision of a licensed physician, practice by licensed vocational nurses, people or acts licensed by any other Board or agency of Texas if the acts are authorized by law, performance in schools of any activities necessary for handicapped students that are routinely performed by the student or the student's family, or nursing tasks performed by nursing students while under the direct supervision of qualified faculty.[18]

Regulation

Unlawful and Prohibited Practices

The Board may refuse to admit an applicant to the examination; to license, certify, or register an applicant; or to recertify an applicant. The Board may also issue warnings or reprimands and suspend or revoke the license of any registered nurse.[19] The grounds for instituting these disciplinary sanctions include:

1. violations of any law or regulation pertaining to professional nursing;
2. fraud or deceit in procuring a license;
3. conviction of a felony or any crime of lesser degree involving moral turpitude;
4. use of any nursing license, certificate, diploma, or permit that has been fraudulently purchased, obtained, or materially altered;
5. impersonation of another person in any licensing examination;
6. assisting any unlicensed person in connection with the unauthorized practice of professional nursing;
7. revocation, suspension, or denial of a license to practice professional nursing in another area;
8. intemperance in the use of alcohol or drugs if the nurse knows or should know that the effects could endanger patients;
9. unprofessional conduct that the Board concludes is likely to

18. Tex. Admin. Code tit. 22, § 218.10(1)-(5) (1986); Tex. Rev. Civ. Stat. Ann. art. 4528 (Vernon Supp. 1987).
19. Tex. Rev. Civ. Stat. Ann. art. 4525(a)-(e) (Vernon Supp. 1987). A suspension may not exceed 2 years.

deceive or injure patients or the public, including, but not limited to:[20]

a. failing to assess a patient's status or take appropriate steps to stabilize the patient;

b. consistently failing to report or document a patient's symptoms, medications, or treatments, or falsifying reports; and

c. violating the confidentiality of a patient;

10. judgment by a court that the nurse is of unsound mind; and

11. lack of fitness to practice due to mental or physical health problems that could result in injury to patients or the public.

Offenses

A registered nurse commits a criminal offense, punishable as a Class B misdemeanor, if the nurse:[21]

1. practices professional nursing while the nurse's license is suspended or revoked;
2. uses the abbreviation "R.N." or any other designation tending to imply the person is a licensed registered nurse when in fact the person is not licensed;
3. fraudulently sells, obtains, or furnishes any nursing diploma, license, or record; or
4. practices under a diploma, license, or record that has been issued, obtained, or signed illegally.

Additionally, registered nurses have a duty to report certain actions to the Board:[22]

1. unprofessional conduct by another registered nurse,
2. the failure of a registered nurse to give adequate care to a patient,
3. the failure of a registered nurse to observe the minimum standards of professional nursing practice, and
4. the impaired status of a registered nurse.

---

20. Tex. Admin. Code tit. 22, § 217.13 (1986).
21. Tex. Rev. Civ. Stat. Ann. art. 4527b (Vernon Supp. 1987). The penalty is a fine of not less than $50 but not more than $500 and/or confinement for not more than 30 days.
22. Tex. Civ. Stat. Ann. art. 4525a §§ 1-6 (Vernon Supp. 1987). The registered nurse must report not only the listed actions, but also any other actions that expose or are likely to expose a patient to unnecessary risks. The registered nurse does not have to report, however, if the nurse reasonably believes that another person has reported the suspected condition.

A registered nurse is subject to sanctions by the Board for failure to report.[23] In conjunction with the duty to report, peer review committees for registered nurses must be established by any facility that employs 10 or more registered nurses.

Disciplinary Procedure

Disciplinary proceedings may be commenced by filing a charge with the Board. Any person may bring charges, which must be written and under oath.[24] The Board is required to notify the registered nurse of the charge and conduct a preliminary investigation to determine its validity. The Board is required to notify the registered nurse of the complaint and its nature at least 10 days before the hearing.[25]

A registered nurse is entitled to a hearing before the Board if the Board refuses to admit the applicant to an examination or to certify, license, or register the applicant. The nurse has a right to counsel at the hearing, as well as a right to call witnesses.[26] A person may appeal a license revocation or suspension to any district court in the person's county of residence within 30 days of a final Board decision. The decision of the Board, however, is not stayed pending the court's judgment unless the person obtains a court order for a stay.

A person may also petition the Board for reinstatement. A person whose license was revoked is required to wait 1 year before petitioning for reinstatement. The Board also has the power to probate any disciplinary order, except revocations or suspensions, by majority vote and to set qualifying terms for the probation.[27] The Board may, however, rescind the probation by a majority vote at any time.[28]

The Board has extensive investigative powers, including the power to issue subpoenas, compel the attendance of witnesses, administer oaths, and initiate prosecution for violations of the law.[29]

---

23. Tex. Civ. Stat. Ann. art. 4525a § 9 (Vernon Supp. 1987). The Board may take any appropriate action, including revocation or suspension of the registered nurse's license. Additionally, a registered nurse may sue for wrongful discharge if any person or organization terminates, disciplines, or discriminates against the nurse following a report to the Board as required by law.
24. Tex. Rev. Civ. Stat. Ann. art. 4525 (Vernon Supp. 1987).
25. *See* Tex. Rev. Civ. Stat. Ann. art. 6252-13a (Vernon Supp. 1987).
26. Tex. Rev. Civ. Stat. Ann. art. 4525(b) (Vernon Supp. 1987).
27. Tex. Rev. Civ. Stat. Ann. art. 4525(d) (Vernon Supp. 1987).
28. The Board must notify the person and hold a hearing if the Board decides to rescind the probation. Tex. Rev. Civ. Stat. Ann. art. 4535(d) (Vernon Supp. 1987).
29. Tex. Rev. Civ. Stat. Ann. art. 4525(e) (Vernon Supp. 1987).

1.3

Certification and Regulation of Psychologists

The Texas State Board of Examiners of Psychologists (Board) regulates the practice and licensure of psychologists in Texas.[1] Psychological services include any service that involves the "application of established principles, methods, and procedures of describing, explaining, and ameliorating"[2] normal behavior and the "evaluation, prevention, and remediation of psychological, emotional, mental, interpersonal, learning, and behavioral disorders of individuals and groups."[3] The Board promulgates the code of ethics, certifies specialties, regulates advertising and continuing education, and establishes criteria for certification and licensure. The Board has the power to revoke, cancel, or suspend licenses and certificates.

Texas State Board of Examiners of Psychologists

The Board consists of nine members who are appointed by the governor with the advice and consent of the Senate.[4] Members serve for 6-year terms. Six members are required to be certified psychologists with 5 years' experience engaged in the practice,

1. Tex. Rev. Civ. Stat. Ann. art. 4512c §§ 1-17 (Vernon Supp. 1987). A psychologist is anyone who "holds himself out to the public by any title or description of services incorporating the words 'psychological', 'psychologist', or 'psychology.' "
2. *Id.*
3. *Id.*
4. Tex. Rev. Civ. Stat. Ann. art. 4512c § 4(a)-(d) (Vernon Supp. 1987).

teaching, or research of psychology. One member is required to be a certified psychological associate with 5 years' experience, and the remaining two members are members of the general public who are not involved with health care.[5]

The Board's duties and powers include:[6]

1. promulgating a code of ethics;
2. certifying health specialties;
3. regulating advertising to prevent false, misleading, or deceptive practices;
4. investigating claims against licensees; and
5. establishing a continuing education program.

Licensure

Licensure is a two-step process, involving certification and granting of a license. The Board certifies applicants who pass the Board's examination if the applicant:[7]

1. has a doctoral degree in psychological studies from an accredited institution;[8]
2. is of the age of majority;
3. has a good moral character;
4. is judged by the Board to be mentally and physically competent to render services skillfully and safely;
5. has not been convicted of a felony or crime involving moral turpitude;
6. does not use drugs or alcohol excessively;
7. has not been guilty of fraud in the application process; and

---

5. The Board certifies psychological associates, graduates of a subdoctoral program requiring a master's degree with a minimum of 27 semester hours from an accredited program. Tex. Rev. Civ. Stat. Ann. art. 4512c § 19 (Vernon Supp. 1987); Tex. Admin. Code tit. 22, § 463.18 (1987).
6. Tex. Rev. Civ. Stat. Ann. art. 4512c § 8(a)-(m) (Vernon Supp. 1987).
7. Tex. Rev. Civ. Stat. Ann. art. 4512c § 11 (Vernon Supp. 1987). Special requirements apply to foreign student applicants. *See* Tex. Admin. Code tit. 22, § 463.17 (1987).
8. An applicant must have a minimum of 90 semester hours and demonstrate competency in four "core" areas: (1) "biological basis of behavior: physiological psychology, comparative psychology, neuropsychology, sensation and perception, psychol-pharmacology;" (2) "cognitive-affective basis of behavior: learning, thinking, motivation, emotion;" (3) "social basis of behavior: social psychology, group processes, organizational and systems theory;" and (4) "individual differences: personality theory, human development, abnormal psychology." Tex. Admin. Code tit. 22, § 463.16(b) (1987).

8. has not assisted any person who is not licensed to practice psychology in Texas in the performance of duties limited to licensed psychologists.

Applicants for certification must also submit at least three reference letters from psychologists.[9] The Board may license an applicant if the applicant is a certified psychologist and has had at least 2 years of supervised experience.[10] All applications must be on Board forms and must be verified.

Certification From Another State

The Board may certify any applicant who has a valid license or certificate from another state if the state's licensure and certification requirements are substantially equivalent to those in Texas.[11] The applicant, however, must pass the Board's jurisprudence examination before the Board may certify the applicant.

Temporary Licenses

Licensed psychologists who are in good standing in another state may obtain a temporary license to practice in Texas.[12] The temporary license may not exceed 30 days and applicants are required to apply at least 30 days prior to the date they expect to work in Texas. The application must specify the exact dates of practice and the services to be rendered, and must provide documentation of the applicant's credentials. The temporary licensing procedure does not apply to applicants who reside in Texas or are in the process of establishing residence in Texas.

Registration

Psychologists must renew their certificates no less than every 2 years.[13] Certificates expire on December 31st of the year following issuance, and the Board is required to notify the psychologist of the upcoming expiration. Psychologists may renew an expired certificate by paying late fees in addition to the normal certification fee if the license has not been expired for more than 2 years. If the certificate has been expired for more than 2 years, the psychologist is required to retake the Board's examination and fulfill all requirements necessary to obtain an original certificate. Psychologists may ask the Board to place a certificate on an inactive list. The

---

9. Tex. Admin. Code tit. 22, § 463.19 (1987).
10. Tex. Rev. Civ. Stat. Ann. art. 4512c § 21(a)-(b) (Vernon Supp. 1987). One year of the experience may be part of the doctoral program, but the other year must be completed after the applicant received the doctoral degree.
11. Tex. Rev. Civ. Stat. Ann. art. 4512c § 15(a)-(b) (Vernon Supp. 1987).
12. Tex. Admin. Code tit. 22, § 465.23 (1987).
13. Tex. Rev. Civ. Stat. Ann. art. 4512c § 17(a)-(c) (Vernon Supp. 1987).

renewal process applies only to doctoral level certificates, licenses, and specialty certificates.[14]

Additionally, every contract for psychological services in Texas is required to contain the name, address, and telephone number of the Board, and a licensee must display in each place of business a sign with the Board's name, address, and telephone number and a statement that complaints against the licensee may be directed to the Board.[15] Every licensed psychologist is also required to display the original license or an official duplicate, along with the current renewal, in a "prominent" place in the office.[16]

Examination

The Board administers the examination, which is required to cover both the applicant's knowledge of psychology and knowledge of Texas laws pertaining to psychology.[17] The examination is held at least once a year, and applicants who fail may retake the examination. An oral examination is also required for certified psychologists to be licensed.[18]

Exemptions

The Psychologists' Certification and Licensing Act does not apply to:[19]

1. persons employed by a governmental agency, public school district, or regionally accredited institution of higher education if the employees perform only the duties required by their positions and do not charge fees over their stated salaries;
2. students, interns, or residents of psychology, provided that tasks are performed under supervision and the students are clearly designated as trainees;
3. activities of other professional groups licensed or certified by the state; Christian Scientist practitioners registered by the church; or ordained religions performing services that are consistent with their code of ethics and training; or
4. marriage and family counselors whose practice is solely limited to marriage and family concerns and who have a master's or

---

14. Tex. Rev. Civ. Stat. Ann. art. 4512c § 17(g) (Vernon Supp. 1987).
15. Tex. Rev. Civ. Stat. Ann. art. 4512c § 8(d)-(e) (Vernon Supp. 1987).
16. Tex. Admin. Code tit. 22, § 463.14 (1987).
17. Tex. Rev. Civ. Stat. Ann. art. 4512c § 14(a)-(d) (Vernon Supp. 1987).
18. Tex. Admin. Code tit. 22, § 463.23 (1987).
19. Tex. Rev. Civ. Stat. Ann. art. 4512c § 22(a)-(d) (Vernon Supp. 1987).

doctoral degree from an accredited institution and abide by the code of ethics.

Regulation

The Board may cancel, revoke, or suspend a license; refuse to renew a license or certificate; or issue reprimands or rehabilitation guidelines if the Board finds that a psychologist or psychological associate:[20]

1. has been convicted of a felony or a crime involving moral turpitude;[21]
2. uses drugs or alcohol to the extent that professional competency is affected;
3. has been guilty of fraud in the rendering of services;
4. has assisted any person not licensed in Texas in the practice of psychology in Texas; or
5. has been found guilty of unprofessional conduct.

An applicant may appeal a Board decision regarding an application for licensure or certification within 30 days of the decision, after which time the applicant must make a new application and pay a new filing fee.[22] The applicant is also entitled to a hearing before the Board. An applicant may apply for reinstatement after 1 year following revocation, cancellation, or suspension. The Administrative Procedure Act and Texas Register Act govern the procedural process of all Board proceedings.

The Board may probate any disciplinary order, including revocations and suspensions, by majority vote. The Board may, however, rescind a probation order by majority vote, provided that the person has at least 10 days' notice and an opportunity for a hearing.[23] Orders revoking probation are not appealable.

After any revocation, suspension, or cancellation, the Board issues a "rehabilitation" plan. The plan may include supervision by a Board-designated psychologist for a certain length of time, educational programs, psychotherapy, reexamination, or physical

20. Tex. Rev. Civ. Stat. Ann. art. 4512c § 23(a)-(f) (Vernon Supp. 1987).
21. Crimes which the Board may consider include, but are not limited to, burglary, rape, child molesting, theft, murder, robbery, substance abuse, or crimes involving fraud or deceit. Tex. Admin. Code tit. 22, § 465.19(d) (1987).
22. Tex. Admin. Code tit. 22, § 463.18 (1987).
23. Tex. Rev. Civ. Stat. Ann. art. 4512c § 23(e) (Vernon Supp. 1987). The person has a right to counsel and a right to call witnesses.

examinations by a Board-designated physician.[24] The Board also has the power to require a mental or physical examination of a psychologist at any time if the Board reasonably believes that the competency of the psychologist is in question and the safety of patients could be jeopardized.[25]

Offenses

Persons who represent to the public that they are certified or licensed psychologists when they are not are guilty of a misdemeanor. Punishment is a fine of not less than $50 but not more than $500 and/or confinement for not more than 30 days.[26]

---

24. Tex. Admin. Code tit. 22, § 465.20(a)-(b) (1987).
25. Tex. Rev. Civ. Stat. Ann. art. 4512c § 24A (Vernon 1976).
26. Tex. Rev. Civ. Stat. Ann. art. 4512c § 25 (Vernon 1976).

1.4

Subdoctoral and Uncertified Psychologists

The Texas State Board of Examiners of Psychologists (Board) regulates the licensure and practice of subdoctoral levels of psychology;[1] thus many rules that apply to psychologists also apply to subdoctoral levels of practice. Subdoctoral licensees are required to use a title with "psychological" followed by "associate," "assistant," "examiner," or "technician."[2] Psychological associates may only practice as an employee under the supervision of a licensed agency or licensed psychologist.[3]

Licensure and Certification

The Board may license and certify an applicant if the applicant:[4]

1. is at least 21 years old,
2. is a resident of Texas,
3. is of good moral character,
4. is a citizen of the United States,
5. passes the Board examination covering psychology and jurisprudence, and
6. has a master's degree in psychology from an accredited institution.[5]

---

1. Tex. Rev. Civ. Stat. Ann. art. 4512c §19 (Vernon Supp. 1987).
2. Tex. Rev. Civ. Stat. Ann. art. 4512c §§ 1-12 (Vernon Supp. 1987).
3. Tex. Admin. Code tit. 22, § 465.7 (1987).
4. Tex. Rev. Civ. Stat. Ann. art. 4512c § 11(b)-(e) (Vernon Supp. 1987); Tex. Admin. Code tit. 22, § 463.1 (1987).
5. Tex. Admin. Code tit. 22, § 463.8 (1987). The applicant must have at least 42 semester hours in psychology, 27 of which must be graduate level hours.

Additionally, the applicant must have a minimum of 450 supervised practical hours during a 12-month period. All applications are required to be on Board forms and must include the applicant's course titles and instructors' names.

Renewal

Licensees are required to renew certificates and licenses no less than once every 2 years. Certificates and licenses expire on May 31st of the year following issuance.[6]

Regulation

The Board may revoke, suspend, or cancel a license or issue reprimands and rehabilitation plans. The disciplinary rules for subdoctoral level psychological associates are the same rules pertaining to doctoral level psychologists (See Chapter 1.3).

---

6. Tex. Rev. Civ. Stat. Ann. art. 4512c § 17(h) (Vernon Supp. 1987). See Chapter 1.3, "Certification and Licensure of Psychologists," for the details of licensure and regulation.

1.5

Certification and Regulation of Social Workers

The Texas Department of Human Services (Department), in conjunction with the Council for Social Work Certification, regulates the practice of social work in Texas.[1] Social work services "consist of the professional application of social work values, principles, and techniques to one or more of the following ends: helping people obtain tangible services; counseling with individuals, families, or groups; helping communities or groups provide social and health services; and participating in formulating relevant public policies . . . requiring knowledge of human development and behavior, of social, economic, and cultural institutions, and of the interaction of all these factors."[2] The Department defines different levels of practice, establishes criteria for certification and renewals, and promulgates and enforces rules pertaining to the practice of social work.

The Council for Social Work Certification (Council) consists of nine members appointed by the Department who serve staggered 3-year terms.[3] The Council advises the Department on ques-

1. Tex. Hum. Res. Code Ann. §§ 50.003, 50.004 (Vernon Supp. 1987) (the Social Work Services Act). Any firms, associations, or businesses which offer social work services must have certified personnel rendering such services and must follow all rules pertaining to the practice of social work. Tex. Hum. Res. Code Ann. §§ 50.010(b), 50.012 (Vernon Supp. 1987).
2. Tex. Hum. Res. Code Ann. § 50.001(a)(3) (Vernon Supp. 1987). Social work is "helping individuals, groups, or communities enhance or restore their capacity for social functioning and creating societal conditions favorable to this goal." *Id.*
3. Tex. Hum. Res. Code Ann. § 50.004 (Vernon Supp. 1987). The council has three certified social workers, three social workers or social work associates, and three members of the general public.

tions relating to the practice and certification of social workers. The Department has the following duties and powers:

1. regulation of advertising to prevent false or misleading practices;[4]
2. adoption of rules for practice and a code of ethics;[5]
3. establishment of criteria for certification;
4. investigation of complaints against certificate holders and issuance of reprimands, revocations, suspensions and probations;
5. designation and certification of specialties; and
6. establishment of continuing education programs and requirements.[6]

Any person certified by the Department, regardless of the certification level, is required to use the appropriate title and designation in connection with the rendering of services and must display the certificate and any renewals at their place of business.[7] Additionally, social workers must display at their place of business a sign informing the public that complaints may be directed to the Department and listing the Department's address and telephone number.

Application Requirements

The Department may certify applicants who pay the appropriate fees and:[8]

1. are at least 18 years of age;
2. have good moral character;
3. successfully complete the Department examination for the level of practice sought;[9] and
4. fulfill the educational and experience requirements for the level of practice sought.

Certified social workers must have a doctoral or master's degree in social work from an accredited institution; social workers must

4. Tex. Hum. Res. Code Ann. § 50.0061 (Vernon Supp. 1987).
5. Tex. Hum. Res. Code Ann. § 50.006 (Vernon Supp. 1987).
6. Tex. Hum. Res. Code Ann. § 50.024 (Vernon Supp. 1987).
7. Tex. Hum. Res. Code Ann. § 50.011 (Vernon Supp. 1987). Certified social workers are designated by that title and "C.S.W.;" social workers by "S.W.;" and social work associates by "S.W.A." The displayed certificates and renewals must be original documents.
8. Tex. Hum. Res. Code Ann. § 50.013 (Vernon Supp. 1987).
9. Tex. Hum. Res. Code Ann. § 50.014 (Vernon Supp. 1987).

have a baccalaureate degree in social work from an accredited institution; and social work associates must have at least one year of work experience and a baccalaureate degree, associate of arts degree, or a high school diploma or its equivalent.[10] Falsification of any information on an application is grounds for denial of certification.

Private Practice

The Department may certify any applicant for private practice if the applicant is a certified social worker with at least 5 years' work experience, 2 years of which were supervised training.[11]

Examination

The Department administers examinations for the three levels of practice at least once a year.[12] Applicants may retake an examination for any level up to three times.

Reciprocity

The Department may certify any applicant who holds a valid license or certificate from another state or territory of the United States as a certified social worker, social worker, or social work associate,[13] as long as the state's or territory's certification or licensure requirements are substantially similar to those in Texas.

Specialty Designation

The Department may certify a certified social worker in good standing as an "advanced clinical practitioner," enabling the applicant to practice in clinical social work.[14] Clinical social work is the "practice of providing direct diagnostic, preventative, or clinical services to individuals, families, and groups whose functioning is threatened or affected by social or psychological stress or health impairment."[15] The Department is required to establish the parameters and requirements of any specialty on the basis of what is best for the public interest and necessity and to establish the rules for conduct and practice in the specialty area. Specialty certificates are renewed annually in the same manner as other social work certificates.

10. Tex. Hum. Res. Code Ann. §§ 50.015, 50.016, 50.017 (Vernon Supp. 1987).
11. Tex. Admin. Code tit. 40, § 85.6003(b) (1987).
12. Tex. Hum. Res. Code Ann. § 50.014 (Vernon Supp. 1987). All examinations are taken and graded anonymously.
13. Tex. Hum. Res. Code Ann. § 50.032 (Vernon Supp. 1987).
14. Tex. Hum. Res. Code Ann. § 50.024 (Vernon Supp. 1987).
15. Tex. Hum. Res. Code Ann. § 50.023 (Vernon Supp. 1987); Tex. Admin. Code tit. 40, § 85.6003(c) (1987).

Renewals

All social workers, regardless of their certification level, are required to renew their certificates annually.[16] Certificates expire on the last day of the month of the certificate holder's birthday. Social workers may renew expired certificates for up to 2 years by paying late charges in addition to the usual renewal fees. If the certificate has been expired for more than 2 years, however, the holder is required to fulfill all requirements for original certification, including reexamination.

Exemptions

The Social Work Services Act does not apply to persons who do not practice social work or do not represent themselves to the public as certified social workers, social workers, or social work associates.[17]

Regulation

The Department may revoke, suspend, or place on probation any certificate; issue reprimands; or refuse to renew or issue a certificate if a social worker or applicant:[18]

1. violates any rule pertaining to social work or assists any person in violating any such rules;
2. engages in unprofessional conduct or any conduct which tends to discredit the profession;
3. engages in false or misleading advertising or other fraudulent activities;
4. allows any person or business not certified by the Department to use the social worker's certificate;
5. violates patient confidentiality;
6. has a license or certificate revoked or suspended in another state or territory or has any disciplinary action taken;
7. is convicted of a felony;
8. refuses to render services to any person solely on the basis of "age, sex, race, religion, national origin, color, or political affiliation."

---

16. Tex. Hum. Res. Code Ann. § 50.023 (Vernon Supp. 1987); Tex. Admin. Code tit. 40, § 85.6009 (1987).
17. Tex. Hum. Res. Code Ann. § 50.002 (Vernon Supp. 1987).
18. Tex. Hum. Res. Code Ann. §§ 50.006(b), 50.021 (Vernon Supp. 1987).

Disciplinary Proceedings

Any person may file a written complaint with the Department, after which the Department is required to notify the certificate holder of the complaint and investigate the allegations.[19] The certificate holder has a right to a hearing before the Department, as well as a right to counsel, if the Department decides to take disciplinary action.[20] The Department's investigative powers include the ability to compel witnesses and the production of records.

The Department may probate any disciplinary order by majority vote. The Department may, however, revoke the probation at any time by majority vote as long as the certificate holder has an opportunity for a hearing before the department. Moreover, a certificate holder may appeal any final decision by the Department within 30 days to the district court in Travis County, Texas.

Violations

Any certificate holder or person who violates any rule of the Social Work Services Act is subject to a civil fine of not less than $50 but not more than $500 for each day of a violation. There is no criminal liability.

---

19. Tex. Hum. Res. Code Ann. § 50.022(a)-(e) (Vernon Supp. 1987). All complaints must be filed under oath.
20. The Administrative Procedure and Texas Register Act controls the specific rules relating to evidence and the nature of the hearings. *See* Tex. Rev. Civ. Stat. Ann. art. 6252-13a (Vernon Supp. 1987).

1.6

Certification and Regulation of School Psychologists

School psychologists are exempt from certification or licensing by the Texas State Board of Examiners of Psychologists.[1] In some states the state Department of Education has an independent structure for regulation of school psychologists exempt from the regular certification and licensing process. Texas does not.

1. Tex. Rev. Civ. Stat. Ann. art. 4512c 22(a) (Vernon Supp. 1987).

1.7a

Certification and Regulation of Professional Counselors

A professional counselor is an MHP who is qualified to offer care for problems less severe than those typically treated by psychiatrists and psychologists. The Texas State Board of Examiners of Professional Counselors (Board) regulates the licensure, certification, and renewal process of professional counselors in Texas.[1] A "licensed professional counselor" may use the title "licensed counselor" and "offer professional counseling services in a private practice to individuals, groups, . . . or government agencies." Counseling includes offering professional services to "develop understanding of personal problems, to define goals, and to plan action reflecting an individual's or group's interests, abilities, aptitudes, and needs as they are related to personal–social concerns, educational progress, and occupations and careers."[2]

Texas State Board of Examiners of Professional Counselors

The Board consists of nine members who are appointed by the Governor with the advice and consent of the Senate.[3] The Board is required to include one counselor educator, four counselors in private practice, and four members of the general public. The Board has the following powers and duties:

1. Tex. Rev. Civ. Stat. Ann. art. 4512g §§ 1-21 (Vernon Supp. 1987).
2. Tex. Rev. Civ. Stat. Ann. art. 4512g § 2(1), (7), (8) (Vernon Supp. 1987).
3. Tex. Rev. Civ. Stat. Ann. art. 4512g §§ 4, 6 (Vernon Supp. 1987).

1. establishment of the criteria for licensure and regulation of licensure;
2. regulation of advertising to prevent false and misleading practices;
3. promulgation of rules and a code of ethics;
4. investigation relating to complaints against licensees;
5. issuance of revocations, suspensions, cancellations, and reprimands; and
6. establishment and regulation of continuing education programs.[4]

Licensure

The Board may license an applicant if the applicant:[5]

1. is at least 18 years old;
2. submits a verified application with the necessary fees to the Board;[6]
3. has completed 45 semester hours at an accredited institution, including 300 hours of supervised practical experience;
4. has 24 months or 2,000 hours of supervised counseling experience; and
5. passes the Board examination.

All licensees are required to display their licenses and renewals in a "prominent" place at their places of business.[7]

Reciprocity

The Board may grant an applicant a license with examination if the applicant holds a valid license or certificate from another state or territory of the United States, provided that the state's or terri-

4. Tex. Admin. Code tit. 22, § 681.253 (1987). Licensed counselors must complete 75 hours of continuing education every 3 years in order to qualify for certificate and license renewal.
5. Tex. Rev. Civ. Stat. Ann. art. 4512g § 10(1)-(5) (Vernon Supp. 1987).
6. The applicant must satisfy certain course requirements, such as obtaining passing grades in human development, group theories and techniques, career and lifestyle development, and counseling theories. Tex. Admin. Code tit. 22, § 681.125 (1987). The applicant must have a master's degree in counseling or concentrated in counseling courses.
7. Tex. Admin. Code tit. 22, § 681.50 (1987). The displayed license must be an original document.

tory's licensure or certification requirements are substantially the same as those in Texas.[8]

Licensure of Specialties

The Board may issue a specialty license to an applicant for any area, except marriage and family counseling, if the applicant can demonstrate compliance with a nationally recognized certification agency's qualifications and passes a Board examination.[9] A licensed professional counselor may not advertise expertise in any specialty unless the counselor is licensed by the Board in that specialty. Licensed professional counselors may not have more than three specialties at one time and must display their specialty certificate at the place of business. Specialty licenses are renewed annually by paying the appropriate fee.

Renewal

Licensed professional counselors are required to renew their licenses annually by paying the renewal fee.[10] A person may renew an expired license for up 90 days by paying late charges in addition to the annual fee. If the delay exceeds 90 days, the license is revoked. The person may petition for reinstatement for up to 1 year, after which the person may only renew the license by fulfilling all requirements for original licensure. Additionally, licensed professional counselors are required to participate in a continuing education program.[11]

Reasons for Denial of a License

The Board may reject an application for licensure if the applicant:[12]

1. lacks the necessary skills to practice competently,
2. misrepresents application information or qualifications,
3. misrepresents the services the applicant will render,
4. engages in sexual intimacies with a client,
5. advertises in a false or misleading manner,
6. breaches patient confidentiality,
7. abuses drugs or alcohol,

---

8. Tex. Rev. Civ. Stat. Ann. art. 4512g § 18 (Vernon Supp. 1987). The applicant must submit a copy of the license or certificate to the Board and fulfill all other licensure requirements. Only the examination requirement is waived.
9. Tex. Rev. Civ. Stat. Ann. art. 4512g § 13 (Vernon Supp. 1987).
10. Tex. Rev. Civ. Stat. Ann. art. 4512g § 14 (Vernon Supp. 1987).
11. Tex. Admin. Code tit. 22, § 681.201(f) (1987).
12. Tex. Admin. Code tit. 22, § 681.244(1)-(10) (1987).

8. uses the professional relationship with a client for personal gain,
9. violates any Board rule or state law pertaining to professional counseling,
10. is convicted of a felony,[13]
11. is committed to a mental health institution.

Exemptions

The Licensed Professional Counselor Act does not apply to:[14]

1. employees of federal, state, county, municipal, or private educational institutions as long as they perform only those duties required by the employment contract;
2. students, interns, or trainees of a counseling program provided the activities are supervised and the person is clearly designated as a trainee;
3. nonresident licensed counselors who do not practice for more than 30 days in any year in Texas;
4. other professionals, such as physicians, psychologists, or nurses, who are performing services consistent with their training and code of ethics;
5. lawyers;
6. persons working with nonprofit organizations or charities; and
7. marriage and family counselors.

Regulation

The Board may revoke or suspend a licensed professional counselor's license if the Board finds that the counselor:[15]

1. has violated any state law or Board regulation pertaining to licensed professional counselors, or
2. has been committed because of mental incompetence.

The Board also reviews and investigates complaints against

---

13. Tex. Admin. Code tit. 22, § 681.45 (1987). Felony conviction is also grounds for license revocation or suspension.
14. Tex. Rev. Civ. Stat. Ann. art. 4512g (Vernon Supp. 1987). Marriage and family counselors are exempt as long as they have a master's or doctoral degree in marriage or family counseling and confine their practice exclusively to family or marriage counseling.
15. Tex. Rev. Civ. Stat. Ann. art. 4512g § 16 (Vernon Supp. 1987).

licensees. If the Board determines that a complaint necessitates a hearing, the Board is required to notify the licensee.

Disciplinary Procedure

Any person may submit a complaint against a licensee to the Board. The Board is required to notify the licensee of all complaints and may hold an investigative hearing.[16] The licensee is required to receive notice of the hearing at least 10 days prior to the hearing and has the right to have counsel present and call witnesses at the hearing. The Board's investigative powers, including the power to issue subpoenas, ensure that the licensee may produce any necessary information or witness at the hearing. Licensees may appeal any final Board decision within 30 days to the district court in Travis County, Texas.[17]

Penalties

Persons who knowingly represent themselves to the public as licensed professional counselors when in fact they are not licensed are guilty of a Class B misdemeanor. The punishment is a fine of not more than $1,000 and/or confinement for not more than 180 days.[18]

---

16. Tex. Rev. Civ. Stat. Ann. art. 4512g § 16(b) (Vernon Supp. 1987); Tex. Admin. Code tit. 22, §§ 681.75, 681.94 (1987).
17. *See* Tex. Rev. Civ. Stat. Ann. art. 6252-13a (Vernon Supp. 1987) (the Administrative Procedure Act and Texas Register Act govern appeals and the procedure for Board hearings).
18. Tex. Rev. Civ. Stat. Ann. art. 4512g § 15(a)-(b) (Vernon Supp. 1987).

1.7b

Endorsement and Regulation of School Counselors

The Texas Board of Education governs the certification of counselors in the Texas school system.[1] Counselors must have a professional counselor certificate for all levels of education from preschool through high school and are also required to have:[2]

1. a valid Texas teacher certificate;
2. 3 years of teaching experience; and
3. a minimum of a master's degree in counseling, focusing on guidance and development of youth, and testing techniques.[3]

To qualify for the basic teacher certificate, an applicant must be:[4]

1. a citizen of the United States,
2. at least eighteen years old, and
3. of good moral character.[5]

---

1. Tex. Educ. Code Ann. §§ 11.26, 13.032 (Vernon 1987).
2. Tex. Admin. Code tit. 19, § 141.241 (1987). Counselors at a Texas state university must fulfill the same requirements as counselors in the public school system. Counselors at private universities normally must meet the same criteria, although the school may alter the requirements to meet its needs.
3. A master's degree is defined as a minimum of 30 graduate level hours in counseling from an approved institution. Additionally, special requirements are necessary for special education or vocational education counselors. Tex. Admin. Code tit. 19, § 141.241 (1987).
4. Tex. Admin. Code tit. 19, § 141.3 (1987).
5. The applicant needs three individual recommendations or a recommendation from an approved college to satisfy the moral character requirement. Further, a conviction of a felony or any crime involving moral turpitude is grounds for refusal to certify. Tex. Admin. Code tit. 19, § 141.3 (1987).

Additionally, the applicant must pass the teacher competency examination given by the Board of Education and be able to speak, read, and write English.[6] Applicants are also required either to take college courses or to pass an examination on the United States and Texas constitutions. All teachers and counselors must register their certificates with the school district of their employment.[7]

The state commissioner of education may issue a valid Texas teacher's certificate or a professional counselor's certificate to an out-of-state applicant who:[8]

1. has a current out-of-state teacher certificate, if the state's certificate is substantially the equivalent of a Texas certificate; or
2. has a current professional counselor certificate or teacher certificate from another state, if the state also requires a professional counselor to hold a teacher certificate.

Exemption From Other Licensure and Certification

A public school counselor is exempt from the requirements for licensed professional counselors, psychologists, and psychiatrists, provided the counselor performs only the services required by the teaching contract, abides by the teaching professional code of ethics, and does not charge for any services rendered. If the counselor desires to engage in private practice, the counselor is required to fulfill the appropriate licensure or certification requirements.[9]

Evaluation and Discipline

The same rules that govern teaching in general in Texas also govern public school counselors.[10] Public school counselors are evaluated annually according to written guidelines.[11] The board of trustees may consider the evaluations when considering the re-

---

6. Tex. Educ. Code Ann. § 13.032 (Vernon 1987).
7. Tex. Educ. Code Ann. § 13.045 (Vernon 1987).
8. Tex. Admin. Code tit. 19, § 141.181 (1987).
9. Tex. Admin. Code tit. 19, § 141.181 (1987).
10. Tex. Educ. Code Ann. § 21.021 (Vernon 1987).
11. The evaluation criteria include observation of the counselor/teacher performance, personal development, and instructional theories and presentation. Tex. Admin. Code tit. 19, § 149.42 (1987). *See also* Tex. Educ. Code Ann. §§ 21.201-21.203 (Vernon Supp. 1987) (rules for teacher contracts).

newal of the teacher's contract. While the professional counselor certificate is valid for life, counselors and teachers follow a contract system with each school district for employment.[12] If the board of trustees for a school district chooses not to renew a contract, it must give the counselor written notice, on or before April 1 of the year in which the contract terminates, stating the reasons for the decision not to renew.[13]

If a contract is not renewed, the counselor is entitled to a hearing with the board of trustees.[14] The counselor may appeal to the Board of Education if the board of trustees upholds its decision not to renew and then to the district court in Travis County, Texas. The board of trustees may, however, terminate a counselor for good cause at any time during a contract term.

Grounds for revocation, suspension, or cancellation of a teacher certificate or professional counselor certificate include:[15]

1. violation of the laws pertaining to teaching or the teaching code of ethics,
2. determination that the counselor/teacher is "unworthy to instruct the youth of Texas," or
3. abandonment of the employment contract.

The board of trustees or the Board of Education may also issue formal reprimands or place a teacher/counselor on probation.

The teacher/counselor is required to receive notice of a pending revocation or suspension and has a right to a hearing before the board of trustees. The teacher/counselor may appeal the trustees' final decision to the district court in Travis County, Texas. The counselor may petition for reinstatement of the certificate upon adequate proof to the Board of Education that the counselor is qualified to be a teacher.

Finally, the Commission on Education, in conjunction with the Board of Education, has the power to investigate claims against a counselor and hold formal hearings concerning any claims. The counselor has a right to counsel at these hearings and a right to call witnesses. The Commissioner of Education makes a recommendation to the Board of Education after the hearing for suspension or revocation, if necessary. If the Board of Education grants the re-

12. Tex. Admin. Code tit. 19, § 141.2 (1987).
13. If the board fails to give the written notice, the contract automatically renews for 1 year. Tex. Educ. Code Ann. § 21.204 (Vernon Supp. 1987).
14. The counselor must make a written request for the hearing within 10 days of receiving the board's notification. The hearing must be held within 15 days. Tex. Educ. Code Ann. § 21.204 (Vernon 1987).
15. Tex. Educ. Code Ann. § 13.046 (Vernon 1987). Suspensions may not exceed 2 years.

vocation or suspension, the counselor may appeal to the district court in Travis County, Texas.[16]

Any willful alteration or change in a teacher/counselor certificate or diploma is a felony, punishable by confinement in the state penitentiary for not less than 2 years but not more than 7 years.[17]

---

16. Tex. Educ. Code Ann. §§ 13.213, 13.214 (Vernon 1987).
17. Tex. Educ. Code Ann. § 4.10 (Vernon 1987).

1.8

Certification and Regulation of Marriage and Family Therapists

Texas does not regulate the licensure and certification of marriage and family counselors directly. Further, marriage and family counselors are exempt from other licensing requirements such as those for psychologist licensing and professional counselor licensing.[1] To qualify for these exemptions, however, marriage and family counselors must "provide counseling exclusively related to marriage and family concerns,"[2] have a master's or doctoral degree in marriage and family therapy from an accredited institution, and adhere to the code of ethics recognized by marriage and family counselors.

1. Tex. Rev. Civ. Stat. Ann. art. 4512c § 22 (Vernon Supp. 1987); Tex. Rev. Civ. Stat. Ann. art. 4512g § 3(7) (Vernon Supp. 1987).
2. *Id.*

1.9

Certification and Regulation of Hypnotists

Hypnosis is often practiced by psychiatrists and psychologists who are regulated as such by their respective regulatory agencies. Hypnosis is not, however, a separately regulated form of therapy. There are no specific provisions for licensure or certification of hypnotists in Texas.

1.10

Licensure and Regulation of Polygraph Examiners

The Polygraph Examiners Board (Board) regulates the licensure and regulation of polygraph examiners in Texas.[1] The law applies to the use of any instrument used to detect deception, covering lie detectors, polygraphs, deceptographs, and related devices. The Polygraph Examiners Act prohibits the use of any instrument that does not visually, permanently, and simultaneously record the cardiovascular and respiratory patterns of the subject. The Board establishes the criteria for licensure, regulates advertising, and promulgates rules for the regulation of polygraph examiners.

Polygraph Examiners Board

The Board consists of six members who have the following powers and duties:[2]

1. enacting and enforcing rules for the administration of the Polygraph Examiners Act;
2. regulating advertising to prevent false and misleading practices;
3. establishing criteria for licensure; and
4. issuing reprimands, revocations, and other disciplinary measures.

1. Tex. Rev. Civ. Stat. Ann. art. 4413(29cc) (Vernon Supp. 1987).
2. Tex. Rev. Civ. Stat. Ann. art. 4413(29cc) §§ 6, 17, 19 (Vernon Supp. 1987).

Licensure

The Board may license an applicant who:[3]

1. has not been convicted of a felony or crime involving moral turpitude,
2. has a baccalaureate degree from an accredited institution or 5 years of investigative experience immediately preceding the application,
3. is a graduate of a Board-approved polygraph examiners' course with a minimum of a 6-month internship; and
4. has passed the Board examination.

Additionally, applicants must obtain a surety or insurance bond for $5,000 as security for any judgment that may be rendered against the licensee for acts relating to professional services.[4] The Board may waive licensure requirements for an applicant who holds a valid license from another state if the state's licensure requirements are substantially the same as the requirements in Texas.

Renewal

Polygraph examiners must renew their licenses annually by paying a renewal fee.[5] Examiners may renew expired licenses for up to 2 years after the expiration date by paying late charges in addition to the normal renewal fee. If a license has been expired for more than 2 years, the license may be renewed only if all requirements necessary to obtain an original license, including reexamination, are satisfied.

Revocation and Reprimand

The Board may refuse to issue or renew a license; cancel, revoke, or suspend a license; or issue a reprimand if a polygraph examiner:[6]

1. fails to inform a subject of the nature of the examination or that participation is voluntary;
2. materially misrepresents information on a licensure application;
3. willfully disregards rules, for example, makes false reports of an examination;

---

3. Tex. Rev. Civ. Stat. Ann. art. 4413(29cc) § 8(a)-(c) (Vernon Supp. 1987).
4. Tex. Rev. Civ. Stat. Ann. art. 4413(29cc) § 8(b) (Vernon Supp. 1987).
5. Tex. Rev. Civ. Stat. Ann. art. 4413(29cc) § 17(a) (Vernon Supp. 1987).
6. Tex. Rev. Civ. Stat. Ann. art. 4413(29cc) § 19(1)-(13) (Vernon Supp. 1987).

4. is convicted of a felony or crime involving moral turpitude;
5. engages in false or misleading advertising;
6. demonstrates incompetency;
7. allows another person who is not licensed to use the polygraph examiner's license;
8. assists a person in a violation of any rule pertaining to polygraph examiners;
9. is judged to be mentally incompetent or a "habitual drunkard" by a court;
10. fails to respond to the Board regarding a complaint or investigation within a reasonable period of time;
11. fails to inform a subject of examination results if the subject requests the information;
12. violates the confidentiality of any examination information.[7]

Disciplinary Procedure

Any polygraph examiner whose license is revoked or suspended or who is denied a license is entitled to a hearing before the Board.[8] The Board is required to investigate complaints, notifying the polygraph examiner at least 10 days prior to a hearing of the date, place, and nature of the hearing.[9] A polygraph examiner may appeal a final Board decision within 30 days, either to the district court in the county where the polygraph examiner resides or the district court of Travis County, Texas.

Penalties

If a polygraph examiner violates the Polygraph Examiners Act or if a person impersonates a polygraph examiner, the person is guilty of a misdemeanor. The punishment is a fine of not less than $100 but not more than $1,000 and/or confinement of not more than 6 months.[10]

---

7. Tex. Rev. Civ. Stat. Ann. art. 4413(29cc) § 19(a)-(c) (Vernon Supp. 1987). All information obtained from an examination is confidential and may only be disclosed to the subject, a person whom the subject designates in writing, the person or business requesting the examination, other polygraph examiners for private consultation, or as the law may require.
8. Tex. Rev. Civ. Stat. Ann. art. 4413(29cc) § 22(a)-(b) (Vernon Supp. 1987).
9. *See* Tex. Rev. Civ. Stat. Ann. art. 6252-13a (Vernon Supp. 1987). Polygraph examiners have a right to counsel and a right to call witnesses on their behalf at the hearing.
10. Tex. Rev. Civ. Stat. Ann. art. 4413(29cc) § 26(a) (Vernon Supp. 1987); Tex. Penal Code Ann. § 12.22 (Vernon 1976). This includes violating the confidentiality requirements regarding examination information.

1.11

Sunset of Credentialing Agencies

Certain regulatory agencies are subject to the "sunset law," which provides for periodic review by the state legislature.[1] Under the sunset law, the statutory authority establishing the agency automatically expires on a certain date. The legislature may reenact the statute or change the statute due to new developments in society or the profession. The Texas law states that "the legislature should review proposed regulatory programs to better evaluate the need for the program" and "regulation should not be imposed on any profession or other occupation unless required for the protection of the health, safety, or welfare of the residents of the state."[2] MHPs who are subject to the sunset law are licensed professional counselors, psychologists, psychological associates, psychiatric nurses, and psychiatrists.[3]

---

1. *See* Tex. Rev. Civ. Stat. Ann. art. 5429k-1 (Vernon Supp. 1987).
2. Tex. Rev. Civ. Stat. Ann. art. 5429k-1 (Vernon Supp. 1987).
3. *See* Tex. Rev. Civ. Stat. Ann. art. 4512c § 4(a) (psychologists); Tex. Rev. Civ. Stat. Ann. art. 4512g § 21 (professional counselors); Tex. Rev. Civ. Stat. Ann. art. 4513a (psychiatric nurses); Tex. Rev. Civ. Stat. Ann. art. 4495b § 5.10 (psychiatrists). All of these statutory schemes expire on September 1, 1993.

Section 2

Forms of Business Practice

2.1

Sole Proprietorships

A sole proprietor is a person who owns a business alone with no formal business form or organization. Unlike a corporation or partnership, an MHP who is a sole proprietor has no special law regulating the practice. (See Chapters 2.2 and 2.3 for discussions of these other business forms.) Instead, general business law, including contract, agency, employment, tax, and state and local licensing laws, govern sole proprietorships. The assets of the proprietorship are the assets of the owner; the liabilities and obligations of the proprietorship are the direct liabilities and obligations of the owner. The owner and all his or her personal and other assets are subject to these proprietary liabilities. There is no limited liability as in a partnership or corporation.

2.2

Professional Corporations

Generally, MHPs may choose to practice in one of three forms of business: sole proprietorships (see Chapter 2.1), partnerships (see Chapter 2.3), and professional corporations. A professional corporation (PC) is similar in many respects to a regular business corporation, thus giving the MHP certain tax and practice benefits. One important requirement is that an MHP must incorporate under the special professional corporation law, rather than under the general business incorporation law.[1] Additionally, physicians have a separate law under which they are required to incorporate, if they so choose, rather than the professional corporation law.[2]

Benefits of Incorporation

Perhaps the major benefit of becoming a PC is tax deductions, since the corporation may deduct expenses for insurance, death benefits, and pension plans. Thus, an employee of the PC receives these benefits tax-free and the corporation receives a business expense deduction. Another major benefit of becoming a PC is that when there is more than one shareholder, the shareholders share liability in addition to having liability limited to the amount

---

1. Tex. Rev. Civ. Stat. Ann. art. 1528e (Vernon Supp. 1988). A "professional corporation" is a "corporation organized . . . for the sole and specific purpose of rendering professional service and which has as its shareholders only individuals who themselves are duly licensed or otherwise authorized within this state to render the same professional service as the corporation." *Id.*
2. *Id.* Also, professionals may form a professional association, which is distinct from either a professional corporation or a partnership. *See* Tex. Rev. Civ. Stat. Ann. art. 1528f (Vernon Supp. 1988).

of the investment in the corporation. Finally, because PCs are required to hold meetings of shareholders, issue reports, and keep records, the members may become more sensitive to the business ramifications of practice.

Incorporation and Operation Practice

A PC may only organize to perform one type of professional service.[3] Every shareholder, director, officer, and employee is required to have a license or certificate to render the particular professional service. The PC, however, may employ ancillary personnel such as bookkeepers, secretaries, and technicians, provided the personnel do not render any service beyond that for which they are qualified.[4] If any member becomes disqualified to render services, or if a person gains possession of the shares (e.g., by inheritance) who is not licensed or certified, the PC is required to purchase the shares at a fair price.

Incorporating as a PC requires filing articles of incorporation with the secretary of the state that state the name of the corporation, the names and addresses of the members, the purpose of the corporation, the directors' names, and the duration of the corporation.[5] The name of the PC is required to reflect the corporate status, and may include "P.C." if desired rather than "Inc.," "Co.," or "Corp." PCs enjoy the same privileges of normal business corporations except for the specific limitations provided for PCs, such as the requirement that members be duly licensed and/or certified.

Liability and Accountability

When an MHP forms a PC, the professional relationship between the MHP and client is not altered.[6] For example, all information that was confidential remains so. Additionally, the corporation and the shareholders are jointly and severally liable for any errors, negligence, or incompetence on the part of any employee. Joint and several liability means that an individual shareholder is not only liable for the acts of employees and officers, but also that the individual shareholder can be held responsible for the entire

3. Tex. Rev. Civ. Stat. Ann. art. 1528e (Vernon Supp. 1988).
4. Tex. Rev. Civ. Stat. Ann. art. 1528e § 15 (Vernon Supp. 1988).
5. Tex. Rev. Civ. Stat. Ann. art 1528e § 4 (Vernon Supp 1988).
6. Tex. Rev Civ. Stat. Ann. art. 1528e § 16 (Vernon Supp 1988).

amount of damages, with an accompanying right to then look to the other shareholders for contribution.

Additionally, a PC may not carry out any act in contravention of the laws relating to the specific profession.[7] Thus, as previously indicated, if any shareholder, officer, or director becomes legally disqualified to render professional services, the corporation is required to purchase the person's shares and terminate all interests with the person, as provided for in the articles of incorporation, bylaws, or stock purchase agreement.

Termination of the Professional Corporation

A PC may be terminated in two ways. If there is a vote by at least two thirds of the shareholders at a meeting, the shareholders can elect to terminate the PC. The shareholders may also give unanimous consent to terminate the PC without a meeting.

7. Tex. Rev Civ. Stat Ann. art. 1528e § 5 (Vernon Supp 1988).

2.3 Partnerships

A partnership is "an association of two or more persons to carry on as co-owners a business for profit."[1] This may be beneficial to participants by allowing the partners to carry on a more complex business due to the pooling of resources. A partnership, however, also creates liability for every other partner for each partner's acts. Even if professionals do not expressly agree to create a partnership, the law may determine that a partnership exists if the professionals share both the profits (and possibly losses) and the control of the business.[2] Therefore, MHPs should be familiar with partnerships even if they are not express partners in a partnership.

Formation of a Partnership

A general partnership is formed when two persons agree to carry on a business as co-owners. In the absence of a formal partnership agreement, partners share in the profits and management of the partnership on an equal basis. However, in most instances, a partnership will be formed by formal agreement. According to the law in Texas, the primary factor in formal partnership formation is an agreement to share the profits of the business, whether or not

1. Tex. Rev. Civ. Stat. Ann. art. 6132b (Vernon 1980). Additionally, Texas law expressly provides for the formation of professional associations if the association files certain information with the secretary of state, such as the members' names, type of service offered, and name and address of the association. Tex. Rev. Civ. Stat. Ann. art. 1528f (Vernon Supp. 1988).
2. Tex. Rev. Civ. Stat. Ann. art. 6132b § 7 (Vernon Supp. 1988).

on an equal basis.[3] Thus, one partner may receive 75% of the profits while the other partner receives only 25%. Usually, a partner's interest corresponds to the capital contribution of the partner in the business, meaning that in the example given one may have originally contributed $75,000 and the other $25,000. However, the percentage of profits for each partner is an element to be decided by the partners during negotiation, and the law does not mandate any certain percentages.

The law provides that profit sharing for the following purposes will not create a partnership without more proof that a partnership exists: loans and/or interest on a loan, wages for employees, debt repayments, annuities, payments for the goodwill or sale of a business, and mineral interest payments.[4]

Finally, a partnership does not have to file any documents with the secretary of state as do corporations. Additionally, it is not required to have any formal written documentation, although the partners may desire documentation and a formal partnership agreement. Thus, even an oral agreement will suffice to create a partnership.

Rights and Duties of Partners

The law imposes on partners certain rights and duties. Partners may agree to alter certain aspects of partnership law by formal agreement, while others such as liability remain fixed. Partners may, however, agree to indemnify each other for certain liabilities. Each partner, for example, is an agent of the partnership with equal management powers unless agreed otherwise.[5] Each partner also has the right to review and receive all partnership information and the right to rely on other partners to share partnership benefits.[6]

Partners may not, however, carry out certain acts without the unanimous consent of all the partners. These acts include disposing of the business' goodwill, submitting a partnership claim to

3. Tex. Rev. Civ. Stat. Ann. art. 6132b § 7 (Vernon Supp. 1988). In certain instances, the law makes exceptions. For example, if the share of the profits is merely for payment of an installment debt, a partnership will not be presumed. *Id.*
4. *Id.*
5. Tex. Rev. Civ. Stat. Ann. art. 6132b § 9 (Vernon Supp. 1988). Thus, every partner may bind the partnership if the transaction is one that is apparently for partnership purposes, unless the person transacting the business with the partner knows that the partner has no power to perform the particular act. *Id.*
6. Tex. Rev. Civ. Stat. Ann. art. 6132b §§ 18, 20-21 (Vernon Supp. 1988). Additionally, unless the partners agree otherwise, the partners share the profits equally. *Id.*

arbitration, acting in a manner that makes carrying on the partnership business impossible, assigning partnership property to creditors or other debt payment, confessing a judgment, and acting in contravention of the partnership agreement.[7]

Additionally, the partnership as an entity and the partners individually are bound by any admission or representation by a partner concerning partnership business.[8] If a partner is notified or has knowledge of an act, except in cases of fraud, the partnership as an entity will be presumed to know of the act.[9] Finally, "where, by any wrongful act or omission of any partner acting in the ordinary course of the business of the partnership or with the authority of his co-partners, loss or injury is caused to any person . . . or penalty is incurred,"[10] the partnership, as well as the partners, is liable for the wrong to the injured party. Partnership liability is joint and several, as in professional corporations, making each partner potentially responsible for the full amount of damages, regardless of whether the particular partner is the one who committed the wrong.[11]

Dissolution of a Partnership

A partnership may or may not dissolve when a partner ceases to be associated with the partnership, depending on the terms of the partnership agreement.[12] A partnership may be dissolved by the following means, unless the partners provide otherwise in a partnership agreement:[13]

1. fulfillment of the specific partnership purpose,
2. the express request of any and/or all partner(s),
3. expulsion of any partner according to the terms of the partnership agreement,
4. a breach of the partnership agreement by any partner,
5. any event that makes it unlawful to continue the partnership business,
6. the death of any partner,

---

7. Tex. Rev. Civ. Stat. Ann. art. 6132b § 9(3) (Vernon Supp. 1988).
8. Tex. Rev. Civ. Stat. Ann. art. 6132b § 11 (Vernon Supp. 1988).
9. Tex. Rev. Civ. Stat. Ann. art. 6132b § 12 (Vernon Supp. 1988).
10. Tex. Rev. Civ. Stat. Ann. art. 6132b § 13 (Vernon Supp. 1988).
11. Tex. Rev. Civ. Stat. Ann. art. 6132b § 15 (Vernon Supp. 1988). An incoming partner is liable for all partnership obligations. *Id.* § 17. This liability, however, is limited to the value of the incoming partner's partnership property, and the incoming partner is not personally liable for any amount not covered by the partnership property. *Id.*
12. Tex. Rev. Civ. Stat. Ann. art. 6132b §§ 29-30 Vernon Supp. 1988).
13. Tex. Rev. Civ. Stat. Ann. art. 6132b §§ 31-32 (Vernon Supp. 1988).

7. the bankruptcy of any partner, or
8. a court decree.

A court may decree that a partnership is required to dissolve if:

1. a partner is declared to be mentally incompetent by a court or becomes incapable of performing partnership duties;
2. a partner performs any act that prejudicially affects the partnership business;
3. a partner "willfully or persistently commits a breach of the partnership agreement, or otherwise so conducts himself in matters relating to the partnership business" so that it is not practicable to carry on the business with that partner;
4. the business can only perform at a loss; or
5. other circumstances indicate that dissolution is a fair resolution for the business.

If a partnership dissolves, the partners may only carry out acts that are necessary to "wind up" the partnership affairs and settle partnership accounts.[14] Thus, the partners may no longer bind the partnership and other partners unless the person transacting business has no knowledge of the dissolution.[15] Dissolution, however, does not terminate a partner's liability, which does not formally end until the partnership business is completely settled.[16]

---

14. Tex. Rev. Civ. Stat. Ann. art. 6132b § 33 (Vernon Supp. 1988)
15. Tex. Rev. Civ. Stat. Ann. art. 6132b § 35 (Vernon Supp. 1988).
16. Tex. Rev. Civ. Stat. Ann. art. 6132b § 36 (Vernon Supp. 1988).

2.4

Health Maintenance Organizations

A health maintenance organization (HMO) is any person or organization who provides health care services to the public on a prepaid basis.[1] The HMO may cover a single service or an overall health care plan. The services are provided by employees or professionals associated with the HMO.

Benefits for Mental Health Services

To provide services for an HMO, an MHP is required to have all necessary state licenses and/or authorization.[2] This requirement includes, for example, physicians, nurses, and hospital staff. The law, however, does not expressly include mental health services, defining coverage instead as medical, emergency, dental, hospitalization, or any service "for the purpose of preventing, alleviating, curing or healing human illness or injury."[3] Thus, mental health services are presumably covered if the services fit any of the categories, or if the HMO contract expressly covers such services.[4]

Additionally, the law does not expressly provide employment criteria other than the licensing/authorization requirement. An HMO, therefore, should be able to employ any MHP it desires

1. Tex. Ins. Code Ann. § 20A.02 (Vernon Supp. 1988). The expenses not covered by the contract price are guaranteed and paid by a sponsoring organization, such as an employer. *Id.*
2. *Id.*
3. *Id.*
4. The law provides that an HMO may cover mental health services, even though they are not required to cover such services. Tex. Admin. Code tit. 25, § 119.7 (1987).

who is duly licensed or authorized. Finally, because the HMO has a separate reimbursement service system, the ordinary insurance rules for coverage do not apply to HMOs.

2.5

Preferred Provider Organizations

Preferred provider organizations (PPOs) are groups of health care providers and/or hospitals that contract with unions, employers, or third parties such as Blue Cross/Blue Shield to provide health services to employees and members at a discounted rate in exchange for an exclusive contract.

In Texas, however, there is no law expressly regulating PPOs. Thus, it is uncertain whether the state's insurance laws cover their services.

2.6

Individual Practice Associations

Individual Practice Associations (IPAs) are groups of health care providers, including MHPs, who contract to provide services on a prepaid basis for health service organizations such as HMOs. IPAs retain their private practice and may, if they choose, provide additional services to private clients. IPAs' work for the provider organization, however, is on a fee-for-service or fee-per-person basis. Texas law does not expressly address IPAs. In the absence of express law, therefore, traditional contract law should apply.

2.7

Hospital, Administrative, and Staff Privileges

The law in many states provides certain requirements for holding a hospital staff, agency, or administrative position. In Texas, for hospitals to be licensed, the medical staff must consist of physicians licensed to practice medicine in Texas.[1] Additionally, to serve on a hospital's staff, an individual must fulfill any criteria set by the hospital's governing body, as well as those set by the Hospital Licensing Agency and Hospital Licensing Advisory Council.

Hospital Staff Privileges

Individuals desiring to obtain staff privileges at a hospital are required to submit an application and seek approval from the hospital's board of managers or directors.[2] Each hospital may adopt rules and requirements relating to "qualifications for medical staff appointments or any categories thereof, termination of appointments, the delineation of clinical privileges or the curtailment of clinical privileges of those who are appointed to the medical staff so long as those rules, regulations, and requirements are determined on a reasonable basis, such as professional and ethical qualifications of the applicant for medical staff membership."[3] The hospital may deny privileges for any nonprohibited reason. Examples of prohibited reasons are sex and race. Thus, the fact

1. Tex. Rev. Civ. Stat. Ann. art. 4437f (Vernon Supp. 1988). Also, a hospital must have at least one or more physicians on the staff in order to obtain a license. *Id.*
2. Tex. Rev. Civ. Stat. Ann. art. 4437f § 17 (Vernon Supp. 1988).
3. Tex. Rev. Civ. Stat. Ann. art. 4437f § 18(5) (Vernon Supp. 1988).

that a physician is licensed to practice medicine in Texas does not guarantee that the physician may serve as staff at a hospital. To admit a patient, a person must be a member of the medical staff and provide for the general care of the patient.

2.8

Zoning for Community Homes

Zoning laws allow cities to regulate growth by permitting regulation of what particular building uses, i.e., commercial or residential, are permitted in an area and even what type of structural design a building may have. Unfortunately, although zoning serves this useful purpose, it has also been used in the past to exclude certain uses or classes of people from an area or city.[1] Some cities, for example, enacted laws which prohibited homes for the mentally retarded from entering the city or which prohibited low-income housing in the city.[2]

Aside from challenging a zoning ordinance on a discriminatory basis if the zoning does not serve a legitimate purpose, the law in Texas also provides that certain residential facilities automatically fulfill any use criteria to preclude exclusionary tactics. For example, a community home for disabled persons who have either substantial physical or mental impairments or both is automatically a "permitted use" in any residentially zoned area in any city.[3]

To qualify as a community home for disabled persons, the home must have no more than six disabled persons, with two supervisory personnel, living at the home at any time and must provide the following services:

1. Such actions are termed "exclusionary zoning" and may be challenged successfully if the particular zoning ordinance does not serve the intended purpose of furthering the public health, safety, and welfare.
2. *See* City of Cleburne v. Cleburne Living Center, 473 U.S. 432 (1985) (city passing ordinance preventing group home for the mentally retarded from entering the city).
3. Tex. Rev. Civ. Stat. Ann. art. 1011n (Vernon Supp. 1988).

1. food and shelter,
2. personal guidance,
3. care,
4. habilitation services, and
5. supervision.[4]

Additionally, a community home may not be located within one-half mile of a previously established community home and is required to obtain a license to operate from the state. The only other restriction on a community home relates to the number of vehicles which the residents may keep on the premises.[5]

4. Tex. Rev. Civ. Stat. Ann. art. 1011n § 3 (Vernon Supp. 1988).
5. *Id.* Additionally, the law provides for community centers for the mentally retarded or mentally deficient. Tex. Rev. Civ. Stat. Ann. art. 5547-203 (Vernon Supp. 1988). These facilities, however, contract with the city for both operation and location and the city may not establish one unless the home would serve at least a population of 200,000. *Id.*

Section 3

Insurance Reimbursement and Deductions for Services

3.1

Insurance Reimbursement for Services

Health insurance carriers may limit reimbursement for mental health services to specific types of treatments or specific MHP services. Because insurers may limit and deny claims by MHPs or their patients unless the law explicitly provides otherwise, each policy may differ and the best assurance of coverage is familiarity with the policy in question.[1]

Every policy in Texas for certain types of insurance has specific definitions for terms such as "major medical expense" and minimum requirements for coverage. A "major medical expense" coverage is required to include reimbursement for physician visits, both in and out of the hospital, for not less than $10 per visit or an annual aggregate of not less than $600.[2] Additionally, the major medical expense insurance must include at least three of the following benefits: in-hospital, private-duty registered nurse services; nursing home care; treatment by a radiologist or physiotherapist; rental of medical equipment; artificial limbs, casts, braces, or other similar care; treatment for mental, emotional, or nervous disorders; and prescription drugs.

Generally, insurers may exclude coverage for alcoholism,[3] veterans hospital services, nursing home or convalescent center services, drug addiction treatment, or mental and nervous disorders treatment from hospital coverage as well as from accident and health insurance policies.[4] The definition of a mental and nervous disorder is "a neurosis, psychoneurosis, psychopathy,

---

1. Tex. Admin. Code tit. 28, § 3.3005 (1987).
2. Tex. Admin. Code tit. 28, § 3.3074 (1987).
3. Tex. Admin. Code tit. 28 § 3.3016 (1987). To exclude treatment for alcoholism, the insurer must expressly exclude the disease by name in the policy.
4. Tex. Admin. Code tit. 28, § 3.3006 (1987).

psychosis, or mental or emotional disease or disorder of any kind."[5]

Accident insurance policies cover "accidental bodily injury sustained by the insured person which is the direct result of an accident, independent of disease or bodily infirmity or any other cause," therefore excluding treatment of mental or emotional disorders.[6] Medicare supplement policies may also exclude coverage of mental or emotional disorders, alcoholism or drug addiction treatment, and suicide treatment.[7]

Finally, the definition of "physician services" includes only services rendered by an individual licensed to practice medicine in Texas. "Nursing services," however, include not only services by registered nurses but by licensed vocational nurses as well.[8]

---

5. Tex. Admin. Code tit. 28, § 3.3016 (1987).
6. Tex. Admin. Code tit. 28, § 3.3304 (1987).
7. Tex. Admin. Code tit. 28, § 3.3305 (1987).
8. Tex. Admin. Code tit. 28, § 3.3304 (1987). Insurers who exclude reimbursement for services by certain professionals must expressly state the exclusions in the policy.

3.2

Mental Health Benefits in State Insurance Plans

Insurers in Texas may issue policies covering crisis stabilization treatment for any acute psychiatric condition that is serious and substantially impairs the patient's "thought, perception of reality, emotional processes, or judgment, or grossly impairs behavior."[1] A licensed professional, whether physician, nurse, counselor, or psychologist, is required to render the services for coverage to apply.

Additionally, any policy for group insurance or any group hospital plan that reimburses costs for services that are within the scope of the practice of a licensed psychologist is required to cover the costs of such services whether rendered by a licensed physician or a licensed psychologist.[2] Moreover, no group policy for accident or sickness that reimburses treatment of mental or emotional disorders incurred at a hospital may exclude coverage for treatment of mental or emotional disorders provided at a licensed psychiatric day treatment center.[3]

1. Tex. Ins. Code Ann. § 3.72 (Vernon Supp. 1987).
2. Tex. Ins. Code Ann. § 21.35A (Vernon Supp. 1987).
3. Tex. Ins. Code Ann. § 3.70-2 (Vernon Supp. 1987). Coverage for psychiatric day center treatment must be no less favorable than the coverage for hospital expenses.

3.3

Tax Deductions for Services

Mental health expenses may be deductible as a personal medical expense deduction or as a business expense deduction. The deduction will depend on the nature of the services rendered and the taxpayer's use of the services.

Mental Health Services as a Medical Deduction

A taxpayer may deduct expenses for medical care not compensated by insurance or otherwise to the extent the expenses exceed 7.5% of the taxpayer's adjusted gross income.[1] Medical care expenses are "amounts paid for the diagnosis, cure, mitigation, treatment, or prevention of disease, or for the purpose of affecting any structure or function of the body."[2] Thus, the taxpayer may deduct expenses for psychologists, psychiatrists, psychotherapists, and "others rendering similar type services" related to medical care.[3] The taxpayer may also include medical expenses of a spouse and dependents.

Moreover, the law provides that:[4]

> The [Internal Revenue] Code and the regulations do not require a taxpayer to ascertain whether a practitioner is qualified, is authorized under state law, or is licensed to practice, before

1. 26 U.S.C. § 213(a) (1987).
2. 26 U.S.C. § 231(d). Additionally, medical care expenses include expenses related to transportation "primarily for and essential to medical care."
3. Rev. Rul. 143, 1953-2 C.B. 129; Rev. Rul. 91, 1963-1 C.B. 54.
4. Rev. Rul. 91, 1963-1 C.B. 54.

obtaining his services or claiming a medical expense deduction. . . . Accordingly, it is held that amounts paid for medical expenses rendered by practitioners, such as chiropractors, psychotherapists, and others rendering similar services, constitute expenses for 'medical care' within the provisions of section 213 of the Code, even though the practitioners who perform the services are not required by law to be, or are not licensed, certified, or otherwise qualified to perform such services.

Mental Health Services as a Business Deduction

If the taxpayer uses mental health services in operating a business, the taxpayer may deduct the expenses as a business expense under section 162 of the Internal Revenue Code.[5] Section 162 provides that "all the ordinary and necessary expenses paid or incurred during the taxable year in carrying on any trade or business" are deductible. "Ordinary" means "common and accepted", while "necessary" means "appropriate and helpful."[6]

5. *See* 26 U.S.C. § 162 (1987).
6. *See* Welch v. Helvering, 290 U.S. 111 (1933).

Section 4

Privacy of Professional Information

4.1

Extensiveness, Ownership, Maintenance, and Access to Records

Psychologists

Extensiveness of Records

The maintenance of patient records is a requirement of good psychological practice and the law. The regulations issued by the Board of Examiners of Psychologists (Board) provide that:[1]

> Accurate, current, and pertinent records of essential psychological services must be maintained. These records may include, but are not limited to, identifying data, dates of services, types of services, and significant actions taken. Providers of psychological services insure that essential information concerning services rendered is appropriately recorded within a reasonable time of their completion.

The regulations do not specify what is essential information concerning the services rendered. It is clear, however, that a complete failure to maintain records is prohibited and that record keeping is deemed by the Board to be an important element of the rendition of competent services.

Maintenance of Records

The regulations requiring record keeping do not state a minimum time that the records must be maintained. The decision to maintain existing records should take into account the possibility of a professional malpractice action. The applicable statute of limita-

1. Tex Admin. Code tit. 22, § 465.22 (1987).

tions for professional malpractice liability is generally 2 years, but one should consider the possibility of its extension in certain cases.[2] Once a decision is made not to maintain existing records, a process of destruction should be undertaken that eliminates the possibility of records becoming available to unauthorized third persons.

Although psychologists in their own practice are not required to maintain their records for a minimum time period, private mental hospitals licensed under the Mental Health Code are authorized to dispose of medical records 10 years after the date of the patient's last treatment.[3] This provision may be read to imply an obligation to maintain these records until that time. This record-keeping requirement is not directly applicable to MHPs whose records are not required to be included in the hospital medical records. Because parallel issues may be presented in these sets of records, however, maintenance of the MHP's private office records for this same length of time in the case of patients who have been hospitalized is prudent.

Client Access

Neither the statutes creating the Board nor the regulations requiring the keeping of records address the question of client access to those records. A Texas court of appeals has ruled, however, that a patient has a common-law right to obtain access to the patient's own medical records.[4] Although this case did not involve records of mental health care, there is nothing in the court's reasoning to suggest a different outcome for those types of records.

Access by the Board of Examiners of Psychologists

The duty of confidentiality that otherwise applies to psychologist–patient communications and records of those communications is not applicable to disclosures to government agencies that are "required or authorized by law."[5] There is nothing explicit in the Board's enabling legislation that bears on its authority to compel disclosure of confidential communications. However, the Board's authority to investigate complaints about licensees[6] and to cancel, revoke, suspend, or refuse to renew a license or certificate[7]

2. Tex. Rev. Civ. Stat. Ann. art. 4590i § 10.01 (Vernon Supp. 1987). In the case of minors and injuries not discovered until after the statute of limitations has run, an additional time for bringing the action exists. Nelson v. Krusen, 678 S.W.2d 918 (Tex. 1984).
3. Tex. Rev. Civ. Stat. Ann. art. 5547-96A (Vernon Supp. 1988).
4. Hutchins v. Texas Rehabilitation Comm., 544 S.W.2d 802 (Tex. Civ. App.-Austin 1976).
5. Tex. Rev. Civ. Stat. Ann. art. 5561h § 4(b)(1) (Vernon Supp. 1987).
6. Tex. Rev. Civ. Stat. Ann. art. 4512c § 8(f), (g) (Vernon Supp. 1987).
7. Tex. Rev. Civ. Stat. Ann. art. 4512c § 23 (Vernon Supp. 1987).

would likely be construed by the courts as an implicit grant of power to compel disclosure of relevant confidential communications in its investigations of violations of its rules and regulations.

Hospital Medical Review Boards

Although the legislature has recognized a limitation on the compelled disclosure of information communicated to a hospital medical or peer review committee (for a discussion of the scope of this limitations, see Chapter 6.4), that legislation does not independently authorize these groups to obtain access to confidential information.[8] The confidentiality provisions applicable to psychologists do, however, provide an exception for disclosure of confidential information that does not identify the patient for "management audits, financial audits, program evaluations, or research."[9]

Liability for Violation

The failure to maintain patient records as required by the Board's regulations may result in the revocation, cancellation, or suspension of a psychologist's license or certification. In addition, because these regulations may be used to define the conduct of a reasonable psychologist in an action for professional malpractice liability, their violation may result in civil liability in an action for monetary damages when an injury to the patient results from a record-keeping failure.

Psychiatrists

Extensiveness of Records

The Medical Practice Act and the regulations issued by the Board of Medical Examiners do not refer to the maintenance of patient records generally. Thus, there is no general requirement that psychiatrists maintain records under Texas statutes or regulations. Notwithstanding the absence of any general record-keeping requirement, numerous other considerations such as reimbursement, specialty Board requirements, and common standards of good practice argue strongly in favor of comprehensive record keeping. The Medical Practice Act does, however, have a requirement for record keeping related to certain drugs. The Act includes the following within the definition of unprofessional conduct:[10]

8. Tex. Rev. Civ. Stat. Ann. art. 4447d (Vernon Supp. 1987).
9. Tex. Rev. Civ. Stat. Ann. art. 5561h § 4(b)(3) (Vernon Supp. 1987).
10. Tex. Rev. Civ. Stat. Ann. art. 4495b § 3.08(4)(B) (Vernon Supp. 1987).

> [F]ailing to keep complete and accurate records of purchases and disposals of drugs listed in the Texas Controlled Substances Act (Article 4476-15, Vernon's Texas Civil Statutes) or of controlled substances scheduled in the Federal Comprehensive Drug Abuse Prevention and Control Act of 1970, 21 U.S.C.A. Section 801 et seq. (Public Law 91-513). A physician shall keep records of his purchases and disposals of these drugs to include without limitation the date of purchase, the sale or disposal of the drugs by the physician, the name and address of the person receiving the drugs, and the reason for the disposing or dispensing of the drugs to the person. A failure to keep the records for a reasonable time is grounds for revoking, canceling, suspending, or probating the license of any practitioner of medicine. The board or its representative may enter and inspect a physician's place(s) of practice during reasonable business hours for the purpose of verifying the correctness of these records and taking inventory of the prescription drugs on hand.

Maintenance of Records

There is no provision in the Medical Practice Act for a minimum period for medical record storage. However, the decision to maintain existing records should take into account the applicable statute of limitations for professional malpractice liability, generally 2 years, and the possibility of its extension in certain cases.[11] Once a decision is made not to maintain existing records, a process of destruction should be undertaken that eliminates the possibility of records becoming available to unauthorized third persons.

Although psychiatrists are not individually in their practices required to maintain their records for a minimum time period, private mental hospitals licensed under the Mental Health Code are authorized to dispose of medical records 10 years after the date of the patient's last treatment.[12] This provision may be read to imply an obligation to maintain these records until that time. This record-keeping requirement is applicable only to institutional care and has no direct application to MHPs not required to include treatment records in the hospital medical records. Because parallel issues may be presented in these sets of records, however, maintenance of the MHP's private office records for this same time in the case of patients who have been hospitalized is prudent.

Client Access

There is no provision in the Medical Practice Act or the Board's regulations concerning patient access to medical records. The

11. Tex. Rev. Civ. Stat. Ann. art. 4590i § 10.01 (Vernon Supp. 1987). In the case of minors and injuries not discovered until after the statute of limitations has run, an additional time for bringing the action exists. Nelson v. Krusen, 678 S.W.2d 918 (Tex. 1984).
12. Tex. Rev. Civ. Stat. Ann. art. 5547-96A (Vernon Supp. 1988).

Medical Liability and Insurance Improvement Act does, however, make provision for the claimant/patient to obtain "complete and unaltered copies of the claimant's medical records from any other party within 10 days from the date of receipt of a written request for such records; provided, however, that the receipt of a medical authorization executed by the claimant herein shall be considered compliance by the claimant with this section."[13] In addition, a Texas court of appeals has ruled that a patient has a common-law right to obtain access to the patient's own medical records.[14] Although this case did not involve records of mental health care, there is nothing in the court's reasoning to suggest a different outcome for these types of records.

Access by The Board of Medical Examiners and Other Physicians

The duty of confidentiality that normally applies to physician–patient communications and records of those communications is excepted in disciplinary investigations and proceedings brought under the Medical Practice Act.[15] Thus, the Board may consider relevant portions of patient records in any disciplinary investigation or proceeding.

Hospital Medical Review Boards

Although the legislature has recognized a limitation on the compelled disclosure of information communicated to a hospital medical or peer review committee, that legislation does not independently authorize these groups to obtain access to confidential information.[16] The confidentiality provisions applicable to psychiatrists do, however, provide an exception for disclosure of confidential information that does not identify the patient for "management audits, financial audits, program evaluations, or research."[17]

Liability for Violation

The failure to keep complete and accurate records of the purchase and disposal of drugs, noted above, is a ground for refusing to

13. Tex. Rev. Civ. Stat. Ann. art. 4590i § 4.01(d) (Vernon Supp. 1987).
14. Hutchins v. Texas Rehabilitation Comm., 544 S.W.2d 802 (Tex. Civ. App.-Austin 1976).
15. Tex. Rev. Civ. Stat. Ann. art. 4495b § 5.08(g)(5), (6) (Vernon Supp. 1987). More specifically, the Board's regulations require the physician to provide the Board with medical records in the following situations: when accompanied by a release from the patient or the patient's legal representative; in response to a request for an explanation of an answer to a question on an application for license renewal; when the physician has been the subject of at least three professional liability lawsuits within a 3-year period, in an investigation of physician impairment; or in an inspection of controlled drug purchases and disposals. Tex. Admin. Code tit. 22, § 179.2.
16. Tex. Rev. Civ. Stat. Ann. art. 4447d (Vernon Supp. 1987).
17. Tex. Rev. Civ. Stat. Ann. art. 4495b § 5.08(h)(3) (Vernon Supp. 1987).

license or renew the license of a physician. In addition, inadequate record keeping of the purchase and disposal of these drugs may subject a physician to criminal prosecution under state and federal controlled substance laws.

4.2

Confidential Relations and Communications

The concept of confidentiality in a professional relationship between an MHP and a client involves an understanding that information communicated in this relationship will not be disclosed to third parties without the client's consent. The source of this understanding is rooted in assumptions about the necessity of confidentiality for effective therapy,[1] professional ethical codes,[2] and a legal recognition of a duty to maintain confidentiality.[3] Confidentiality and the duty to maintain it are not absolute, however. In the courtroom, the duty of confidentiality is not a legally recognized excuse to fail to obey a court order to disclose information relevant in a case. Rather, that issue is addressed under the law of privilege, discussed in Chapter 4.3. And, outside the courtroom, the duty of confidentiality is not necessarily a sufficient excuse to fail to take actions that may be necessary to protect the patient or others in society.

Psychologists

Scope of the Duty

The duty of psychologists to maintain confidentiality is not expressly mentioned in the statutes creating the Board of Examiners of Psychology (Board). The only oblique reference to confidential-

1. D. Shuman and M. Weiner, *The Psychotherapist–Patient Privilege: A Critical Examination* (1987).
2. American Medical Association, *The Principles of Medical Ethics*, 245 J. AM. MED. ASSOC. 2187-8 (1981); American Psychological Association, *Ethical Principles of Psychologists*, 36 AM. PSYCHOL. 633, 635 (1981).
3. Tex. Rev. Civ. Stat. Ann. art. 4495b § 5.08(l) (Vernon Supp. 1987).

ity in these statutes is a provision that a psychologist's license or certification may be revoked, canceled, or suspended for unprofessional conduct as defined by the Board.[4] The regulations issued by the Board contain two relevant provisions.

The first provision incorporates into the Board's rules relating to professional conduct the American Psychological Association's Code of Ethics:

> A violation of the code of ethics is unprofessional conduct and is a violation of the Board's rules.[5]

Principle 5, the relevant provision of the American Psychological Association Ethical Principles of Psychologists incorporated by this rule, provides that:

> Psychologists have a primary obligation to respect the confidentiality of information obtained from persons in the course of their work as psychologists. They reveal such information to others only with the consent of the person or the person's legal representative, except in those unusual circumstances in which not to do so would result in clear danger to the person or to others. Where appropriate, psychologists inform their clients of the legal limitations of confidentiality.[6]

The other relevant reference to confidentiality in the Board's rules provides that:

> A psychologist may not intentionally reveal information about a patient or client without written authorization by the patient, client, or guardian, or without a proper court order, or unless a state or federal statute requires it. A psychologist is bound by the provisions of Texas Civil Statutes article 5561h, unless some other state or federal law requires the psychologist to reveal the information.[7]

Article 5561h describes, among other things, a duty applicable to psychologists to keep confidential "records of the identity, diagnosis, evaluation, or treatment of a patient/client" when the patient consults the psychologist for the "purposes of diagnosis, evaluation, or treatment of any mental or emotional disorder."

Limitations on the Duty

Article 5561h, which defines a psychologist's duty of confidentiality, also provides for exceptions to that duty. The exceptions that apply outside of the courtroom are:[8]

---

4. Tex. Rev. Civ. Stat. Ann. art. 4512c § 23 (a) (5) (Vernon Supp. 1987).
5. Tex. Admin. Code tit. 22, § 461.3 (1987).
6. American Psychological Association, *Ethical Principles of Psychologists*, 36 AM. PSYCHOL. 633, 635 (1981).
7. Tex. Admin. Code tit. 22, § 465.2 (1987).
8. Tex. Rev. Civ. Stat. Ann. art. 5561h § 4(b)(1)-(6) (Vernon Supp. 1987). There is some degree of confusion over whether this provision survived the adop-

1. disclosures to governmental agencies authorized by law;
2. disclosures to medical or law enforcement personnel when there is probable imminent physical or emotional harm to the patient or physical harm to others;
3. disclosures for audits, evaluations, and research that do not identify patients;
4. disclosures consented to in writing by the patient or the patient's guardian or personal representative;
5. disclosures to third party payers; and
6. disclosures to other professionals jointly involved in the patient's treatment or diagnosis.

Similarly, Principle 5 of the American Psychological Association's Ethical Principles of Psychologists recognizes an exception to confidentiality when maintaining confidentiality would pose a clear danger to the patient or others.

Liability for Violation

An unauthorized breach of confidentiality is a basis for revocation, cancellation, or suspension of a psychologist's license or certification. In addition, it may provide the basis for a civil action seeking damages or an injunction against further disclosure. However, disclosure pursuant to a court order is absolutely privileged, and such a disclosure is immune from an action for damages.[9]

Psychiatrists

Scope of the Duty

The duty of a physician to maintain confidentiality is governed by a provision of the Medical Practice Act that the individuals revising the statutes for publication thought were repealed by the Rules of Evidence adopted by the Supreme Court of Texas and the Court of Criminal Appeals.[10] According to the Board, however, these provisions have been repealed only insofar as they address privilege issues, but not issues of confidentiality that are not addressed by the courts' Rules of Evidence. The confidentiality requirement

---

tion of the civil and criminal rules of evidence in Texas. Although the revisers assumed that the rules of evidence, which repealed article 5561h and section 5.08 of the Medical Practice Act to the extent that they were inconsistent, completely repealed these laws, the better position is that the rules of evidence only repealed the privilege rules contained in these laws and not the confidentiality provisions.

9. Leigh v. Parker, 740 S.W.2d 101 (Tex. Civ. App.-Austin 1987).
10. Tex. Rev. Civ. Stat. Ann. art. 4495b § 5.08 (Vernon Supp. 1987).

of the questionable section of the Medical Practice Act provides that "communications between [sic] one licensed to practice medicine, relative to or in connection with any professional services as a physician to a patient, is confidential and privileged and may not be disclosed except as provided in this section."[11]

Limitations on the Duty

Section 5.08 of the Medical Practice Act provides eight exceptions to the duty of confidentiality:[12]

1. disclosures to governmental agencies authorized by law;
2. disclosures to medical or law enforcement personnel when there is probable imminent physical or emotional harm to the patient or physical harm to others;
3. disclosures for audits, evaluations, and research that do not identify patients;
4. disclosures bearing on charges and services when necessary to collect a fee;
5. disclosures consented to in writing by the patient or the patient's guardian or personal representative;
6. disclosures to third party payers;
7. disclosures to other professionals jointly involved in the patient's treatment or diagnosis;
8. disclosures not identifying an individual patient in an official inquiry into a state school or hospital.

Liability for Violation

An unauthorized breach of confidentiality is a basis for revocation, cancellation, or suspension of a physician's license to practice. In addition, it may provide the basis for a civil action seeking damages or an injunction against further disclosure.[13] However, disclosure pursuant to a court order is absolutely privileged and is thus immune from an action for damages.[14]

11. Tex. Rev. Civ. Stat. Ann. art. 4495h § 5.08(a) (Vernon Supp. 1987).
12. Tex. Rev. Civ. Stat. Ann. art. 4495b § 5.08 (h)(1)-(8) (Vernon Supp. 1987).
13. Tex. Rev. Civ. Stat. Ann. art. 4495b § 5.08(l) (Vernon Supp. 1987).
14. Leigh v. Parker, 740 S.W.2d 101 (Tex. Civ. App.-Austin 1987).

4.3 Privileged Communications

The laws of confidentiality and privilege both address the privacy of communications between the client and the MHP. Confidentiality, discussed in Chapter 4.2, does not address issues of court-ordered disclosure and does not limit the power of a judge to order disclosure of relevant communications. Rather, that subject is treated in this chapter under the law of privilege.

Because of the division of authority for civil and criminal cases in the Texas courts, there are different rules of privilege in civil and criminal cases. In civil cases, there is a physician–patient privilege and a "confidentiality of mental health information" privilege. In criminal cases, a physician–patient privilege or mental health information privilege is not recognized. There is, however, a privilege for persons being treated for alcohol or drug abuse. And, for work done by an MHP for a client in connection with legal representation of that client, the attorney–client privilege may limit the power of a judge to compel disclosures of those communications.

Civil Proceedings

Physician–Patient Privilege

The physician–patient privilege applies to confidential communications between a physician and a patient made in the context of professional services rendered by the physician.[1] Although psy-

1. Tex. R. Evid. 509.

chiatrists, as physicians, are included within this privilege, nonmedical doctors, including psychologists, are not.

Confidentiality of Mental Health Information

This privilege applies to confidential communications between certain MHPs and their patients relating to the diagnosis, treatment, or evaluation of mental or emotional disorders.[2] The MHPs included are licensed physicians, persons licensed or certified by the state to treat mental or emotional disorders,[3] and persons involved in the treatment of drug abuse.

Assertion and Waiver of the Privilege

It should not be assumed that a court will raise the question of a privilege by itself. Therefore, particularly in situations in which the client is absent, it will be necessary for the MHP to raise the issue of privilege with the court. When this occurs, the court will be required to decide whether the communications were privileged when made, whether an exception to the privilege applies, and whether the patient has waived the privilege.

The court's determination of the validity of the privilege initially focuses on whether the professional's credentials meet the legal requirements for the operation of the privilege; whether the patient sought professional mental health services for diagnosis, evaluation, or treatment; and whether the communication between these persons took place in confidence.[4] The next question, the exceptions to the privilege, is discussed under the following topical heading.

The protections of the privilege may also be waived by the patient expressly or impliedly. Once the privilege has been waived by the patient, there is no independent right of an MHP to refuse to disclose the communications.

Limitations on the Scope of the Privilege

Both the physician–patient privilege and the confidentiality of mental health information contain exceptions. The exceptions contained in the physician–patient privilege include:[5]

---

2. Tex. R. Evid. 510.
3. See Section 1 for a discussion of MHP licensure and certification.
4. A communication may still be deemed confidential if it is disclosed to a third person who is "present to further the interest of the patient in the diagnosis, examination, evaluation, or treatment, or persons reasonably necessary for the transmission of the communication, or persons who are participating in the diagnosis, examination, evaluation, or treatment under the direction of the professional, including members of the patient's family." Tex. R. Evid. 510(a)(4); Tex. R. Crim. Evid. 509(a)(3).
5. Tex. R. Evid. 509(d)(1)-(7).

1. judicial or administrative proceedings brought against the physician by the patient;
2. disclosures consented to in writing by the patient or the patient's legal guardian or representative;
3. disclosures necessary to substantiate a claim for medical services;
4. disclosures relevant to the patient's attempt to collect damages for an impairment;
5. disclosures relevant in a disciplinary proceeding under the Medical Practice Act;
6. disclosures relevant in a lawsuit having to do with the parent–child relationship;
7. civil commitment proceedings;
8. proceedings involving claimed abuse or neglect of an institutionalized patient.

The exceptions contained in the confidentiality of mental health information section are largely the same as those set forth above, with three significant differences: (a) the confidentiality of mental health information has no exception for civil commitment proceedings; (b) it does have a specific exception for court-ordered examinations if the patient was first warned that the examination would not be privileged (one appellate court has required, in addition, that the subject of the examination be informed of a right to consult with counsel before submitting to the examination)[6]; and (c) it has no exception for disciplinary proceedings.

Criminal Proceedings

The physician–patient privilege and mental health information privilege do not apply in criminal cases.[7] The only limitation on compelled judicial disclosure of confidential communications between clients and MHPs recognized in criminal cases concerns treatment or examination of alcohol and drug abusers. A communication to any person involved in the treatment or examination of alcohol or drug abuse by a person being treated voluntarily or being examined for admission to treatment for alcohol or drug abuse is not admissible.[8] Therefore, an MHP can be compelled to disclose client communications relevant to an issue in a criminal

6. Lanett v. State, 750 S.W.2d 302 (Tex. Civ. App.-Dallas 1988)
7. Tex. R. Crim. Evid. 509.
8. Tex. R. Crim. Evid. 510.

proceeding, unless the communications concern voluntary treatment or examination for alcohol or drug abuse.

When an MHP works with an attorney on some aspect of the criminal case, the communications between the client and the MHP may be protected under the attorney–client privilege. If the MHP examines the client at the request of the attorney to assist the attorney in preparing or presenting the criminal case—for example, to evaluate whether the client would make an effective witness or whether an insanity defense should be raised—and the MHP provides a report only to the attorney and is not to be called as a witness at trial by that attorney, the attorney–client privilege prevents the prosecution from learning the contents of the MHP's communication with the client or the attorney.[9]

9. Ballew v. State, 640 S.W.2d 237 (Tex. Cr. App. 1982).

4.4

Search, Seizure, and Subpoena of Records

During a criminal investigation of an MHP or a client, a court may order a search and/or seizure of articles and records within the possession of the MHP. Normally, such an order is in the form of a subpoena or a search warrant. Under either method, an MHP should be aware of the law because these are major exceptions to the normal rules regarding confidentiality and privileged communications.

Search and Seizure

Under the fourth amendment to the United States Constitution, citizens are protected from unreasonable searches and seizures. A search is reasonable when conducted under a properly granted warrant, supported both by evidence to establish probable cause and a sworn affidavit. Additionally, Texas law reiterates this right.[1] Texas defines a search warrant as "a written order, issued by a magistrate and directed to a peace officer, commanding him to search for any property or thing and to seize the same and bring it before such magistrate."[2] The law also states that a court may not issue a search warrant unless it is supported by sufficient facts to "satisfy" the court that there is probable cause for the issuance

1. Tex. Code of Crim. Proc. Ann. § 1.06 (Vernon 1986). One significant fact regarding subpoenas and search warrants is the fact that merely because evidence is seized does not mean that the evidence will ultimately be admissible during a trial.
2. Tex. Code of Crim. Proc. Ann. § 18.01(a) (Vernon Supp. 1987).

and a sworn affidavit relating these facts filed with the court.[3] A search warrant may also direct a peace officer to arrest a person if the facts within the warrant support the conclusion that the party committed an offense or to search a person.[4]

Additionally, to be valid, a search warrant must sufficiently describe the property or person to be searched and/or seized and contain the following elements:[5]

1. a statement that it is issued in the name of the State of Texas,
2. a command authorizing a peace officer to conduct the search, and
3. the date and hour of issuance with the signature of the issuing magistrate.

Items that may be properly searched and seized include:

1. stolen property or other property for which acquisition is a crime;
2. property made for or commonly used in committing a crime;
3. arms or munitions for riots;
4. weapons that are illegal to possess;
5. gambling equipment or paraphernalia;
6. obscene materials for commercial distribution;
7. drugs made or kept illegally;
8. property for which possession is illegal;
9. instruments used in committing a crime;
10. "property or items, except the personal writings by the accused, constituting evidence of an offense" or showing that a particular party committed a crime; and
11. persons.

Further, when the search is for property or items constituting evidence of an offense or a party's guilt, the search warrant must also state the specific offense that has been committed and that the evidence sought is located at or in the possession of the person or place to be searched.[6]

An MHP may object to a search, but should do so only after seeking the advice of a lawyer. MHPs should also be aware that a police officer is authorized to use reasonable force when necessary

3. *Id.* Further, the party seeking the warrant may not rely merely on the party's own statement, but must provide the supporting facts or evidence to the court.
4. Tex. Code of Crim. Proc. Ann. § 18.03 (Vernon 1986).
5. Tex. Code of Crim. Proc. Ann. §§ 18.02, 18.04 (Vernon 1986).
6. Tex. Code of Crim. Proc. Ann. § 18.01 (Vernon 1986).

to execute the warrant.[7] Officers must, however, prior to using such force, identify themselves and state the purpose of the search or arrest if the purpose is not readily apparent. To use force, the officer must also reasonably believe that the search is lawful and that the warrant is valid.[8]

Subpoena

A subpoena is a written order from a court commanding a person to appear at a certain time to testify as a witness in a judicial proceeding.[9] A subpoena duces tecum is a written order from a court ordering a party to bring specified written records or other items and appear before the court. A sheriff or other government official may deliver a subpoena, which should be read in the presence of the person served. After the reading, the officer is required to return to the court and state the time and manner of service. If the subpoena is not served, the officer must provide an explanation for the failure.

Before a court may issue a subpoena or a subpoena duces tecum, either the defendant or the prosecution in the criminal case is required to make a written, sworn application to the court stating that the witnesses and materials are necessary to the case. The application for a subpoena should state the name and location of the witness and which party, the state or defendant, requested the witness.[10] Additionally, for a subpoena duces tecum to be valid, it must provide a reasonably accurate description of the desired papers. If one party subpoenas a witness, another subpoena is not necessary since the opposing side is entitled to question the witness.

A subpoena should not be disobeyed. If a witness fails to obey and appear at the stated time, the court may fine the witness up to $500 in a felony case or up to $100 in a misdemeanor case.[11] Disobedience includes failure to attend the hearing at the specified time, failure to attend at any other specified time, and refusal to

7. Tex. Code of Crim. Proc. Ann. § 9.51(a) (Vernon 1986).
8. *Id.* The use of deadly force is severely limited to situations in which the officer reasonably believes that the person may cause death or severe bodily injury upon escape. *Id.*
9. Tex. Code Crim. Proc.Ann. § 24.01 (Vernon Supp. 1988). Additionally, the board of medical examiners, board of nurse examiners, Texas Department of Health, and other state boards have the power to subpoena witnesses during investigations. These boards also have the power to request and receive records pertaining to the matters under investigation.
10. Tex. Code Crim. Proc. Ann. § 24.03 (Vernon Supp. 1988). The court is authorized to allow traveling expenses for a witness who resides outside the county where the case is pending.
11. Tex. Code Crim. Proc. Ann. § 24.05 (Vernon Supp. 1988).

produce any evidence in the witness's possession that was subpoenaed. If the witness later produces the evidence or appears, the court in its discretion may remit any fine. The court, however, may also order the witness to pay the costs incurred by the parties by reason of the failure to attend at the proper time. Finally, a court may issue a writ of attachment commanding a peace officer to "take the body of a witness" and bring the witness before the court if a witness fails to respond to a properly served subpoena.[12]

12. Tex. Code Crim. Proc. Ann. § 24.11 (Vernon Supp. 1988).

4.5

State Freedom of Information Act

The Texas version of the Freedom of Information Act makes all information collected and maintained by governmental bodies public information.[1] This provision would, without any further limitation, permit general public access to files of patients in governmental health care facilities. However, an exception to the act excludes from its application information that is deemed confidential by constitution, statute, or judicial decision.[2] Thus the confidentiality provisions applicable to communications between MHPs and their clients should preclude public access to this information under the state open records law when this information is contained in the records of state governmental bodies.

1. Tex. Rev. Civ. Stat. Ann. art. 6252-17a (Vernon Supp. 1987).
2. Tex. Rev. Civ. Stat. Ann. art. 6252-17a § 3(a)(1) (Vernon Supp. 1987).

Section 5

Practice Related to the Law

Section 5A

Families and Juveniles

5A.1

Competency to Marry

Texas, unlike many states, does not have an explicit requirement for the mental condition of individuals desiring to marry.[1] Individuals wishing to marry formally, however, must obtain a marriage license, have proof of identity and age, and be at least 18 years old.[2] Individuals under 18 but above 14 years of age may marry if they have either parental consent or a court order.[3] Any individual under 14 may marry only with a court order granting permission for the marriage.[4] The court may grant permission for marriage only if it determines that the marriage will be in the best interest of the individual. This is a question on which an MHP may be able to assist the court.

1. It is grounds for annulment, however, if a party lacks the mental capacity to consent to or understand the nature and consequences of marriage. See Chapter 5A.4 for a discussion of annulment.
2. Tex. Fam. Code Ann. §§ 1.02, 1.51 (Vernon 1986).
3. Tex. Fam. Code Ann. § 1.51 (Vernon 1986). The parental consent must be on the state form supplied and sworn before the county clerk no more than 30 days before the ceremony.
4. Tex. Fam. Code Ann. § 1.53 (Vernon 1986).

5A.2

Guardianship for Adults

Courts are empowered to appoint guardians for individuals who are unable to care for themselves physically or are not able to manage their own affairs and property. These include minors, incapacitated persons, and habitual drunkards. MHPs may become involved in guardianship proceedings if a court orders or a party requests an evaluation of either the person requiring a guardian (the prospective ward) or the potential guardian. Additionally, MHPs may provide treatment to the ward.

Temporary Guardians

A court may appoint a temporary guardian for an incapacitated person or a habitual drunkard without notice or hearing if it finds that the person requires an immediate guardian before a hearing on a permanent guardian can be held.[1] A situation requiring this could include a need for prompt medical treatment of an incapacitated person. The powers of a temporary guardian are limited to those specifically ordered by the court.

A petition for temporary guardianship is required to include the name and address of the applicant and the person requiring the guardianship and the name and address of the proposed temporary guardian. The court is required to appoint counsel to represent the person in question ("the respondent") at the earliest possible time. The appointment without notice is valid for 10 days, following which a hearing is required to be held. If the court finds

1. Tex. Prob. Code Ann. § 131 (Vernon Supp. 1987).

that "there is imminent danger that the physical health or safety of the respondent will be seriously impaired and/or that respondent's estate will be seriously damaged or dissipated unless immediate action is taken," it may continue the appointment of the temporary guardian. A temporary guardianship may not exceed 60 days. If necessary, the parties may petition during the 60-day period for a limited or permanent guardianship.

Permanent Guardianship

To appoint a guardian, the court must first find that the potential ward is a minor, a person of unsound mind, or a habitual drunkard and that the potential guardian is qualified. The court must also find that the proposed action and proposed guardian will adequately protect the rights of the ward. If the permanent guardian dies, resigns, or is removed, the court is required to appoint a replacement based on the same considerations.

Courts must consider only the best interests of the potential ward in the appointment of a permanent guardian. Any person may petition a court to appoint a permanent guardian. The petition must include the name, age, and address of the potential ward; facts supporting the necessity of a guardian; the name and relationship of the proposed permanent guardian; and a description of any property involved, if possible.[2] After receiving the petition, the court is required to notify all concerned parties and to appoint a guardian ad litem to represent the interests of the potential ward. Any person interested in the trial may attend to contest that the action will not be in the best interests of the potential ward. A jury trial is not required, but a jury may be requested on behalf of the respondent.

Guardianship Hearing

The court is required to appoint a guardian ad litem to represent the interests of the party believed to be of unsound mind. Unsound mind is intended to include those incapable of caring for themselves and/or managing their property, as when they are insane or have mental deficiencies. Proof of an unsound mind, however, requires more than mere proof of old age or mental weakness. If the finder of fact finds that the person is of unsound

2. Tex. Prob. Code Ann. § 111 (Vernon 1980).

mind, the court may appoint a permanent guardian for the incompetent individual.[3]

Who May Serve as Guardian

If an incompetent person has a spouse, the spouse is preferred as guardian.[4] If there is not a spouse or the spouse is disqualified or unwilling to serve, the closest relative of the incompetent may be appointed as guardian.

Certain individuals may not serve as guardians. Those who may not serve as guardians include minors, incompetents, and persons "whose conduct is notoriously bad."[5] Individuals who are parties to a suit that may affect the welfare of the person for whom the guardianship is sought and individuals who are indebted to or who assert a claim against the property of the individual requiring a guardian are also disqualified to serve as guardians. Finally, people who lack adequate education or experience of are otherwise incapable of managing property or the ward may not serve as guardians.

Duties of the Guardian

A guardian of the person of an adult is required to take charge of the ward and care for the ward's support, including food, shelter, and medical care. A guardian of the property of an adult is required to care for the property as "a prudent man would take of his own property."[6] The guardian, therefore, is required to collect any debts or rents due to the ward, bring suits for and defend suits against the ward, and generally manage the ward's financial affairs. Additionally, the guardian is required to make an annual accounting to the court concerning the ward's property.

A guardian may exercise some limited powers without a court order, including insuring the ward or the ward's property, paying taxes, voting stock, and releasing liens that are paid in full.[7] Other actions, however, require a court order; these include purchasing or selling property, compromising claims, or compounding bad or doubtful debts.

---

3. Tex. Prob. Code Ann. § 416 (Vernon 1980). While a jury determination that the person is of unsound mind allows the court to appoint a guardian, the verdict does not result in loss of liberties or confinement to an asylum. Confinement requires a separate hearing. The court may order a new trial and set aside the jury verdict of incompetency for up to 10 days upon a showing of good cause.
4. Tex. Prob. Code Ann. § 109 (Vernon 1980).
5. Tex. Prob. Code Ann. § 110 (Vernon 1980).
6. Tex. Prob. Code Ann. § 230 (Vernon 1980).
7. Tex. Prob. Code Ann. § 234 (Vernon 1980).

Termination of the Guardianship

Any person, including the guardian, may petition for termination of the guardianship.[8] The petition must be in writing and must assert that the incompetent person has been restored to a sound mind. If the facts are not disputed, the court may terminate the guardianship without a jury trial. If the facts are disputed, however, a jury is required to determine whether the person is now of sound mind to terminate the guardianship. A guardian is immediately required to return all property to the former ward after termination of the guardianship.

Limited Guardianship for Adults

If the court finds an incapacitated person totally unable to care for himself or herself, it may appoint an unlimited (plenary) guardian. If it finds the incapacitated person totally able to care for himself or herself it should dismiss the proceedings. However, if it finds that the incapacitated person has the capacity to care for himself or herself in part but not completely, it may appoint a limited guardian with powers limited to the ward's incapacity. A limited guardianship is designed to encourage self-reliance, and the guardian has powers only to the extent necessary to deal with the physical or mental incapacity of the person. An incapacitated person is defined as "an adult individual who, because of a physical or mental condition, is substantially unable to feed, clothe, or shelter himself, to care for his own physical health, or to manage his property or financial affairs."[9] An incapacitated person is not legally incompetent and, therefore, retains all legal rights except those granted to the limited guardian.

A court may not order a limited guardianship unless the court has received a written statement from a physician, either chosen by the parties or appointed by the court, describing the condition of the alleged incapacitated person.[10] If the basis of the incapacity is mental illness, the court may also consider evaluations of the incapacitated person's social, intellectual, and behavioral condition from an MHP.

The person claimed to be incapacitated is required to attend the guardianship hearing, unless the court determines that this is not in that person's best interest. Further, the person is entitled to counsel and a jury trial.[11] The standard of proof by which the court

8. Tex. Prob. Code Ann. § 426 (Vernon 1980).
9. *Id.* The incapacity must be evidenced by recurring acts within the preceding 6 months, rather than by isolated events.
10. Tex. Prob. Code Ann. § 130F (Vernon Supp. 1987).
11. Tex. Prob. Code Ann. § 130G (Vernon Supp. 1987). The court must appoint counsel if necessary.

must decide whether to appoint a limited guardian is that the evidence be "clear and convincing." This standard is more rigorous than the usual standard in civil cases, that is, that there be a preponderance of the evidence. The order appointing a limited guardian is required to specify the exact powers given to the limited guardian.[12]

A limited guardian may not admit the incapacitated person to a residential care facility without the incapcitated person's consent. Moreover, a limited guardian is required to file an annual report concerning the management of the incapacitated person's affairs and the condition of the person.[13] The report must inventory all the property, including all debts and liens, over which the limited guardian has power.

12. Tex. Prob. Code Ann. § 130H (Vernon Supp. 1987).
13. Tex. Prob. Code Ann. § 130J (Vernon Supp. 1987).

5A.3

Conservatorship for Adults

In many states, a separate conservatorship law allows a court to appoint someone to manage the estate of a person no longer able to manage his or her property or financial affairs. Texas has no separate scheme for conservatorship apart from the guardianship provisions discussed in Chapter 5A.1.

5A.4

Annulment

An annulment is a judicial termination of a voidable marriage. A divorce is a judicial termination of a valid marriage. MHPs are not necessarily directly involved in annulments; however, their knowledge of this proceeding may assist them in counseling clients.

Grounds and Procedure for Annulment

An annulment may be obtained on several grounds, including minority, incapacity, or failure to observe statutory requirements for a valid marriage. A parent, conservator, or next friend may petition for an annulment if the married person is under 14 years of age for up to 90 days after the 14th birthday of the party or up to 90 days after the petitioner knew or should have known of the marriage.[1] If the married person is between 14 and 18 years of age, the parent, conservator, or next friend may petition for an annulment unless there was a court order or parental consent permitting the marriage within the same time limits.

If a party lacked the mental competency to consent to or understand the nature and consequences of the marriage ceremony, the person's guardian or next friend may petition the court for an annulment.[2] Additionally, the competent person to the marriage may petition for an annulment based on mental incompetency, provided that at the time of the marriage that person

1. Tex. Fam. Code Ann. § 2.41 (Vernon 1986). An individual may not petition for annulment if there was a court order permitting the marriage.
2. Tex. Fam. Code Ann. § 2.45 (Vernon 1986).

neither knew or had reason to know of the mental condition of the other.

A marriage is also voidable if the parties did not observe the mandatory 72-hour waiting period required after issuance of the marriage license before participating in a cermonial marriage.[3] If a party was under the influence of alcohol or narcotics at the time of the marriage ceremony, thus having no capacity to consent, the marriage is voidable.[4] Finally, a marriage is voidable by a party who was induced to enter into the marriage by fraud, duress, or force.[5]

Parties may petition for annulment in the county where the petitioning party resides or both of the parties reside, and the procedure parallels the procedure for divorce (see Chapter 5A.5). However, a party may petition for an annulment in Texas only if one of the parties to the marriage is a resident of Texas or the marriage took place in Texas and both parties are still living.

3. Tex. Fam. Code Ann. § 1.82 (Vernon Supp. 1987).
4. Tex. Fam. Code Ann. §§ 2.42, 2.43 (Vernon Supp. 1987). Additionally, the parties must not have lived together after the ceremony to meet this ground for annulment. Another ground for annulment is impotence if the other party had no prior knowledge of the condition.
5. Tex. Fam. Code Ann. § 2.44 (Vernon Supp. 1987).

5A.5

Divorce

In Texas, parties may obtain a divorce upon showing that the marriage has become insupportable. Thus, allegations of fault such as abuse or adultery are not necessary. Instead the focus is on the viability of the marriage.

MHPs may become involved in a suit for divorce if the spouses voluntarily seek out their services to resolve marital difficulties or if the court requires the parties to submit to counseling with a court-appointed counselor to determine whether there is "a reasonable expectation of reconciliation."[1] The court-appointed counselor is required to file a written report with the court stating whether, in the counselor's opinion, a reasonable expectation of reconciliation exists between the parties and whether further counseling would benefit the parties. The written report, however, may not be used as evidence in the divorce proceeding or in determining custody of children. Instead, the report is solely to aid the court in its determination of whether to grant the divorce.[2] A counselor who engages in court-ordered counseling is not permitted to testify as a witness in the divorce or a custody proceeding. Finally, any files or work product of the counselor may not be used in either a divorce or custody proceeding.

Either spouse may petition for a divorce on the ground that the marriage "has become insupportable because of discord or conflict of personalities that destroys the legitimate ends of the

1. Tex. Fam. Code Ann. § 3.54 (Vernon Supp. 1987).
2. Tex. Fam. Code Ann. § 3.54 (Vernon Supp. 1987). The parties to the divorce may also obtain a copy of the report. The court may order further counseling and grant a continuance for the divorce action if the judge believes that further counseling will be beneficial. If the court does order further counseling, another written report is required.

marriage relationship and prevents any reasonable expectation of reconciliation."[3] Fault-based grounds for a divorce, which are not commonly used, include cruelty,[4] adultery, conviction of a felony or confinement for a year, and abandonment for a year. There are also nonfault grounds that are rarely used: living apart for 3 years and confinement of a party in a mental hospital with no prospect of recovery.[5] To petition for a divorce, the petitioning spouse is required to have lived in Texas for at least 6 months. Also, the spouse must petition for the divorce in the county where either one of the spouses resides.[6]

---

3. Tex. Fam. Code Ann. § 3.01 (Vernon 1975).
4. Tex. Fam. Code Ann. § 3.02 (Vernon 1986). This includes emotional and mental injury as well as physical injury.
5. Tex. Fam. Code Ann. §§ 3.03-3.07 (Vernon 1986).
6. Tex. Fam. Code Ann. § 3.21 (Vernon 1986).

5A.6

Child Custody After Marital Dissolution

MHPs may become involved in child custody proceedings if the parties request or the court orders an evaluation to assess parental capacity. MHPs may also become involved if the court orders one or both parents to participate in counseling. The court may order counseling if there is a history of difficulties and conflicts over possession of the child. The court may either appoint the counselor or approve a counselor chosen by the parents. Additionally, the court may order the parents to pay the expenses of counseling.

In a suit affecting the parent–child relationship (i.e., divorce or child custody hearing), the court may appoint one of the parents as managing conservator for any children of the marriage.[1] The managing conservator is the custodial parent. The court is required to appoint the managing conservator considering the qualifications of both parents, without regard to sex. The court is also required to consider any evidence of intentional and excessive use of force by the parent against any person under 18 years of age. A managing conservator retains all parental rights, duties, and privileges of the parent–child relationship to the exclusion of the other parent, subject to that other parent's rights as a possessory conservator (e.g., visitation and consent to emergency medical care).[2]

The court may not deny a parent access to a child unless the court finds that the access will endanger the physical or emotional

1. Tex. Fam. Code § 14.01 (Vernon Supp. 1987). A "managing conservator" is the parent with primary care of the children, while a "possessory conservator" is a parent who has a right to "possess" or visit the child at certain times. Individuals other than parents may serve as conservators, a situation discussed in Chapter 5A.12.
2. Tex. Fam. Code Ann. § 14.02 (Vernon 1986).

welfare of the child and that access is not in the best interests of the child.[3] The court is required to specify the times and conditions of possession. The court is also required to decree the specific rights and powers of the possessory conservator.

The court may also appoint joint managing conservators, discussed in detail below. The court is required to specify the powers and duties of each parent as a joint managing conservator. Further, the court is required to order that the parents exchange "information concerning the health, education, and welfare of the child, and, if possible, confer before making decisions concerning" such matters.[4]

Parents also have the right to file a settlement agreement with the court for conservatorship, support, and the details of visitation rights.[5] The purpose of allowing the parents this control is to promote peaceful resolution of the issues. If the court determines, however, that the agreement is not satisfactory, it may request a revision or make its own orders. If the court accepts the terms of the agreement, the terms become part of the divorce decree. Thus, the terms become judicially enforceable obligations.

Joint Managing Conservatorship

Joint managing conservatorship is the sharing of parental rights and duties, but it does not require equal periods of physical possession. Although the principal reason for providing joint conservatorship is often "face-saving" for the parent who would not be appointed managing conservator, the statute states that the purpose of appointing joint managing conservators is to "assure that children will have frequent and continuing contact with parents who have shown the ability to act in the best interest of the child and to encourage parents to share in the rights and responsibilities of raising their children after the parents have separated or divorced."[6] A court may not order a joint managing conservatorship, however, if there is evidence and a history of child neglect or physical or sexual abuse against any child, the other parent, or a spouse. Normally, the court will appoint one joint conservator to maintain the primary residence for the child. The court may also order that certain rights and privileges belong exclusively to one parent.

If the parents file a joint conservatorship agreement with the

3. Tex. Fam. Code Ann. § 14.03 (Vernon 1986). The court may also grant rights of access to grandparents if the parties request such access in the custody suit.
4. Tex. Fam. Code Ann. § 14.02 (Vernon Supp. 1987).
5. Tex. Fam. Code Ann. § 14.06 (Vernon 1986).
6. Tex. Fam. Code Ann. § 14.021 (Vernon Supp. 1987).

court, the agreement must specify where the child will live and the parent who will have primary responsibility; the rights and duties of each parent regarding care, support, and education; and that there will be minimal disruption of the child's schooling, association with friends, and daily routines. Further, the agreement may have a dispute resolution provision to assure that future disagreements are handled in a reasonable manner.

If the parents do not file an agreement, the court may nonetheless appoint joint managing conservators if it finds that such an arrangement is in the best interest of the child. The court is required to consider the physical, emotional, and psychological needs of the child; the abilities of each parent to reach mutual agreements concerning the child and give the child priority; whether the parents can agree with each other and accept a relationship between the child and the other parent; and the proximity of the two potential homes. Any child who is at least 14 years old may express a preference to the court for or against the appointment of joint managing conservators.

Child Custody Hearing Procedure

Texas has adopted the Uniform Child Custody Jurisdiction Act.[7] Thus, the law in Texas on jurisdiction over child custody determinations is the same, with some variations, as in at least 48 other states. A court has jurisdiction over child custody matters if Texas is the home state of the child at the time of the suit or within 6 months prior to the suit, or the child and at least one parent have significant connections with Texas. Physical presence of the child and/or a parent alone is not enough to give a court jurisdiction. If the conservator and child leave Texas for 6 months, Texas ceases to be the home state.

The court is required to give all parties notice by personal service, certified mail, or any method ordered by the court calculated to give actual notice and an opportunity to be heard. The court has the power to compel the attendance of any party within the state, including the child. Further, even if a parent is outside the state but receives actual notice of a custody suit, the parent's failure to appear may result in an adverse decision by the court against the parent. A custody decree is final to all parties who receive notice of the hearing as to all the issues presented in the particular action. Thus, the order may only be modified by court order. Texas must, of course, recognize valid custody decrees from other states.

7. *See* Tex. Fam. Code Ann. §§ 11.21-11.64 (Vernon 1986).

5A.7

Reporting of Adult Abuse

Texas law requires any person, including an MHP, with a reasonable belief that an elderly or disabled person has been abused, exploited, or neglected to report that information to the Department of Human Resources.[1] Failure to report is punishable as a Class B misdemeanor, which may involve a fine of not less than $100 but not more than $1,000 and/or confinement for not more than 180 days.[2]

Terms and Definitions

An "elderly person" is anyone 65 years of age or older, and a "disabled person" is a person "with a mental, physical, or developmental disability who is 18 years of age or older or under 18 years of age and who has had the disabilities of minority removed."[3]

"Abuse" is defined as "the willful infliction of injury, unreasonable confinement, intimidation, or cruel punishment with resulting physical harm or pain or mental anguish or the willful deprivation by a caretaker or one's self of goods or services which are necessary to avoid physical harm, mental anguish, or mental illness."[4] "Exploitation" is "the illegal or improper act or process of a caretaker using the resources of an elderly or disabled person for monetary or personal benefit, profit, or gain." And "neglect" is

---

1. Tex. Hum. Res. Code Ann. § 48.036 (Vernon Supp. 1987).
2. Tex. Penal Code Ann. § 12.22 (Vernon 1976).
3. Tex. Hum. Res. Code Ann. § 48.002 (Vernon Supp. 1987).
4. Tex. Hum. Res. Code Ann. § 48.002(2) (Vernon Supp. 1987).

"the failure to provide for one's self the goods or services which are necessary to avoid physical harm, mental anguish, or mental illness or the failure of a caretaker to provide such goods or services."[5]

Who Must Report

Any person with "reasonable cause to believe that an elderly or disabled is in the state of abuse, exploitation or neglect"[6] is required to report that knowledge to the Department of Human Services. Therefore, any MHP, whether licensed or not, is required to report suspected abuse as long as there is a reasonable basis for believing the abuse is occurring or has occurred.

Additionally, employees of mental health facilities are required to report abuse of patients or clients occurring at any facility.[7] The employee is required to report within 2 hours of the incident to the head of the facility.[8] The head of the facility is then required to investigate all claims, take appropriate actions, and report the abuse to the Texas Department of Mental Health and Mental Retardation.

When and How to Report

Any person reasonably suspecting abuse, exploitation, or neglect is required to report either orally or in writing to the Department of Human Services (Department).[9] The report must contain the name, address, and age of the elderly or disabled person; the name and address of the person responsible for the elderly or disabled person; the condition of the elderly or disabled person; and the basis of the reporting person's knowledge.[10] If the suspected abuse

5. Tex. Hum. Res. Code Ann. § 48.002(3),(4) (Vernon Supp. 1987).
6. Tex. Hum. Res. Code Ann. § 48.036(a) (Vernon Supp. 1987).
7. Tex. Admin. Code tit. 25, § 405.366 (1987). Neglect and exploitation must also be reported. Client abuse provides grounds for disciplinary action against the employee. Disciplinary actions may include dismissal, suspension, or written reprimand. Neither the facility, nor any employee, may retaliate against an employee who makes such a required report.
8. Tex. Admin. Code tit. 25, § 405.366 (1987). Failure to report within the time limit is grounds not only for disciplinary action but for criminal prosecution as well.
9. Tex. Hum. Res. Code Ann. § 48.036 (Vernon Supp. 1987). There is not a time limit within which to make the report, except within institutions.
10. Tex. Hum. Res. Code Ann. § 48.036 (Vernon Supp. 1987). The report must also contain any other relevant or helpful information the reporter has.

occurred in a state facility, the report must be made to the state agency governing the facility.[11]

The Department is required to investigate all reports of suspected abuse or neglect to determine if abused persons need protective services, if they are physically or financially capable of obtaining necessary services on their own behalf, and what services are available in their particular community.[12] The Department is required to visit the abused person's residence, accompanied by a peace officer if necessary to gain entry.[13] The Department is required to report any finding of physical abuse to the appropriate law enforcement agency. And, if the report suggests that the abused person requires protective services immediately, the Department is required to act within 24 hours to begin the investigation.

Immunity from Liability

Any person who files a report of suspected abuse, who testifies in any judicial proceeding regarding abuse, or who aids in any investigation by the Department relating to abuse is immune from both civil and criminal liability for those actions. If the report is made in bad faith, however, no immunity exists.[14]

Confidentiality of Records

All records of the Department of Human Resources or other state agencies pertaining to abuse reports and investigations are unavailable for public inspection.[15] A court may order the Department to make records available, however, for good cause and may order any means necessary to protect the identity of individuals contained in the report, if necessary.

11. Tex. Hum. Res. Code Ann. § 49.036 (Vernon Supp. 1987). Any state agency receiving such a report must promptly and thoroughly investigate the claim and report to the Department of Human Services.
12. Tex. Hum. Res. Code Ann. § 48.038 (Vernon Supp. 1987). Protective services may include social work services, day or home care, legal assistance, health care, or a psychiatric or health evaluation.
13. Tex. Hum. Res. Code Ann. § 48.038 (Vernon Supp. 1987). Either the county court or probate court may issue orders permitting entries.
14. Tex. Hum. Res. Code Ann. § 48.039 (Vernon Supp. 1987).
15. Tex. Hum. Res. Code Ann. § 48.083 (Vernon Supp. 1987).

Emergency Order for Protective Services

If an elderly or disabled person lacks the capacity to consent to protective services, the Department may obtain a court order permitting the services.[16] The petition to the court must include a medical report stating that the elderly or disabled person is suffering from abuse which is a threat to life and is physically or mentally incapable of consenting to services.

Additionally, the court may order removal of the elderly or disabled person to a safer environment, treatments, or any other services that are necessary to remove the threat to life. Any physician who treats an elderly or disabled person under an emergency order is not liable for any damages except those due to the physician's own negligence.

16. Tex. Hum. Res. Code Ann. § 48.061 (Vernon Supp. 1987).

5A.8

Reporting of Child Abuse

Any person, whether an MHP or not, who believes that a child's mental health, physical health, or welfare "has been or may be adversely affected by abuse or neglect"[1] is required to report the abuse to the Texas Department of Human Services. The department has forms for reporting abuse which are available at all licensed hospitals throughout the state. The law specifies that hospitals, nurses, and physicians are required to fill out the report; however, the duty to report encompasses MHPs, whether licensed or not.

Abuse includes "mental or emotional injury to a child that results in an observable and material impairment in the child's growth, development, or psychological functioning;" physical injury; sexual conduct with the child; obscene or pornographic photography involving the child; and the failure to take reasonable efforts to prevent any of these actions.[2] Neglect includes abandonment; leaving a child where there is a substantial risk of harm with no supervision; failure to seek medical care; failure to provide food and shelter; and "placing a child in or failing to remove the child from a situation that a reasonable person would realize requires judgement or actions beyond the child's level of maturity, physical condition, or mental abilities and that results in bodily injury or substantial risk of immediate harm to the child."[3]

1. Tex. Fam. Code Ann. § 34.01 (1975).
2. Tex. Fam. Code Ann. § 34.012 (Vernon Supp. 1987).
3. *Id.*

Requirements for the Report

Persons with knowledge of child abuse or neglect are required to make both an immediate oral and subsequent written report to a state or local law enforcement agency and the Texas Department of Human Services. The report is required to indicate the name and address of the child, as well as the name and address of the persons responsible for the child. Anonymous reports are accepted, but discouraged.[4]

As indicated, in addition to an immediate oral report, a person with knowledge of abuse or neglect is required to make a written report within 5 days after discovering the abuse or neglect. If the reporting party is a professional, the oral report must occur within 48 hours of discovery. A "professional" is "an individual who is licensed or certified by the state, or who is an employee of a facility licensed, certified, or operated by the state, and who in the normal course of official duties, or duties for which a license or certification is required, has direct contact with children."[5] Examples of professionals listed in the statute include teachers, nurses, physicians, and day-care employees.

Investigation of the Report

A state or local agency receiving a report of suspected abuse or neglect is required to investigate the claims. The investigation is required to address the nature and extent of any abuse, the persons responsible for the abuse, the names and conditions of other children in the same home, the parents' competency, the adequacy of the home environment, and the nature of the parent–child relationship.[6] The final report goes to the juvenile court and, if grounds exist, to the appropriate law enforcement agencies. Subsequently, the juvenile court may initiate an action to intervene or ultimately to terminate the parent–child relationship (see Chapter 5A.10).

The investigation may include a psychiatric or psychological evaluation of the child and any other children in the home. If the

4. Tex. Fam. Code Ann. § 34.02 (Vernon 1975).
5. Tex. Fam. Code Ann. § 34.02 (Vernon 1980). Texas teachers must receive training in the recognition of and response to signs of child abuse. Tex. Educ. Code Ann. § 13.032 (Vernon Supp. 1987). Thus, professional school counselors receive the training and must report as professionals any suspected abuse. *See* Chapter 1.6 for a discussion of licensure and certification of school counselors.
6. Tex. Fam. Code Ann. § 34.05 (Vernon 1975).

parents or responsible parties do not consent to such an examination, the juvenile court may order the examination.

If the investigation reveals that immediate removal from the home is necessary to protect the child, the investigators may initiate an action for temporary custody and care of the child.

Immunity from Liability

Any person who makes a report of child abuse or neglect in good faith is immune from civil and criminal liability for that action.[7] The immunity extends to testifying as a witness in any proceeding regarding the abuse.

Confidentiality and Privilege

All information in any report of suspected abuse is confidential and may only be used for the purpose of investigating the report.[8] Further, all reports, records, and investigation files concerning child abuse are confidential.[9] A court may order disclosure, however, if the reports and records are necessary for a judicial proceeding regarding the abuse.

In child abuse proceedings, the only recognized privilege is that between attorneys and clients.[10] Thus, evidence may not be excluded on the basis of any privilege except the attorney–client privilege. MHPs may not validly claim a physician–, psychiatrist–, psychotherapist–, or psychologist–client privilege.

Failure to Report

Failure to report child abuse or neglect may result in conviction of a Class B misdemeanor, which is punishable by a fine not to exceed $1,000 and/or confinement in jail for not greater than 180 days.[11]

---

7. Tex. Fam. Code Ann. § 34.03 (Vernon 1980).
8. Tex. Fam. Code Ann. § 34.011 (Vernon 1980).
9. Tex. Fam. Code Ann. § 34.08 (Vernon 1980).
10. Tex. Fam. Code Ann. § 34.04 (Vernon 1980).
11. Tex. Fam. Code Ann. § 34.07 (Vernon 1986). *See also* Tex. Penal Code Ann. § 12.22 (Vernon 1974).

5A.9

Abused and Neglected Children

MHPs may become involved with abused and neglected children in several ways. If professionals suspect abuse, they have a duty to report the suspected abuse or neglect to the Texas Department of Human Services. Also, MHPs may participate in the investigation of suspected abuse. If the juvenile court determines that foster care or termination of parental rights is necessary to protect the child, an MHP may evaluate the child or the prospective or biological parents and recommend or provide therapy.

Temporary Custody of a Child

A court may issue an order to take temporary custody of a child or issue a restraining order to prevent a parent or other person from seeing a child if the court determines from a sworn petition that an immediate danger to the physical health or safety of the child exists.[1] Additionally, law enforcement officers or juvenile probation officers may take immediate custody of a child if:[2]

1. the child is in immediate danger and the sole purpose of taking custody is to deliver the child to the parent or guardian,

2. a parent or guardian releases the child to the officer,

---

1. Tex. Fam. Code Ann. § 17.02 (Vernon 1986). Courts may also order temporary custody during the pendency of an appeal to protect a child in suits affecting the parent–child relationship.
2. Tex. Fam. Code Ann. § 17.03 (Vernon 1986).

3. there is reason to believe the child is in immediate danger and there is no time to get a temporary custody order, or
4. there is reason to believe the child is a victim of sexual abuse.

If an officer takes possession of a child, the officer is immediately required to initiate an action to appoint a guardian ad litem for the child and an action to intervene or terminate the parent–child relationship, if necessary, within 60 days. The officer or agency having custody of the child must also give the parents or guardian written notification of the custody. The notice is required to state the reason the child is in custody, the name of the agency the parents may contact, a summary of the parents' legal rights, and a statement that the parents have the right to hire an attorney.[3] The notice must be given as soon as possible, but not later than the first working day after taking custody.

The court is required to conduct a temporary custody hearing within one working day after either custody of the child is obtained or the child returns to the parents or guardian. The hearing may be ex parte, meaning that only one side is present and heard.[4] However, a full adversary hearing must occur within 10 days if the original hearing was ex parte, and an ex parte custody order may not exceed 10 days. If the evidence is such that a reasonable person would believe that a danger to the child exists, the court may order temporary custody. Additionally, the court may make any orders necessary to protect the child. If the court finds there is not a danger to the child, the child is required to be returned to the parent(s)' or guardian's custody.

Options for Abused Children

If the court determines that the child has been abused or neglected, the court may initiate a suit to terminate the parent–child relationship involuntarily.[5] Additionally, a party may request the court to terminate the relationship or the natural parents may voluntarily relinquish custody and care of the child.

After finding abuse or neglect, the court has several options. It may place the child in foster care or in an agency home, or appoint a managing conservator such as a grandparent or anyone who has had substantial contact with the child, with whom the child would live.

3. Tex. Fam. Code Ann. § 17.031 (Vernon Supp. 1987).
4. Tex. Fam. Code Ann. § 17.02 (Vernon 1986).
5. See Chapter 5A.13 for a discussion of foster care and Chapter 5A.10 for a discussion of termination of parental rights.

5A.10

Termination of Parental Rights

Parental rights may be voluntarily relinquished, subject to effectuation by a court order, or terminated involuntarily by a court.[1] Before a court orders a termination of parental rights, however, it may order a social study of the child and the home environment. Thus, MHPs may be directly involved in the process of termination.

Petition for Termination

If a parent files a petition for voluntary termination (which is rarely done), the court may grant the request if termination is in the best interest of the child.[2] Parties who may bring suit for involuntary termination include the child through a representative, guardians, custodians, managing conservators, or any governmental unit or agency.[3] Additionally, grandparents, stepparents, and other parties seeking adoption may sue to terminate the parent–child relationship. The court is required to appoint counsel and a guardian ad litem to represent the child in all cases and may appoint counsel for indigent parents. The suit must be filed in the county where the child resides.

The court may, but is not required to, order a social study of the child's conditions and circumstances and the home environ-

1. Tex. Fam. Code Ann. § 15.03 (Vernon 1986).
2. Tex. Fam. Code Ann. § 15.01 (Vernon 1986). Additionally, the parents may file before the birth of the child any time after the first trimester of a pregnancy. In this case, the formal voluntary relinquishment hearing does not occur until the child is at least 5 days old. *See* Tex. Fam. Code Ann. § 15.021 (Vernon Supp. 1987).
3. Tex. Fam. Code Ann. § 11.03 (Vernon 1986).

ment in any suit affecting the parent–child relationship.[4] Any qualified state agency or qualified MHP may perform the social study, which must be filed with the court. The parties are entitled to receive a copy of the report in contested cases.

The court has the power to compel the attendance of witnesses, including the author of the social study. The court may close the actual termination hearing to the public, allowing only interested parties to attend, if it finds that closing the hearing is in the best interest of the child. Additionally, the court may give preferential treatment to a termination hearing by moving it ahead of other civil suits on the court docket. Finally, if the court terminates the parent–child relationship, it is required to appoint a managing conservator for the child.[5] The judicial termination has the effect of removing all parental rights and privileges, except that the child may still inherit from the intestate parent unless the court orders otherwise.[6]

Reasons for Involuntary Termination

The court may order involuntary termination of the parent–child relationship if termination is in the best interest of the child and the parent has:[7]

1. abandoned the child and expressed an intent not to return;
2. voluntarily left the child alone or with another person for at least 3 months without expressing an intent to abandon, yet failing to provide adequate support for the child;
3. knowingly placed or allowed the child to remain in surroundings that endanger the child's physical or emotional well-being;
4. exposed the child to conduct that endangers the child's physical or emotional well-being;
5. failed to support the child according to the parent's ability for at least a year ending within 6 months of the date the suit is filed;
6. abandoned the child without any means to identify the child;
7. voluntarily, and with knowledge of pregnancy, abandoned the mother or failed to adequately support the mother and remained separated from the child;

---

4. Tex. Fam. Code Ann. § 11.12 (Vernon 1986).
5. Tex. Fam. Code Ann. § 15.07 (Vernon 1986).
6. Tex. Fam. Code Ann. § 12.04 (Vernon 1986). Parental rights that are extinguished include the right to have physical possession of a child; provide for the care, discipline, and moral training of the child; manage the child's finances; and consent to the child's marriage or enlistment in the armed forces.
7. Tex. Fam. Code Ann. § 15.02 (Vernon 1986).

8. refused to submit to a lawful and reasonable court order pertaining to child abuse; or
9. been the major cause of either the child's failure to enroll in school or the child's absence from the home without parental consent for a significant period of time.

Additionally, the court may order termination of the parent–child relationship with respect to any parent if a child is born alive after an abortion.[8] However, a parent who had no knowledge of the abortion or consented solely to save the life of the mother is not subject to such involuntary termination.

The Texas Department of Human Services (Department) may also request involuntary termination of the parent–child relationship.[9] A court may grant the request if the court finds that (a) the parent has a mental or emotional illness or deficiency that renders the parent unable to fulfill the physical, emotional, and mental needs of the child and that there is a reasonable probability that the illness or deficiency will last until the child is 18; (b) the Department has been the permanent managing conservator of the child for the preceding 6 months; and (c) the termination is in the best interest of the child. The hearing, when the Department files for termination, may not occur for at least 180 days after the petition is filed.

Voluntary Relinquishment

Parents who petition for voluntary relinquishment must file with the court a written affidavit, signed before two competent witnesses.[10] MHPs may be used to ascertain whether the affidavit was voluntary. The affidavit must contain:

1. the name, age, and address of the parent who is relinquishing rights;
2. the name, age, and birthday of the child;
3. the names and addresses of the child's guardians, if any;
4. a statement as to whether the parent is or is not under a duty to pay child support and the amount;
5. a description of the child's property, if any;
6. a statement that termination is in the best interest of the child, and one of the following:

---

8. Tex. Fam. Code Ann. § 15.022 (Vernon Supp. 1987). Abortion is defined as "an intentional expulsion of a human fetus from the body of a woman induced by any means for the purpose of causing the death of the fetus." *Id.*
9. Tex. Fam. Code Ann. § 15.024 (Vernon Supp. 1987).
10. Tex. Fam. Code Ann. § 15.03 (Vernon 1986).

a. the name and address of the other parent,

b. a statement that the other parent is dead or has no parental rights, or

c. a statement that the child is not the legitimate child of the father;

7. a statement that the parent has been told of the parent's rights, duties, and privileges; and
8. a statement as to whether the relinquishment is revocable or irrevocable.

The affidavit may also contain a designation of a managing conservator or a consent to place the child for adoption. Any relinquishment is revocable for up to 60 days after execution, unless either the relinquishment states that it is irrevocable or the appointed managing conservator is the Texas Department of Human Services or a licensed placement agency.

Also, any person except the child's natural mother may file an affidavit of waiver of interest in a child.[11] The waiver of interest waives the person's right to notice in any suit concerning the child and may also be used against the person if the person later attempts to obtain possession of the child or establish rights to the child in any manner. While the affidavit may not be used in any suit "brought by another person to establish the affiant's paternity of the child,"[12] it does act to disclaim any parental interest in the child. The affidavit must be verified and witnessed by two competent persons. The affidavit may also contain a statement that the party does not admit to being the father of the child or having had sexual relations with the mother of the child. If a person files a waiver of interest, a court may terminate all rights of an alleged father that exist or may exist if he fails to respond to a paternity suit.[13]

11. Tex. Fam. Code Ann. § 15.041 (Vernon Supp. 1987).
12. *Id.*
13. Tex. Fam. Code Ann. § 15.023 (Vernon Supp. 1987).

5A.11

Guardianship for Minors

A minor whose parents have died or are otherwise unable to care for the minor may be appointed a legal guardian. An MHP may be involved in the determination of a particular guardian's appropriateness or subsequent treatment for the minor.

Petition for Guardianship

Any person may petition a court to appoint a permanent guardian.[1] The petition is required to include facts about the person requiring the guardian, such as name, address, and age; facts supporting the need for a guardian; the name and relationship of the proposed guardian; and a description of any property involved, if possible. After receiving the petition, the court is required to notify the concerned parties and appoint a guardian ad litem and counsel for the minor to represent the minor's interests, if necessary. Any person may appear to contest the selection of the guardian, or any action by the court, on the basis that it will not be in the child's best interests. Guardianship hearings do not require a jury. If the court finds that the potential ward is a minor and that the rights of the minor will be adequately protected by the appointment of the proposed guardian, the court may appoint a permanent guardian.

If the permanent guardian dies, resigns, or is removed, the court is required to appoint another permanent guardian if the

1. Tex. Prob. Code Ann. § 111 (Vernon 1980). Suits should be in the county where the child resides.

child is still a minor.[2] The new guardian must qualify as a guardian and the appointment must be in the best interests of the child.

Who May Serve as Guardian

Courts are required to appoint a guardian or conservator considering only the best interests of the child.[3] If a minor has parents living, the parents are the natural guardians of the minor. If the parents do not live together, the court may appoint one parent a managing conservator in a custody proceeding on the basis of which parent is best qualified to care for the child. Additionally, the natural parents may select a guardian to care for a minor in case of their death, and a court will honor such a selection if the designated person is qualified. If the parents did not select a guardian, the nearest relative is the first choice for a guardian, after which the court may appoint any person who is qualified. If there is more than one eligible relative, the court is required to select the most qualified to care for the minor.

Certain individuals may never serve as guardians, including minors, incompetents, and persons "whose conduct is notoriously bad."[4] Persons who are parties to a suit that may affect the welfare of the minor may not serve as guardians. Persons who are indebted to the minor or who assert an adverse claim against the minor's property may not serve as guardians. Finally, people who lack education or experience to manage either property or the minor may not serve as guardians.

Additionally, if a minor is at least 14 years of age, the minor may select the guardian, subject to approval by the court, by filing a written request with the court.[5] When a minor reaches the age of 14, the minor may select a different guardian, again subject to approval by the court, by filing a written request in the same manner. In such instances, the court's approval is sometimes withheld.

Duties of the Guardian

Guardians of the minor's person are required to take charge of the minor and provide for the minor's support and education. The

2. Tex. Prob. Code Ann. § 119 (Vernon 1980).
3. Tex. Prob. Code Ann. § 109 (Vernon 1980).
4. Tex. Prob. Code Ann. § 110 (Vernon 1980).
5. Tex. Prob. Code Ann. § 118 (Vernon 1980).

guardian must treat the minor humanely, attend to the minor's education, and, if possible, see that the minor learns a trade or profession.[6]

Guardians of the minor's property are required to care for the property as "a prudent man would take of his property,"[7] including maintenance and repair. Thus, the guardian is required to collect any debts or rents due to the minor, bring and defend suits for or against the minor, and manage the profits from the property. Guardians must take an oath and give a bond if property is involved. They must also make an annual accounting to the court concerning the ward and any property. Guardians may exercise some powers without obtaining a court order, including insuring the ward or the ward's property, paying taxes, voting stock, and releasing liens which are paid.[8] Other actions require a court order, however, such as purchasing or selling property, compromising claims, or compounding bad or doubtful debts.

---

6. Tex. Prob. Code Ann. § 229 (Vernon 1980).
7. Tex. Prob. Code Ann. § 230 (Vernon 1980).
8. Tex. Prob. Code Ann. § 234 (Vernon 1980).

5A.12

Conservatorship for Minors

Conservatorship of a minor or other person in need of a guardian is, in many jurisdictions, a description of a guardianship of the property as contrasted with the person of the minor or incompetent. In Texas, no separate proceedings exist to appoint the guardian of a minor's property rather than a minor's person. Either or both may occur under the proceedings described in Chapter 5A.11.

Conservatorship as it relates to minors in Texas does have a special usage, however, in child custody determinations. In that context, the term is used to refer to a determination of parental rights. The managing conservator is the custodial parent and the other parent is the possessory conservator. Those determinations are discussed in Chapter 5A.6.

5A.13

Foster Care

The Texas Department of Human Services regulates foster care for illegitimate, dependent, neglected, and delinquent children.[1] If a court terminates the parent–child relationship or appoints the Texas Department of Human Services or another licensed agency as managing conservator, the court may place a child in a foster home, a group home, or an institution.[2]

Each foster home is required to obtain a license from the Texas Department of Human Resources, which requires proof that the home meets the safety and health requirements.[3] The Texas Department of Human Services (Department) may pay foster parents for the costs of caring for a foster child in certain instances, or the foster parents may be eligible for the Department's dependent children program or child welfare services. The expenses for which the Department may pay include medical care for the child. The parents or guardians, however, remain liable to the state for the expenses incurred by the Department, state, or county for foster care. Additionally, before a child may be placed in foster care, the Department is required to do a study of the potential foster parents.[4] The study must include the reasons why place-

1. Tex. Hum. Res. Code Ann. § 41.021 (Vernon 1986).
2. Tex. Fam. Code Ann. § 18.01 (Vernon Supp. 1987). Also, if the parents voluntarily relinquish custody of a child, the court may order any of the options.
3. Tex. Hum. Res. Code Ann. § 42.041 (Vernon 1986). The Department is required to inspect the home at least once a year and has a right to make unannounced visits.
4. Tex. Admin. Code tit. 40, § 83.236 (1987). Persons performing the study must have a master's degree in social work with at least 1 year of experience in child or family services, or a graduate or bachelor's degree in social work or behavioral science with at least 2 years' experience.

ment in foster care is necessary; the potential parents', biological parents', and child's expectations and feelings toward foster care; the child's school and previous placement history, if any; and a description of the short- and long-term goals of the care.

Placement Hearing

The court must give all interested parties at least 10 days notice prior to the hearing. The Texas Department of Human Services, the potential foster parents, the natural parents, managing conservators or guardians, and any state or other person having an interest in the child should receive this notice. Additionally, the placement hearing may not be earlier than 5½ months after the filing of the placement petition, or later than 12 months after the court terminates the parent–child relationship.

The Texas Department of Human Services is required to investigate the potential foster parents before the hearing and has the power to obtain the criminal records of any prospective foster parent. The court is required to appoint a guardian ad litem for the child and counsel, if necessary, to represent the interests of the child. Normally, the child is required to attend a placement hearing unless the court orders otherwise.

At the placement hearing, the court is required to determine which of the available options—foster care, agency home care, or rehabilitative care—is in the best interest of the child. The court may also return the child to the natural parents or guardians. If the court terminates the parent–child relationship, or the parents voluntarily relinquish their parental rights, however, the court must initiate steps for permanent placement or adoption in addition to the temporary placement in foster care.

5A.14

Adoption

MHPs may become involved in adoptions by a court order or a party's request to evaluate the child or the prospective parents. The potential parents are required to meet certain criteria, and the rights of the natural parents must be fulfilled, for a valid adoption.

Adoption Requirements

Any adult may adopt a child if the necessary requirements are met.[1] The Texas Department of Human Services has established certain criteria for prospective adoptive parents. These criteria include evaluations of the following factors:[2]

1. *Age.* Maturity and life expectancy are considered. The person should have a life expectancy that will allow the person to raise the child to adulthood.
2. *Marriage.* The evaluation considers not only whether a person is married, but also the length of the marriage. Normally, a couple is required to have been married for at least 2 years. If the person is single, the study considers the person's ability to provide for a child alone.
3. *Fertility.* Fertility studies are not routine and are considered necessary only in relation to the couple's ability to accept a child who is not their own.

---

1. Tex. Fam. Code Ann. § 16.02 (Vernon 1986). Also, if the petitioning parties are married, both parties must attend the adoption hearing unless the court orders otherwise.
2. Tex. Admin. Code tit. 40, § 49.1502 (1987).

4. *Handicaps.* Handicaps are considered to the extent that the particular handicap could interfere with adequately caring for the child.
5. *Residence.* Normally a couple may only adopt if they live in a community long enough for the agency to complete the study. The evaluation considers the stability of the home.
6. *Race/ethnicity.* The parents should normally be the same race or ethnicity as the child, so that the child will develop the appropriate ties.
7. *Financial status.* The evaluation considers both past and present management of funds, as well as the person's or couple's ability to provide for the child's maintenance and support.
8. *Health.* Both the potential parents' physical and mental health are considered and must be adequate to assure that the parents may adequately care for the child. Additionally, one goal is to protect the child from another loss of a parent by death or incapacity and to prevent repetition of abuse or neglect.
9. *Religion.* There is no specific religious requirement. The evaluation will consider, however, the potential parent's ability and willingness to respect and encourage the child's affiliations and provide the child with religious or ethical opportunities.
10. *Discipline.* Potential parents are evaluated on their willingness and ability to individualize discipline and respect differences between children. Further, corporal punishment is discouraged and the department has specific rules if spanking will be used.
11. *Criminal history.* The child placement agency checks not only the potential parents' criminal history, but that of any person who is at least 18 years old and lives in the potential home. Crimes are evaluated in terms of the dangers to placement, rearing, and protection of the child. Further, if the person has been convicted of a felony offense, crime against a person, public indecency, or drug charge, the potential parent must give the agency proof of rehabilitation.

An adult may adopt a child who is under the age of 18 and not married.[3] In processing applications, the placement agency is required to apply certain priorities, in the following order: requests for specific children; requests for children who are characteristic of the children within the agency's region; and requests for children who will probably be requiring placement in the future.

The party, or parties if married, are required to file suit in the

3. Tex. Fam. Code Ann. § 16.01 (Vernon 1986).

county where the child resides.[4] If the child has natural parents, there must first be a decree terminating the parent–child relationship or an action to terminate the relationship joined with the adoption suit.[5] The petitioning party must be either a stepparent, an adult who has had possession of the child for a 30-day period immediately prior to the suit, an adult who has had actual possession of the child for at least 2 months during the preceding 3-month period, or an adult who has had substantial contact with the child. Additionally, before the court may grant an adoption, the child is required to live with the potential parents for at least 6 months.[6]

After the parties file suit, the court is required to order a social study of the prospective parents and the child.[7] The study considers the child's condition and circumstances and the home environment of the prospective parents. Any qualified state agency may perform the study or the court may appoint a qualified individual. The report must be completed within 60 days and filed with the court. In a contested case, the parties may also receive a copy of the report.

Additionally, before a court may grant an adoption, a study concerning the health, social, educational, and genetic history of the child is required to be completed and filed with the court.[8] A parent, guardian, or state agency in charge of the child completes the report, which should include:

1. the child's health history, including birth, neonatal, medical, psychological, psychiatric, and dental history;
2. the social history, to the extent known, including the child's relationship with parents, siblings, and extended family, or anyone who had possession of the child;
3. the educational history, including the results of testing and any special educational needs;
4. the genetic history, including, to the extent known, information about the parents (their health prior to and at the time of the adoption; cause and age of death; height, weight, hair, and eye color; nationality or ethnic background; and educational and

---

4. If the child resides with parents, guardians, or conservators, their place of residence is also the child's. Tex. Fam. Code Ann. 11.04 (Vernon 1986).
5. See Section 5A.10 for a discussion of grounds for terminating the parent–child relationship. If the petitioning party is married to a natural parent, the termination decree is not necessary. Tex. Fam. Code Ann. § 11.03 (Vernon 1986).
6. Tex. Fam. Code Ann. § 16.04 (Vernon 1986). The court may shorten the period if it finds that the action will be in the best interests of the child.
7. Tex. Fam. Code Ann. § 16.031 (Vernon 1987).
8. Tex. Fam. Code Ann. § 16.032 (Vernon 1986). All adoption records and reports are maintained for a minimum of 99 years.

professional achievement levels) and the existence of any other children.

The report is edited to protect the confidentiality of the natural parents and their families. Either the state agency or a court, however, may release the report to the adoptive parents, managing conservators or guardians, the adopted child when the child reaches the age of majority, or the adopted child's surviving spouse or children upon adequate proof of identity and legal entitlement.

If the child's natural parents have voluntarily relinquished parental rights or had their rights involuntarily terminated by court order, the conservator must give written consent to the adoption.[9] Also, if the child is at least 12 years old, the child must consent to the adoption. The court, however, may waive the requirement for the child's or managing conservator's consent if the court determines the action will be in the best interests of the child.

9. Tex. Fam. Code Ann. § 16.05 (Vernon 1986). Also, if the petitioning party is married, both the husband and the wife must attend the adoption hearing unless the court orders otherwise.

5A.15

Delinquency and In Need of Supervision Determinations

A juvenile court may determine that a child 10 to 17 years of age is delinquent or in need of supervision.[1] Delinquent conduct includes violations of criminal law punishable by imprisonment or violations of juvenile court orders. Conduct indicating a need for supervision includes three or more violations of criminal laws, other than traffic offenses, punishable by fine only; unexcused absence for 10 days or more from school within a 6-month period; absence from the home for a significant period without the consent of the parents or guardians; and violations of the laws pertaining to driving under the influence of alcohol or drugs.[2] The purpose of these provisions is to "remove from children committing unlawful acts the taint of criminality and the consequences of behavior and to substitute a program of treatment, training, and rehabilitation."[3]

A law enforcement officer may elect to issue a warning to a child and child's family instead of taking the child into custody for delinquent conduct.[4] If an officer does take custody of a child, the officer is required to do one of the following, without delay:[5]

1. release the child to the parents or guardians, if they promise to bring the child before the court at the proper time;
2. bring the child to an officer of the juvenile court;

---

1. Tex. Fam. Code Ann. § 51.01 (Vernon Supp. 1987).
2. Tex. Fam. Code Ann. § 51.03 (Vernon 1986). Delinquent behavior does not include minor traffic violations.
3. Tex. Fam. Code Ann. § 51.01 (Vernon 1986).
4. Tex. Fam. Code Ann. § 51.16 (Vernon 1986). A warning is a formal written statement about the conduct, which must be approved by a juvenile court.
5. Tex. Fam. Code Ann. § 52.01 (Vernon 1986).

3. take the child to a detention facility pending a hearing before the juvenile court; or
4. take the child to a medical facility if the child has a serious condition requiring prompt treatment.

If a child is referred to juvenile court authorities for detention, the juvenile court is required to conduct a preliminary investigation and hearing to determine if there is probable cause to believe that the child committed the delinquent conduct or conduct indicating a need for supervision.[6] If the court finds probable cause, it is required to set a date for a formal hearing. The court must release the child pending the formal hearing unless the child is likely to leave the county, the parents are likely to remove the child from the county, the parents or guardian is not giving the child adequate care and protection, the child has no parents or guardian, the child is accused of a felony and there is a possible danger to the community, or the child has a history of delinquency or crime and is likely to commit an offense if released.[7]

The hearing may be held in either the county in which the child resides or the county where the conduct allegedly occurred.[8] The court is required to appoint counsel for the child if the child does not have counsel and a guardian ad litem for any child who does not have parents or a guardian to represent the child's interest at the hearing. The child has a right to trial by jury at this adjudication hearing on the issue of delinquency or in need of supervision unless the child waives this right.[9]

The state must prove delinquent or in need of supervision conduct beyond a reasonable doubt. If the judge or jury finds the child did not engage in the conduct alleged, the case is dismissed. If the child is found to have engaged in the conduct alleged, a disposition hearing is then held. At the disposition hearing, the court may consider, in addition to the evidence presented at the adjudication hearing, a social study or professional assessment.[10] If the court determines that the child needs rehabilitation, or the

6. Tex. Fam. Code Ann. § 53.01 (Vernon 1986).
7. Tex. Fam. Code Ann. § 53.02 (Vernon 1986). If the child remains in custody, the formal hearing must be within 2 days. Otherwise, the trial must be within 10 days.
8. Tex. Fam. Code Ann. § 51.08 (Vernon 1986). If the court does not release the child pending the formal hearing, the child may not be confined with adults. Further, a child may not be photographed or fingerprinted unless the charge is a felony and the case is transferred to criminal court.
9. Tex. Fam. Code Ann. § 54.03 (Vernon 1986).
10. Tex. Fam. Code Ann. § 54.03 (Vernon 1986). If there is a trial by jury, the jury may not receive a social study at any time during the trial.

child or the community requires that a disposition be made, the court may:[11]

1. place the child on probation for up to 1 year, with additional 1-year extensions possible until the child is 18;
2. place the child on probation in a foster home or suitable institution;
3. require restitution for the victim of the delinquent conduct; or
4. commit the child to the Texas Youth Commission.[12]

Before the court may place the child outside the home, however, it is required to determine that all reasonable efforts were made to prevent removal.

The court may order treatment by MHPs as part of the rehabilitation program. Another option to the court is to impose a period of not more than 6 months for voluntary rehabilitation and adjustment in the place of a formal delinquency hearing.[13] If the child is committed to the Texas Youth Commission, the facility may require and provide psychiatric care for the child.[14] Further, delinquency records may only be used as evidence either in subsequent delinquency proceedings or in sentencing determinations in a criminal court.[15]

---

11. Tex. Fam. Code Ann. § 54.03 (Vernon 1986). Any disposition, except commitment to the Texas Youth Commission, may be modified by petitioning the court for a modification hearing. If the delinquent conduct was capital murder, murder, aggravated kidnapping, aggravated sexual assault, or attempted murder, the sentence may be for up to 30 years, beginning in the Texas Youth Commission and followed by transfer to the Department of Corrections.
12. Commitment to the Texas Youth Commission is essentially the same as commitment to a prison for adults, with the modifications necessary in view of the youth and rehabilitative prospects of the children.
13. Tex. Fam. Code Ann. § 53.02 (Vernon 1986).
14. Tex. Hum. Res. Code Ann. § 61.076 (Vernon Supp. 1987).
15. Tex. Fam. Code Ann. § 51.13 (Vernon 1986). Thus, the records may not be used as evidence in regular civil or criminal proceedings. Further, a judgment of delinquency does not impose civil liability on the child or act as a conviction of a crime.

5A.16

Competency of Juveniles to Stand Trial

A psychiatrist or psychologist may become involved in delinquency or in need of supervision proceedings if evidence of the child's mental illness or mental retardation is brought to the attention of the court and the court orders an examination for competency to stand trial in the juvenile proceeding.[1] Unfitness to proceed may be due to either mental illness or mental retardation. The court is required to hold a competency hearing if a bona fide question is raised, before which a psychologist or psychiatrist is to examine the child. If mental retardation is suspected, the examination is required to be conducted at a facility approved by the Texas Department of Mental Health and Mental Retardation. The examination may include temporary hospitalization for observation and testing if necessary.

If the court finds that the child lacks the capacity to understand the nature of the proceedings or to assist in his own defense, the child is not subject to delinquency or in need of supervision proceedings in juvenile court, or transfer to criminal court. However, the court may order commitment for mental health or mental retardation services.

1. Tex. Fam. Code Ann. § 55.01 (Vernon 1986).

5A.17

Non-Responsibility Defense

A psychiatrist or psychologist may become involved in delinquency or in need of supervision proceedings if the court orders or a child seeks an examination for non-responsibility (i.e., insanity) in the juvenile proceeding. To prove this defense, the juvenile must demonstrate that at the time of the delinquent conduct, "as a result of a mental disease or defect, he lack[ed] substantial capacity either to appreciate the wrongfulness of his conduct or to conform his conduct to the requirements of law."[1] If it is shown by a preponderance of the evidence that this test has been met, the proceedings are required to be dismissed and the child may be temporarily committed for mental health care or mental retardation services. If the child is determined to be responsible, the proceedings are to continue as if the question had never been raised.

The test for non-responsibility in juvenile court is broader than the test for the insanity defense in adult criminal court.[2] The former adult insanity defense test, which was changed in 1983, was also broader than the current M'Naghten test, which focuses on mental illness resulting in a cognitive incapacity. Following the change in the adult standard, no change was made in the juvenile standard.

---

1. Tex. Fam. Code Ann. § 55.05 (a) (Vernon 1986).
2. *See* Tex. Penal Code Ann. § 8.01 (Vernon 1987).

5A.18

Transfer of Juveniles to Stand Trial as Adults

A child under 15 is not subject to criminal prosecution in Texas state court for most offenses.[1] Those offenses for which a child under 15 is subject to prosecution include perjury if the child understood the nature and influence of the oath; traffic violations except driving under the influence of alcohol or narcotics; and misdemeanors punishable by fine only.

A juvenile court may waive its jurisdiction over a child and transfer the case to criminal court in certain instances. The juvenile court may transfer the case if the offense charged is a felony, the child was at least 15 years of age at the time of the alleged crime, and the court determines that "there is probable cause to believe that the child before the court committed the offense and that because of the seriousness of the offense or the background of the child the welfare of the community requires criminal proceedings."[2] The juvenile court is required to hold a hearing, without a jury, to determine if the case should be transferred. Further, the court is required to appoint counsel to represent the child, if the child does not already have counsel, and a guardian ad litem.

An MHP may become involved in the transfer hearing. Prior to the hearing, the court must order a "complete diagnostic study, social study, and full investigation of the child, his circumstances, and the circumstances of the alleged offense."[3] The MHP may also be called as a witness at the transfer hearing. A copy of the social study and all other written records must be provided the child's

1. Tex. Penal Code Ann. § 8.07 (Vernon Supp. 1987). Additionally, the death sentence is not applicable to children under the age of 17.
2. Tex. Fam. Code Ann. § 54.02 (Vernon Supp. 1987).
3. Tex. Fam. Code Ann. § 54.02 (Vernon 1986).

attorney as well as the court. The court, however, may order the attorneys not to reveal the contents to the child or the child's parents if the disclosure could materially harm the rehabilitation and treatment of the child or substantially decrease the chances of receiving information from the same or similar sources in the future.

The court is required to consider a number of factors in determining a discretionary transfer to criminal court. These include:

1. whether the offense was against a person or property,
2. whether the offense was aggressive and premeditated,
3. whether the evidence is sufficient to support a grand jury indictment,
4. the maturity of the child,
5. the previous history and general record of the child, and
6. the chances of adequately protecting the public and the likelihood of rehabilitating the child in the juvenile system.

If the court transfers the case to criminal court, the child is treated in all respects as an adult. Before the final transfer, however, the court may also order an examining trial.

5A.19

Voluntary Admission and Civil Commitment of Minors

Voluntary Admission for Mental Health Services

A request for voluntary admission of a minor to a mental health facility must be written and signed by the person to be admitted if that person is 16 years of age or older. At the age of 16 years, a minor may be admitted without the additional consent of a parent or guardian. If the request is made on behalf of someone under 16, it must include the consent of the parent, managing conservator, or guardian, and the minor.[1] The mental health facility must determine whether the minor has the capacity to consent. If not, involuntary rather than voluntary hospitalization must be pursued.

The criteria for voluntary admission require a determination by the head of the facility that, based on a preliminary examination, the person suffers from a mental illness and will likely benefit from treatment. A voluntary patient is required to submit to the custody of the facility until discharged or 96 hours after a written request for release is filed with the head of the facility. No application for involuntary commitment may be filed against a voluntary patient unless the patient is absent without authorization or unable or unwilling to commit to care.

1. 1980 Op. Att'y Gen. M.W. 180.

Voluntary Admission for Mental Retardation Services

The consent of the parents or guardian of a minor child is required for voluntary treatment of the retarded minor. An application for voluntary mental retardation services may be filed in writing. If a child is admitted, there must be at least an annual review assessing the child's needs. The parents have a right not only to be informed of the child's progress and review results, but also to participate actively in the planning of treatments. Moreover, the parents or the child has a right to withdraw from the care at any time. After the parents or child requests discharge, the residential care facility may not keep the child for longer than 96 hours. The only exception is if the director of the facility determines that release will endanger either the child or the public and files a petition for court-ordered commitment.

Involuntary Commitment for Mental Health Services

Minors not willing or able (along with parent or guardian) to consent to voluntary hospitalization may be subject to court-ordered mental health services under the same procedures as those applicable to adults (see Chapter 5E.4).

5A.20

Education for Gifted and Handicapped Children

Any educational institution supported entirely or in part by state funds in Texas is required to provide equal educational opportunities to all students within its jurisdiction.[1] The Texas State Board of Education develops and oversees special education for handicapped children, which is available for all children between the ages of 3 and 21 years.[2]

Special education may include "special services" by professionals or paraprofessionals in the classroom or special resource rooms, or "related services," which are developmental, supportive, or evaluative services designed to assure the proper development of the student but which are not necessarily instructional by themselves. Related services may include counseling with the student and the student's family, psychological or psychiatric services, physical therapy, social work services, or medical diagnostic services.[3] Additionally, special education may include residential placement at facilities under the control of the Texas Department of Mental Health and Mental Retardation or the Texas Schools for the Blind or Deaf.

Eligibility for special education services is determined both from diagnostic tests and other general criteria. Both the criteria and test results are referenced with established national levels as part of an evaluation. The general criteria, defined by statute, are definitions of specific classes of students and their associated traits or conditions. The classes include:[4]

1. Tex. Educ. Code Ann. § 1.04 (Vernon Supp. 1987).
2. Tex. Educ. Code Ann. § 21.501 (Vernon Supp. 1987).
3. Tex. Educ. Code Ann. § 21.502(1)(B) (Vernon Supp. 1987).
4. Tex. Educ. Code Ann. § 21.503 (Vernon Supp. 1987).

1. *handicapped students:* students with physical, auditory, visual, mental or emotional, speech, or multiples of such disorders, whose disabilities are "so limiting as to require the provision of special services in place of or in addition to instruction in the regular classroom;"[5]
2. *physically handicapped students:* students whose body members or functions are so impaired as to require special education;
3. *mentally retarded students:* students with "significantly subaverage general intellectual functioning existing concurrently with deficiencies in adaptive behavior and manifested during the developmental period such that they cannot be adequately educated in the regular classes;"[6]
4. *emotionally disturbed students:* students "whose emotional condition is psychologically or psychiatrically determined to be such that they cannot be adequately and safely educated in the regular classes;"[7]
5. *learning-disabled students:* students:
   a. who show a significant discrepancy between actual academic achievement and intellectual abilities in one or more areas, such as reading, mathematics, or spelling;
   b. for whom the discrepancy is not primarily the result of a physical handicap, mental retardation, emotional disturbance, or cultural or economic disadvantage; and
   c. for whom the disability exists to such a degree that regular classes will not provide an equal and appropriate education without special services;
6. *auditorially handicapped students:* students whose hearing is so impaired that they cannot safely or properly be educated in regular classrooms without special education;
7. *visually handicapped students:* students whose sight is so impaired that they cannot be safely or properly taught in regular classrooms without special education;
8. *speech handicapped students:* students whose speech is so impaired that they cannot receive an adequate education in regular classrooms without special services; and
9. *autistic students:* students whose speech, language, perception, mobility, and development rate are so impaired that they cannot be adequately taught in regular classrooms without special services.

---

5. *Id.*
6. *Id.*
7. *Id.*

MHPs may become involved in determining if the child meets the general criteria or in an individual evaluation or testing. Also, MHPs may provide continuing treatment or counseling to the child and/or the child's family as part of the special education program.

School personnel, the child's parents or guardian, or other concerned persons or organizations may initiate an assessment to determine if a child needs special education services.[8] Before the student may be placed in special education classes, however, the student is required to be given either a verbal or written individual intelligence test. The test must be in the language in which the student is the most fluent and capable. After all testing is complete, a written report of the child's capabilities and performance is required to be filed with the school, which in conjunction with the local school board determines whether to place the child in a special education program. The results of skills or achievement tests are confidential, and only the student, the student's parents or guardian, and the school personnel directly involved with the student may receive the results.[9]

Further, the student, if believed to be mentally retarded, has the right to a prompt and comprehensive diagnosis and evaluation.[10] If the parents cannot afford the evaluation, the Texas Department of Mental Health and Mental Retardation is required to pay the expenses. The evaluation must be adapted to the cultural background and language capabilities of the student. After the evaluation is complete, if the parents disagree with the findings and recommendations, they have a right to an independent evaluation and an administrative hearing.[11]

As part of the special education program, each school district may also establish a guidance center to assist children in place of attendance at the regular school.[12] The guidance center may offer psychological testing and treatment to the students in addition to educational services. Before the student may be admitted, however, the school is required to notify the parents or guardian and obtain consent for any testing or counseling. The school is also

8. Tex. Educ. Code Ann. § 21.5031 (Vernon Supp. 1987).
9. Tex. Educ. Code Ann. § 21.556 (Vernon 1986). Other state agencies or private citizens may receive aggregates of the reports provided the names of the students and the teachers are removed from the record prior to release.
10. Tex. Rev. Civ. Stat. Ann. art. 5547-300 (Vernon Supp. 1987).
11. Tex. Rev. Civ. Stat. Ann. art. 5547-300 (Vernon Supp. 1987). The hearing is before the Texas Department of Mental Health and Mental Retardation. The parents have a right to counsel and a right to full access to the evaluation records prior to the hearing. The department's decision is appealable to a state court.
12. Tex. Educ. Code Ann. § 21.601 (Vernon 1986).

required to inform the parents or guardian of the reasons why the student was assigned to the guidance center.

The parents or guardians are entitled to visit the center, inspect the center's materials, and receive the results of any testing or treatments. Moreover, once a student is assigned to a guidance center, the parents or guardians are required to participate in the program. At a minimum, the parents are required to sign an agreement that includes a statement of the program's goals; a requirement that the parents attend certain meetings for review of the student's progress; and an acknowledgment that they understand and accept the responsibilities of attendance and the general program. Finally, if the parents or guardians refuse to participate or cooperate in the program, the superintendent of the school district may petition a court for an order requiring the parents to comply.

5A.21

Consent, Confidentiality, and Services for Minors

Minors may only consent to certain treatments without parental or guardian consent.[1] Two categories of minors, however, may give consent to treatment without regard to their age. Minors who serve actively in the armed forces of the United States and minors who are at least 16 years of age, reside separately from parents or guardians, and manage their own financial affairs may consent to all treatments.

Minors may consent to treatment by a licensed physician for drug addiction or drug-related conditions and pregnancy or pregnancy-related conditions.[2] If a licensed physician renders services under these conditions, the physician is not liable for damages except those due to the physician's negligence. The physician may advise the minor's parents or guardian of the treatment without the consent of the minor. Further, the physician is entitled to rely on a written statement from the minor about the capacity to consent.

Additionally, minors may consent to counseling by a physician, psychologist, counselor, or social worker for sexual abuse, physical abuse, or suicide prevention.[3] The MHP may advise the parents or guardians of the treatment without the minor's consent and may rely on the minor's written statement regarding capacity to consent. The MHP is not liable for damages except any damages due to the professional's own negligence. If the minor refuses treatment, however, the MHP may not treat the minor without a

1. Tex. Fam. Code Ann. § 35.03 (Vernon 1986).
2. Tex. Fam. Code Ann. § 35.03 (Vernon 1986). The law allowing minors to consent to treatment for pregnancy does not include abortions.
3. Tex. Fam. Code Ann. § 35.03 (Vernon 1986).

court order. Parents or guardians are not obligated to pay for any services rendered by an MHP without their consent.

Finally, a licensed physician who has reasonable grounds to believe that a child has been subject to abuse or neglect may examine the child without the consent of the child or the child's parents or guardian.[4] The examination may include X-rays and blood tests if necessary. If the child is at least 16 years old, however, a physician may not examine the child without either the child's consent or a court order. Physicians who examine a child suspected to be the victim of abuse or neglect are not liable for damages except those related to the physician's negligence in the examination.

4. Tex. Fam. Code Ann. § 35.04 (Vernon 1986).

5A.22

Consent for Abortion

Texas does not have a special law regarding consent by minors to abortion. Therefore, the consent rules prescribed by the legislature require that unless the child is an emancipated minor or an active member of the armed forces, parental consent or consent from a properly authorized person is necessary before a physician may perform an abortion on a minor.[1] Specifically, the statute pertaining to consent by minors states that:

> A minor may consent to the furnishing of hospital, medical, surgical, and dental care by a licensed physician or dentist if the minor . . . is unmarried and pregnant, and consents to hospital, medical, or surgical treatment, *other than abortion,* related to her pregnancy.[2]

Thus, the minor may consent to treatment for pregnancy but not an abortion. Further, the statute gives the physician the option of informing the child's parents about the pregnancy without the consent of the child, provided the physician treats the child.[3]

The United States Supreme Court, however, has ruled that as a matter of constitutional law parental consent may not be made an absolute requirement for an abortion if a court finds either that a minor is mature enough to make the decision about abortion or that requiring parental consent would not be in the best interests of the minor.[4] Thus, while the rule in Texas set by the legislature

1. See Chapter 5A.21 for a discussion of who may consent for minors and what services minors may legitimately consent to themselves.
2. Tex. Fam. Code Ann. § 35.03 (Vernon 1986) (emphasis added).
3. *Id.* Additionally, the United States Supreme Court has held that a statute requiring parental notice prior to a minor's abortion is not unconstitutional. *See* H.L. v. Matheson, 450 U.S. 398 (1981).
4. Bellotti v. Baird, 443 U.S. 622, *reh'g denied,* 444 U.S. 887 (1979).

requires parental consent, a minor is constitutionally entitled to consent to an abortion without parental consent if one of these exceptions is met.

5A.23

Evaluation and Treatment of Children at the Request of a Noncustodial Parent

When the custodial parent or guardian cannot be reached and has not given notice to the contrary, the following persons may give consent to medical care for a minor:[1] grandparents, adult brothers and sisters, adult aunts and uncles, educational facilities if there is written authorization from the parent or guardian, any court, any adult who cares for the minor if there is written authorization from the parent or guardian, and any adult who is responsible for the minor due to a juvenile court order if the adult has "reasonable grounds to believe the minor is in need of immediate medical treatment."[2] In addition, the Texas Youth Commission may consent to treatment of any minor committed to it provided the parent or guardian is notified and does not indicate otherwise.

A consent for medical treatment of a minor by someone other than the custodial parent or guardian must be written and must contain:[3]

1. the name of the minor;
2. the name of 1 or both parents, guardian, or conservator;
3. the name of the person giving consent and the relation to the minor child;
4. the nature of the treatment to be given; and
5. the date treatment is to begin.

---

1. Tex. Fam. Code Ann. § 35.01 (Vernon 1986). *See* Section 5A.21 for a discussion of express provisions allowing a minor to consent and abuse cases where even the minor's consent is unnecessary.
2. Tex. Fam. Code Ann. § 35.01 (Vernon 1986).
3. Tex. Fam. Code Ann. § 35.02 (Vernon 1986).

Section 5

Practice Related to the Law

Section 5B

Other Civil Matters

5B.1

Mental Status of Licensed/Certified Professionals

Regulatory boards or courts may request MHPs to evaluate a member of another profession. This usually occurs during a disciplinary proceeding, because the requirement for mental health and competence normally arises as an issue of continued professional competence rather than as part of the initial licensing requirements. Occasionally, however, mental incapacity is also grounds for the initial denial of a license. In either case, the MHP is usually asked to evaluate both the mental competence of the professional and the effect of the professional's health on the ability to perform duties safely.

It should be noted that this section deals only with the mental competence of specific MHPs or related professionals for which the statutory schemes expressly mention mental health. There may be occasions when MHPs are asked to evaluate other professionals and their professional capacity.

Attorneys

Applicants for a license to practice law may be denied a license if the Board of Law Examiners finds that the applicant's present mental or emotional condition will prevent the applicant from performing any duties to clients, courts, or the legal profession in general in a satisfactory manner.[1] Additionally, an applicant for licensure who is "mentally ill" is not permitted to take the state licensing examination.[2] The grievance committee of the board also

1. Tex. Gov. Code Ann. § 81.028 (Vernon Supp. 1988).
2. Tex. Gov. Code Ann. § 82.027 (Vernon Supp. 1988).

has the power to investigate alleged "incapacity" of a licensed attorney and revoke or suspend the attorney's license, disbar the attorney, or issue private reprimands.[3] Finally, if a court declares an attorney legally incompetent, the attorney is suspended from practice.

Dentists

Dentists may face disciplinary action in the form of license suspension, revocation, or probation; fines; or other official reprimands if they are judged to be insane by a court.[4] Mental incompetence is also grounds for denying a license. Additionally, the law requires that dentists be "physically and mentally" capable of performing their duties safely.[5] The statute, however, does not elaborate on this requirement.

Pharmacists

Pharmacists may face license revocation, denial, restriction, suspension, retirement, or cancellation; fines; or reprimand if they are found to be incapable of engaging in pharmacology "with reasonable skill, competence, and safety to the public."[6] While the statute does not further define this standard, it does provide that the licensing board or a court may require the pharmacist to submit to either a physical or mental examination to determine the pharmacist's competence.[7]

Physical Therapists

Physical therapists may have their licenses revoked or suspended, or be denied a license, if they are declared to be mentally incompetent by a court.[8]

---

3. Tex. Gov. Code Ann. § 81.074 (Vernon Supp. 1988).
4. Tex. Rev. Civ. Stat. Ann. art. 4549 § 3(a) (Vernon Supp. 1987).
5. Tex. Rev. Civ. Stat. Ann. art. 4549 § 3(k) (Vernon Supp. 1987).
6. Tex. Rev. Civ. Stat. Ann. art. 4542a-1 § 26(a)(4) (Vernon Supp. 1988).
7. *Id.* Additionally, drug and alcohol addiction are grounds for disciplinary action. *Id.* § 26(a)(7).
8. Tex. Rev. Civ. Stat. Ann. art. 4512e § 19(a)(6) (Vernon Supp. 1988).

Physicians

Physicians, or applicants for licensure, must be able to practice medicine safely. Thus the law expressly provides that grounds for license denial, revocation, or suspension include drug or alcohol addiction and any physical or mental condition that renders a physician incapable of practicing safely (see Chapter 1.1). Additionally, physicians may have their licenses revoked or suspended if they are judged by a court to be mentally incompetent.

Psychiatric Nurses

Psychiatric nurses may face license revocation or suspension, or other sanctions, if they have a physical or mental condition that renders them incapable of practicing nursing safely; are found to be of unsound mind by a court; or if they abuse drugs or alcohol to the extent that they cannot practice safely (see Chapter 1.2).

Psychologists

To obtain a license, psychologists must have both the physical and mental competence to practice safely. Additionally, it is grounds for license revocation or suspension if psychologists abuse drugs or alcohol to the extent that they cannot practice safely (see Chapter 1.3).

5B.2

Workers' Compensation

Workers' compensation law provides a statutory scheme awarding damages to employees for injuries incurred in the course of employment and death benefits to certain survivors in the event of work-related death. It also provides compensation for occupational diseases, such as asbestosis. Under the workers' compensation scheme, the employer either purchases insurance or is self-insured to provide for these benefits. Employees are eligible for these benefits regardless of their contributory fault or the fault of any other party as long as the injury or disease meets the statutory criteria of occurring during, or being related to, the employment.[1] In return, however, the employee gives up the common-law right to sue the employer.[2]

MHPs may become involved in workers' compensation claims either at the request of an employee for services or at the request of the Industrial Accident Board, which is the agency empowered to investigate and adjudicate disputed workers' compensation claims.

Benefits and Scope of Coverage

The workers' compensation law covers all employees, with few exceptions. The exceptions include domestic servants, farm la-

1. Tex. Rev. Civ. Stat. Ann. art. 8306 § 1 (Vernon Supp. 1988).
2. Tex. Rev. Civ. Stat. Ann. art. 8306 § 3 (Vernon Supp. 1988). Employees, however, may preserve their common-law right to sue an employer if they provide written notice to the employer at the time of hiring that they desire to preserve these claims. *Id.* § 3a.

borers, ranch laborers, and employees of any firm or person operating railway systems.[3] Moreover, employees may not waive their rights to workers' compensation.[4]

Generally, the statute provides coverage for injuries or diseases sustained in the course of employment or related to the nature of the employment. It does not cover injury caused by an act of God, intentional injury by a third party unrelated to the employment, injury occurring while the employee is intoxicated, or injury occurring while the employee is intentionally trying to injure self or a third party.[5] Additionally, to receive the benefits, the employer must be a subscriber to the workers' compensation insurance association or self-insured. When employers do not provide workers' compensation insurance, employees retain the right to sue the employer for injuries sustained in the course of employment.

Expenses covered by workers' compensation include the costs of medical services, nursing, hospital services, prosthetic devices, chiropractic services, and medicines.[6] Compensation also covers reasonable expenses for physical rehabilitation and other expenses necessary to return an employee to normal physical capacity to the extent possible.[7] The law, however, only covers "reasonable" expenses. If a physician or facility charges over the amount considered reasonable by the Industrial Accident Board, the additional expenses are not covered. Aside from the specific items covered, workers' compensation also provides coverage for partial or total disability, occupational diseases, and death.

Additionally, for certain conditions resulting in time off from work, workers' compensation pays an employee's average weekly wages.

For partial incapacity, the employee is entitled to receive weekly compensation for lost wages equal to 60% of the average weekly wages, less any wages currently received, for up to 300 weeks.[8] For total and permanent disability, the employee is entitled to receive lifetime benefits equal to 66⅔% of the average weekly wages for specified conditions.[9] For other nonlisted, totally incapacitating conditions, the employee is entitled to receive the same percent, but only for up to 401 weeks following the injury. Normally, these payments are weekly. In certain situations, how-

3. Tex. Rev. Civ. Stat. Ann. art. 8306 § 2 (Vernon Supp. 1988).
4. Tex. Rev. Civ. Stat. Ann. art. 8306 § 14 (Vernon Supp. 1988).
5. Tex. Rev. Civ. Stat. Ann. art. 8309 § 4 (Vernon 1982).
6. Tex. Rev. Civ. Stat. Ann. art. 8307 § 5 (Vernon Supp. 1988).
7. Tex. Rev. Civ. Stat. Ann. art. 8306 § 7 (Vernon Supp. 1988).
8. Tex. Rev. Civ. Stat. Ann. art. 8306 § 11 (Vernon Supp. 1988).
9. Tex. Rev. Civ. Stat. Ann. art. 8306 § 10 (Vernon Supp. 1988). These conditions include such things as loss of sight in both eyes, loss of both hands or both feet, and paralysis of both legs or arms due to spinal injury. *Id.* § 11a.

ever, claims may be settled by a lump sum payment.[10] Employees bear the burden of proving that a total and permanent incapacity exists if the condition is not one expressly provided for by the law.

The statutory scheme also provides coverage for occupational diseases. These are defined as diseases "arising out of and in the course of employment which cause damage or harm to the physical structure of the body and such other diseases or infections as naturally result therefrom."[11] Examples of occupational diseases include asbestosis, silicosis, and diseases occurring from other chemical or X-ray exposure. Benefits include the out-of-pocket expenses for treatment and diagnosis, and possibly a percent of weekly wages if the employee is no longer capable of working at the same job or of working at all. Occupational stress arising out of the course of or related to employment is one area of coverage in which MHPs have particular expertise.

Finally, the statute provides death benefits to surviving spouses, minor children, and parents. Dependent brothers, sisters, grandparents, and adult children may also receive these benefits in certain circumstances.[12] These benefits are paid directly to the recipient and include weekly payments equal to 66⅔% of the employee's average weekly wages over the period for which the employee was reasonably expected to work. The benefits also include funeral expenses up to $2,500. If death followed partial or total incapacity, the previous award for the incapacity is deducted from the death benefit award. Moreover, when children reach the age of majority, or the surviving spouse remarries, the payments terminate.

Procedure

The employee is required to report the injury or disease to the employer within 30 days after the injury or the first clear sign of an occupational disease occurs.[13] After receiving this report, the employer then has a duty to file a written report with the Industrial Accident Board (Board) and the insurance company within 8 days. This report must include the employee's name, age, sex, and occupation; the name and nature of the employer's business; the nature of the work that the employee was performing at the time

10. Tex. Rev. Civ. Stat. Ann. art. 8306 § 15 (Vernon Supp. 1988). For example, if the insurance company refused to pay and forced the employee to litigate, a lump sum payment is authorized.
11. Tex. Rev. Civ. Stat. Ann. art. 8306 § 20 (Vernon Supp. 1988).
12. Tex. Rev. Civ. Stat. Ann. art. 8306 § 8a (Vernon Supp. 1988).
13. Tex. Rev. Civ. Stat. Ann. art. 8307 § 4a (Vernon Supp. 1988).

of injury; the date of the injury; and a description of the nature and extent of the injury.

After the Board receives this report, it is required to forward to the employee the forms necessary to process the claim and a statement relating the proper procedure to follow and the employee's rights.[14] The employee has the sole right to select the physician or facility for any services or treatments required.[15] Additionally, an employer may not retaliate or discriminate against any employee who files a workers' compensation claim.[16]

If the incapacity is one that does not have a predetermined wage percent, however, the Board determines what amount the employee should receive.[17] The Board considers several factors, including the nature and extent of the injury, the presence of previous conditions, the age of the employee, and the occupation of the employee. If the insurance company does not contest the claim, payments for wages and expenses begin within 20 days after the company receives the notice.

If either the employee or insurance company contests an award, the Board has a full hearing on the matter. When the insurance company disagrees with an award, it is required to file a written notice with the Board stating the reasons why the injury should not be covered. At the hearing, the Board has the power to compel witnesses, administer oaths, and admit evidence. The Board also has the power to compel an employee to submit to an examination by a Board-selected physician.[18] The employee has the right to appear before the Board with counsel and to have access to all the medical reports upon which the Board or insurance company will rely. If the Board upholds an award and the insurance company still refuses to pay the claim, the Board has the power to assess a penalty against the company in addition to the award amount.[19]

During the application process, physicians, chiropractors, and hospitals have a duty to provide the Board with written reports concerning the nature and extent of an employee's injury and progress.[20] The insurance company may refuse to pay a claim if these reports are not filed.

Finally, if an employee disagrees with a final Board ruling, the

14. Tex. Rev. Civ. Stat. Ann. art. 8307 § 7b (Vernon Supp. 1988).
15. Tex. Rev. Civ. Stat. Ann. art. 8306 § 7 (Vernon Supp. 1988).
16. Tex. Rev. Civ. Stat. Ann. art. 8307c (Vernon Supp. 1988).
17. Tex. Rev. Civ. Stat. Ann. art. 8306 § 18a (Vernon Supp. 1988).
18. Tex. Rev. Civ. Stat. Ann. art. 8307 §§ 4, 18a (Vernon Supp. 1988). In the event the Board orders an examination, the employee has the right to have an examination by a physician of the employee's choice as well, and both reports are evidence at the hearing.
19. Tex. Rev. Civ. Stat. Ann. art. 8306 § 18a (Vernon Supp. 1988).
20. Tex. Rev. Civ. Stat. Ann. art. 8307 § 7 (Vernon Supp. 1988).

employee may file an appeal with the state district court in the county where the employee resides within 20 days after the final Board ruling.[21] The court may overrule the Board; however, it may not award any amount exceeding that which the employee could have received under the workers' compensation scheme.[22] Further, the court may only award amounts that have actually been incurred at the time of the trial. The employee may receive future expenses that may be incurred only by following normal application procedures.

The court, however, may award reasonable attorney fees against the insurance company, plus up to 12% of the allowable compensation as a penalty or accelerate the periodic payments to create a lump sum settlement.

21. Tex. Rev. Civ. Stat. Ann. art. 8307 § 5 (Vernon Supp. 1988).
22. *Id.*

5B.3

Vocational Disability Determinations

The Board of the Texas Rehabilitation Commission administers the vocational rehabilitation program, which is funded by both the state and federal governments.[1] Vocational disability benefits and training are available to persons who have a physical or mental disability so that they may obtain a "gainful occupation" or attain "maximum personal independence."[2] The program is available to any person who meets the established criteria, regardless of race, color, sex, religion, age or national origin.[3] Services include counseling, therapeutic training, and evaluative examinations. MHPs may become involved if they are counselors employed by the state.

Eligibility Requirements

A counselor determines the initial eligibility of an individual, based on two criteria. The person must have a physical or mental disability that creates a substantial handicap to employment, and there must be a reasonable expectation that vocational rehabilitation services will benefit the person and increase the person's employability.[4] Counselors should not consider the age of the applicant as long as the applicant meets these requirements. If a

1. Tex. Hum. Res. Code Ann. § 112.001-.032 (Vernon Supp. 1988). Tex. Admin. Code tit. 40 § 103.1 (1988). *See also* Texas Const. art. 16 § 6; art. 3 § 51(a) for the constitutional basis providing a right to vocational rehabilitation services.
2. Tex. Admin. Code tit. 40, § 101.2 (1988).
3. Tex. Admin. Code tit. 40, § 101.4 (1988)
4. Tex. Admin. Code tit. 40, §§ 103.2, 103.41 (1988).

counselor determines that a person is not eligible for vocational rehabilitation services, the counselor is required to give the person written notice of the denial and explain the reasons for the denial.[5] The applicant may then appeal the counselor's decision to an area or regional manager. At the eligibility hearing, the applicant has a right to have counsel present, call witnesses, and have access to pertinent evidence.[6]

After an applicant is found to be eligible, the counselor, working with the applicant, develops a written rehabilitation program personalized to the applicant's needs.[7]

Diagnostic Studies

A counselor should first conduct a preliminary evaluation to determine eligibility for vocational rehabilitation.[8] If the counselor finds that the applicant is eligible, a thorough diagnostic study should follow. This thorough study "consists of a comprehensive evaluation of pertinent medical, psychological, vocational, education, and other related factors which bear on the individual's handicap to employment and rehabilitation needs"[9] to determine the nature and extent of services needed by the individual.

If a counselor cannot determine whether an applicant is eligible after performing a thorough study, the commission may provide for an extended evaluation.[10] This extended evaluation may last up to 18 months, during which time the commission may provide counseling and vocational training to facilitate a determination of whether the applicant would benefit from vocational rehabilitation services.

Counseling Services

Not only do counselors make the determination of whether an applicant is eligible, they also provide "counseling, guidance, and referral services" throughout vocational rehabilitation.[11] The law defines counseling as "a process in which a vocational rehabilitation counselor works in a face-to-face relationship with a client in order to help the client understand both his problems and his

---

5. Tex. Admin. Code tit. 40, § 103.44 (1988).
6. Tex. Admin. Code tit. 40, § 101.11 (1988).
7. Tex. Admin. Code tit. 40, § 103.16 (1988).
8. Tex. Admin. Code tit. 40, § 103.4 (1988).
9. Tex. Admin. Code tit. 40, § 103.4 (1988).
10. Tex. Admin. Code tit. 40, § 103.15 (1988).
11. Tex. Admin. Code tit. 40, § 103.5 (1988).

vocational potential."[12] Additionally, counselors, psychologists, and psychiatrists may provide mental restoration services or short-term psychiatric services if an applicant has a mental condition warranting these services. All services end when the person completes the vocational rehabilitation program. In special cases, however, the commission may provide post-employment services if the services are necessary to maintain the person's employability and are intended to "overcome regressive, emergent, or latent problems after the case is closed."[13]

Services Available to Applicants

Once an applicant is found to be eligible, the applicant may receive the following benefits:[14]

1. physical restoration services, which may include speech or hearing therapy, psychological services, or prosthetic devices;
2. mental restoration services, including psychiatric or psychological treatment;
3. vocational or other training services, including classroom education at universities, business schools, technical schools, or on-the-job training;
4. interpreter services for the deaf or other training or devices to increase employability;
5. maintenance, that is, cash payments to cover basic living requirements;
6. transportation;
7. telecommunications, sensory aids, or other technological aids or devices;
8. placement in employment suitable to the applicant's abilities;
9. post-employment counseling if necessary;
10. occupational tools, equipment, supplies or licenses; or
11. extended rehabilitation services to persons who are severely handicapped, with the goal being achievement of personal independence rather than entering the "competitive labor market."

Fees and Expenses

Depending on the applicant's financial ability, the applicant may be required to pay all or part of the cost for certain services.[15]

---

12. Tex. Admin. Code tit. 40, § 103.5 (1988).
13. Tex. Admin. Code tit. 40, § 103.13 (1988).
14. Tex. Admin. Code tit. 40, § 103.6-.14 (1988).
15. Tex. Admin. Code tit. 40, § 103.21 (1988).

Diagnostic services, counseling, guidance, and referral services, however, are not subject to this requirement. Instead, persons rendering services are paid as state employees by the commission.

5B.4

Emotional Distress as a Basis for Civil Liability

Persons who suffer emotional or mental distress as a result of another's wrongful acts may sue for this injury, either as a separate cause of action or part of a larger claim relating to damages. Several factors bear on this cause of action, including the cause of the distress, the type of injury, and the motives of the person causing the injury. MHPs may become involved by evaluating the person alleging the injury and the injury itself. For example, the cause, symptoms, severity, duration, and treatment may be relevant to a suit.

Emotional Distress as an Element of Damages

Aside from a separate lawsuit for emotional distress, a person may recover damages for emotional anguish or distress suffered as a result of another compensable injury. For example, if a defendant negligently causes physical injury to another in an automobile accident, the injured party may also recover for the mental suffering associated with the injuries. Additionally, individuals may recover mental damages for the death of a spouse or child when another person wrongfully causes their death.[1] MHPs may be called upon to evaluate a claim for mental suffering and conditions related to the underlying injury.

1. Sanchez v. Schindler, 651 S.W.2d 249 (Tex. 1983). In *Sanchez*, the court stated that the mental anguish resulting from the loss of a child could not realistically be separated from the injury to the family relationship.

Additionally, other legal claims may either directly or indirectly involve elements of emotional distress as part of the recovery. For example, false imprisonment, slander, or invasion of privacy, which involve an injury to a person's reputation or personal sense of worth, may involve mental suffering. The distinguishing element of these claims is that the person does not have to prove emotional distress to recover damages. Instead, emotional distress may, if present, constitute an element of damages.

Intentional Infliction of Emotional Distress

Texas recognizes a separate right to recover for the consequences of an intentional infliction of emotional distress.[2] The elements of this cause of action are:[3]

1. the defendant must act intentionally or recklessly,
2. the defendant's conduct must be "outrageous" or "extreme,"
3. the defendant's actions must cause the plaintiff emotional distress, and
4. the emotional distress must be severe.

Further, the plaintiff does not have to suffer any physical injury in addition to the emotional distress to recover damages. Cases of intentional infliction of emotional distress may involve, for example, debt collections where the creditor or collection agency harasses or threatens the debtor in an extreme fashion or insurance companies' flagrant refusal to pay on legitimate policy claims.[4]

Negligent Infliction of Emotional Distress

In certain situations, people may also recover damages for negligent infliction of mental anguish if:[5]

---

2. Tidelands Auto. Club v. Walters, 699 S.W.2d 939 (Tex. Civ. App.-Beaumont 1985, writ ref'd n.r.e.). Texas has adopted the Restatement of Torts 2nd view.
3. *Id.* at 942.
4. *Id.*; Credit Plan Corp. v. Gentry, 516 S.W.2d 471 (Tex. Civ. App.-Houston 1974), *rev'd on other grounds*, 528 S.W.2d 571 (Tex. 1975).
5. St. Elizabeth Hosp. v. Garrard, 730 S.W.2d 649 (Tex. 1987) (permitting plaintiff to sue for negligent infliction of emotional distress after the hospital disposed of the couple's stillborn child in an unmarked grave without the couple's consent); Williams v. Steves Indus., Inc., 678 S.W.2d 205 (Tex. Civ. App.-Austin), *aff'd*, 699 S.W.2d 205 (Tex. 1978); Apache Ready Mix Co. v. Creed, 653 S.W.2d 79 (Tex. Civ. App.-San Antonio 1983).

1. the defendant should have reasonably foreseen that the plaintiff would suffer mental anguish,
2. the plaintiff did suffer mental anguish as a result of the defendant's acts, and
3. the defendant's injurious acts involved the plaintiff or a member of the plaintiff's family.

This claim is limited in that the injured person must be a child, parent, spouse, sister, or brother of the plaintiff, if not for injury to the plaintiff alone. If individuals are not formally married but merely live together in the form of a common-law marriage, they may not recover damages for mental anguish based on this theory.[6] The courts have removed some limitations on a negligent infliction of emotional distress claim in recent years. For example, the courts no longer require that the party seeking recovery have physical injury or physical manifestations of the mental anguish, such as sleeplessness or weight loss, to sue.[7]

---

6. Hastie v. Rodriquez, 716 S.W.2d 675 (Tex. Civ. App.-Corpus Christi 1986, writ ref'd n.r.e.).
7. St. Elizabeth Hosp. v. Garrard, 730 S.W.2d at 649.

5B.5

Insanity of Wrongdoers and Civil Liability

Although insanity does not excuse civil responsibility in the same manner as it does criminal responsibility, it may in some limited instances affect civil responsibility. Additionally, there may be special procedural safeguards necessary to assure that the mentally disturbed person receives a fair trial. Finally, the person's mental condition at the time of the wrong may determine whether insurance will cover the damages. Therefore, MHPs may become involved in these suits if a party requests an evaluation of the alleged wrongdoer's mental status.

Liability of an Insane Person

In Texas, insanity in an adult does not affect civil liability for injuries to another.[1] Thus the insane person is liable even though the mental condition may have prevented the person from foreseeing the consequences of an action. An exception occurs, however, when the wrong requires that the person act with intent to cause wrong.[2] If the person's mental state prevented the person from being capable of forming an intent to injure, the person is not liable for the injury. Additionally, a person who was mentally

1. *See* Ross v. York, 233 S.W.2d 347 (Tex. Civ. App.-El Paso 1950). The person is still liable for the injury because the main purpose of the tort system is to compensate a victim for the injury rather than to punish the wrongdoer. *Id.* at 349.
2. *Id.*

disordered at the time of the wrong is not liable for exemplary (i.e., punitive) damages.[3]

Insanity and Liability Insurance

Insurance policies frequently exclude coverage for acts of the insured that were intentional. This may also exclude coverage of associated legal expenses of defending the suit. If, however, the insured was insane at the time of the wrong or mentally incapable of forming the necessary intent, courts hold that the policy exclusion does not bar coverage and that the insurance company is required to pay the claim.[4] To invoke this exception, the insured must prove the mental condition by a preponderance of the evidence. For example, if there is proof that more probably than not the insured was insane at the time the insured killed another person, the insurance policy is required pay the claim.[5]

The test for criminal insanity is discussed in Chapter 5D.9.

Procedural Safeguards for an Insane Person

If a person has been determined mentally incompetent and has had a guardian appointed, the guardian must be served with the documents commencing the lawsuit rather than the incompetent person.[6] In other instances, such as when the person has been committed, the law provides that another person and/or the guardian must both be served. For example, the head of the mental institution is required to be served with notice of a lawsuit against a committed person.[7] Unless a court determines that spe-

---

3. *Id.* at 349. Punitive or exemplary damages are damages in addition to and beyond that necessary to compensate a victim for the wrong, with the main purpose being punishment and determent. Black's Law Dictionary 1110 (rev. 5th ed. 1979).
4. *See, e.g.*, Jefferson Standard Life Ins. Co. v. Myers, 284 S.W. 216 (Tex. Civ. App.-1926); Butcher v. State, 284 S.W. 219 (Tex. Crim. App.-1926).
5. *Id.*
6. Tex. Prob. Code Ann. § 130 (Vernon 1984). For limited guardians, the court may order that the limited guardian has the power to bring and defend suits. *Id.* § 130H.
7. Tex. Rev. Civ. Stat. Ann. art. 5547-74 (Vernon Supp. 1988). The head of the facility then notifies either the guardian, the patient, or both, considering the best interests of the patient.

cial circumstances exist, however, a person is presumed to be legally competent.[8]

If a person does not have a guardian, appointment of a guardian ad litem may be necessary to protect the person's interests. The court may appoint a guardian ad litem when a mentally incompetent person is a defendant to a suit and has no legal guardian within the state.[9] The court may also appoint a guardian ad litem even if the mentally incompetent person has a guardian if the court determines that the guardian will not protect the interests of the mentally incompetent person adequately.[10] In addition to having a guardian ad litem, a next friend may represent a mentally incompetent person.[11] Guardians ad litem and next friends, however, have limited powers relating solely to the particular case and do not have control or power over other aspects of the mentally incompetent person's affairs.

---

8. Tex. Rev. Civ. Stat. Ann. art. 5547-83 (Vernon Supp. 1988).
9. Tex. R. Civ. Proc. 173.
10. *Id.*
11. Tex. R. Civ. Proc. 44.

5B.6

Competency to Contract

Individuals who enter into a contract are required to have a minimum level of mental capacity for the contract to be enforceable. This includes an agreement to buy or sell property. Mental capacity frequently becomes an issue when one of the parties to the contract or a relative or legal representative of the party desires to be relieved of the duty to perform the contract. Parties may therefore request that an MHP examine and evaluate a person's mental capacity either to prove or disprove the person's mental capacity.

Legal Test of Competency to Contract

Applications of the legal test for mental capacity will vary with the particular contract involved, since a person may be capable of making some decisions and incapable of making others.[1] Thus, the degree of incompetence necessary in any situation will vary. Generally, a person must have the mental capacity sufficient to contemplate and understand the nature and effect of the act in which the person is engaged to make a valid contract.[2] The test for mental capacity in a contract to buy or sell property is whether the person understands that by making the contract, the title and rights to the property will be acquired or lost.[3] Courts often require a stronger showing of mental incapacity to void a contract, as

1. Smith v. Guerre, 175 S.W. 1093 (Tex. 1915); Gieseck v. Ross, 243 S.W.2d 873 (Tex. Civ. App. 1951).
2. Lemons v. Davis, 306 S.W.2d 224 (Tex. Civ. App.-Fort Worth 1957, writ ref'd n.r.e.).
3. McCleskey v. McCleskey, 7 S.W.2d 657 (Tex. Civ. App.-1928).

compared with the showing necessary to invalidate a will based on lack of testamentary capacity.[4]

Determination of Competency to Contract

If a person of unsound mind enters into a contract, the contract is not automatically void.[5] Instead, the person alleging the nullity of the contract is required to prove that the person in question was incompetent at the time the contract was made. Further, the question of incompetence is a question of fact for a jury to determine after hearing the evidence. Mere proof of mental infirmity, however, may not suffice to void a contract.[6] Until proven otherwise, the law presumes that every person has the mental capacity to contract.[7]

The most critical evidence is the person's state of mind at the time the contract was made, although evidence of mental incapacity at other times is relevant.[8]

Effect of Incompetency

Even if the person attempting to void a contract proves that the other party was mentally incompetent at the time the contract was made, the contract may not be void. If the contract was for "necessaries," i.e., food, shelter, clothing, medical services, or other items without which the person cannot exist, there remains a duty to pay for the goods or services.[9] However, recovery may only be obtained for the reasonable value of the goods, rather than the actual price if greater. In these cases, the person seeking to recover the value of the contract is required to join the incompetent person as a party to the suit. Further, even if the party contracting with an incompetent entered into the contract in good faith with no knowledge of the incompetence, the contract may still be voidable.[10]

The party contracting with an incompetent person may recover, however, the "consideration," or value given as a condition

---

4. Prather v. McClelland, 76 S.W. 543 (Tex. 1890).
5. Gaston v. Copeland, 335 S.W.2d 406 (Tex. Civ. App. Houston 1960, writ ref'd n.r.e.).
6. Decker v. Koenig, 37 S.W.2d 378 (Tex. Civ. App.-1931, writ dism'd w.o.j.).
7. Swink v. Dallas, 36 S.W.2d 222 (Tex. 1931).
8. Cole v. Waite, 246 S.W.2d 849 (Tex. 1951).
9. Legler v. Legler, 189 S.W.2d 505 (Tex. Civ. App.-1945, writ dism'd w.o.m.).
10. Williams v. Sapieha, 61 S.W.2d 115 (Tex. 1901).

to setting aside the contract so that the parties are returned to their original positions. To recover the value, the competent party, who must have been a party to the contract, must show that:[11]

1. the other party had not been judged by a court to be mentally incompetent prior to the contract; and
2. the contract was entered into in good faith.

Finally, the incompetent person, or his successors after death, may ratify a contract after it is made, thus making the contract enforceable and valid.[12] A party may prove ratification by conduct of the incompetent person, words of the person, or failure to disavow the contract within a reasonable time after mental competence is restored.[13]

---

11. Humphries v. Kirkley, 410 S.W.2d 196 (Tex. Civ. App.-Houston 1966).
12. Granberry v. McBride, 138 S.W.2d 283 (Tex. Civ. App.-1940).
13. Oram v. General Am. Oil Co., 513 S.W.2d 533 (Tex. 1974).

5B.7

Competency to Sign a Will

To make or amend a will, individuals are required to have the mental capacity, referred to as "testamentary capacity," to understand the nature of the legal act they are performing. If a person does not have testamentary capacity, a court may hold the will invalid and distribute the person's estate according to the state's intestate succession laws. In intestate succession, the estate passes to specified heirs without regard to the terms of that will.

Parties contesting a will may request an MHP who treated or evaluated the person to testify. (See Chapters 4.2 and 4.3 for limitations on the use of this information.) Additionally, an MHP may give a professional opinion of the person's capacity based on witnesses' reports or other evidence.

Requirements for Testamentary Capacity

In Texas, anyone who meets certain criteria is entitled to make a will. A person must be of "sound mind"[1] to make a will. Additionally, at the time a will is made the person must:

1. be at least 18 years of age,
2. currently be or have been married, or
3. be a member of the United States armed forces.

Possessing a sound mind or testamentary capacity means that:[2]

1. Tex. Prob. Code Ann. § 57 (Vernon 1980).
2. Rich v. Rich, 615 S.W.2d 795, 796 (Tex. Civ. App.-Houston [1st Dist.] 1981).

> The person at the time of the execution of the will has sufficient mental ability to understand the business in which he is engaged, the effect of his act making the will, and the general nature and extent of his property. He must also be able to know his next of kin and natural objects of his bounty. He must have memory sufficient to collect in his mind the elements of the business to be transacted and to hold them long enough to perceive at least their obvious relation to each other, and to be able to form a reasonable judgment as to them.

A person does not, however, have to understand all the details and "true value of his property."[3] Further, the test is directed to the day the person makes the will, although evidence of prior or subsequent behavior may be relevant.[4]

Generally, there are several conditions that may affect testamentary capacity. Proof of insanity at the time invalidates a will. Proof that a person suffered from an "insane delusion" or mental condition aside from insanity, however, will not invalidate the will unless the party contesting the will shows that the condition affected the testator when the will was made.[5] Showing that a person was very old and/or feeble will not invalidate the will without a further showing that these conditions affected the person's capacity when the will was made.

Proving Testamentary Capacity

Parties who contest a person's testamentary capacity have the burden to prove the lack of capacity. Testamentary capacity is a question of fact for a jury to determine based on the evidence, whether from experts such as MHPs or lay witnesses who knew the person and testify about the person's behavior.

---

3. *Id.*
4. *Id.*
5. *Id.* at 797-98. For example, one court stated that "a man may believe himself to be the supreme ruler of the universe" and yet make a valid will which courts will uphold if he understood the nature of the act of making a will and made a sensible disposition of his property. *Id.*

5B.8

Competency to Vote

A "qualified voter" in Texas is any person who is at least 18 years of age, is a United States citizen, is a resident of Texas, is registered to vote, has not been adjudged mentally incompetent, and is not a convicted felon.[1] A person convicted of a felony may, however, still be qualified to vote if he has received a pardon and has had at least 2 years of successful probation since the pardon or if the pardon expressly released the disability to vote.

---

1. Tex. Elec. Code Ann. § 11.002 (Vernon Supp. 1987).

5B.9

Competency to Obtain a Driver's License

A person may not obtain a driver's license if rendered incapable of driving safely due to alcohol or drug abuse or found by a court to be mentally incompetent.[1] If, however, a court later determines that the person is mentally competent, the person may obtain a license. Additionally, if a person has a physical or mental disability that will prevent the person from exercising reasonable control over a vehicle while driving, the person may not obtain a license.

1. Tex. Rev. Civ. Stat. Ann. art. 6687b (Vernon Supp. 1987).

5B.10

Product Liability

The term "product liability" refers to a legal claim permitting a person to recover for personal injuries or property damages arising out of the use of a product. The three bases for product liability suits are strict liability, warranty, and negligence.[1] This chapter, however, will deal only with the strict liability basis. Under the strict liability theory, the person must show that the product was in a defective condition and was unreasonably dangerous to a user to recover damages without regard to fault.

MHPs with expertise in the human factors relating to people's abilities relative to a particular product and the requirements for product design within a specified environment may become involved in evaluating a product.

Elements of a Product Liability Claim

Under strict product liability, the focus is solely on the product itself and not on the manufacturer's conduct. A party may recover against a seller of a product (which typically includes the manufacturer, wholesaler, and/or retailer) for both personal injuries and property damage caused by use of a product if the product is in a defective condition and unreasonably dangerous. Additionally, the product must have been defective at the time it left the manufacturer.

There are two tests for determining whether a product is

1. Negligence refers to a standard of conduct below that which a reasonably prudent man would use in a specific situation, and warranty is based on breach of a promise or representation.

unreasonably dangerous. First, under the consumer expectation test, a product is unreasonably dangerous if it is dangerous to an extent beyond that which an ordinary consumer with ordinary knowledge common to the community would expect.[2] For example, since a consumer should expect a knife to be sharp, a knife is not unreasonably dangerous because of that sharpness alone. The other test used to determine if a product is unreasonably dangerous is the risk/utility test.[3] Under the risk/utility test, the jury may consider whether "the utility of the product outweigh[s] the magnitude of the danger" to the extent that a reasonable person would not sell the product if the person knew of the dangers.[4] Under this test, even if a consumer would have no expectations of the product's dangerousness, if the jury determines that the product's utility is outweighed by its dangers, the product is unreasonably dangerous.

The seller of the product must also engage in the business of selling the product, and the product must reach the consumer without substantial change in its condition from the manufacturer.[5]

There are several defenses to strict product liability claims. A seller is not liable for injury if the product, from its design to warnings, was based on state-of-the-art techniques and knowledge. The mere fact that a product has been used over a long period of time without injury to consumers, however, does not release a seller from liability.[6] Further, the seller is not liable for changes in the product's condition made after the seller sold the product if the changes were not reasonably foreseeable to the seller. Finally, the manufacturer is not liable if the consumer fails to heed warnings and use the product in the intended manner, unless the different use was reasonably foreseeable by the seller.

2. Syrie v. Knoll Int'l, 748 F.2d 304, 306 (5th Cir. 1984).
3. Pavlides v. Galveston Yacht Basin, Inc., 727 F.2d 330, 337 (5th Cir. 1984).
4. *Id.* at 337.
5. McKisson v. Sales Affiliates, Inc., 416 S.W.2d 787 (Tex. 1967). Texas has adopted the Restatement of Torts § 402A view for strict product liability.
6. Hovenden v. Tenbush, 529 S.W.2d 302 (Tex. 1975).

5B.11

Unfair Competition

While competition is generally encouraged in our nation, certain competition is viewed as unfair and may result in liability. Unfair competition involves a business competitor's use of the name, symbol, label, or other property used by another business to induce consumers to buy a product based on the false belief that the two products are the same. MHPs may be asked to evaluate marketing techniques as part of a party's claim of unfair competition, which may include conducting consumer surveys about product confusion.

Legal Test of Unfair Competition

One type of unfair competition occurs when a competitor attempts to pass off goods as those of a better established and better known competitor. Included in this area are claims such as trademark infringement, which covers the use of specific names, symbols, and other devices. The competitor must take some action to mislead consumers regarding the product and consumers must actually be misled for a party to recover. Thus, the party alleging the unfair competition is required to prove either an exclusive right to use the name or symbol, as by showing trademark registration, or that the product similarity causes "confusion."[1] Confusion means that consumers may associate the particular name, symbol, or product with that of another business. Determining similarity is a

1. Jud Plumbing Shop v. Jud Plumbing & Heating, 695 S.W.2d 75 (Tex. Civ. App.-San Antonio 1975).

question of fact for a jury and will vary depending on the nature of the subject in question.[2]

Trademark Confusion

A trademark is "a name, symbol, device, slogan or any combination thereof which, whether registered or not, has been adopted and used by a person to identify his goods and distinguish them from the goods manufactured or sold by others."[3] The trademark must be affixed to a product or the product's package. Federal law provides limited protection for trademarks; however, Texas law also provides for registration of trademarks.[4] Not all words and symbols are necessarily capable of protection under the registration law. Further, the party alleging the wrong bears the burden to prove product similarity and confusion and that the infringement was knowingly done.[5] Generally, the test is whether the resemblance of the products is sufficiently close to deceive an ordinary purchaser and induce the belief that the goods originated with the owner of the trademark.[6]

Additionally, trademark infringement depends on the similarity, connection, and relation among the product, clients, and other factors and not merely on the similarity of the name alone. If the products are so different, for example, that there is no likelihood of confusion, a party's claim will fail.[7]

Similarly, business names are defined by law as "trade names" and are therefore protected from appropriation by another business.[8] A trade name is a name or title rather than a sign, word, or symbol. To be protected by law, the name must indicate a particular class of goods or dealer. Even ordinary words, such as "House Doctor," may be protected if they are associated with a specific business such as one specializing in home maintenance service.[9]

Product Confusion

Any business may use the common characteristics of a product. However, a business may not adopt the ornamental or distinctive

2. Garcia v. Beck, 286 S.W.2d 234 (Tex. Civ. App.-Austin 1955).
3. Tex. Bus. & Com. Code Ann. § 16.01 (Vernon Supp. 1987).
4. Tex. Bus. & Com. Code Ann. §§ 16.01-16.28 (Vernon Supp. 1987).
5. Tex. Bus. & Com. Code Ann. § 16.26 (Vernon Supp. 1987).
6. Hudgens v. Goen, 673 S.W.2d 420 (Tex. Civ. App.-Fort Worth 1984).
7. Hudgens v. Goen, 673 S.W.2d 420 (Tex. Civ. App.-Fort Worth 1984); George H. Dentler & Sons v. Fuller's Food Prod., 183 S.W.2d 768 (Tex. Civ. App.-1945, writ refused).
8. Miller v. Lone Star Tavern, Inc., 593 S.W.2d 341 (Tex. Civ. App.-Waco 1979); Jud Plumbing Shop v. Jud Plumbing & Heating, 695 S.W.2d 75 (Tex. Civ. App.-San Antonio 1975).
9. Walters v. Building Maintenance Serv., 291 S.W.2d 377 (Tex. Civ. App.-Dallas 1956, reh'g denied).

features of another's product if the similarity in the goods will cause consumer confusion.[10] While each case depends on particular facts and circumstances, courts will consider the form, shape, and color of the package or product, as well as pictures, words, or other labels to determine if there is sufficient similarity to prove a claim of unfair competition.

10. Wissman v. Boucher, 240 S.W.2d 278 (Tex. 1951).

5B.12

Employment Discrimination

Both federal and state law provide that employers may not engage in discriminatory employment practices.[1] This discussion treats only the Texas law. In Texas, "employer" is defined as a "person engaged in an industry affecting commerce who has 15 or more employees for each working day in each of 20 or more calendar weeks" and includes schools, universities, state agencies, and political subdivisions of the state.[2] MHPs should be aware of these laws not only as potential employers, but also in their practice if they engage in industrial counseling and test construction for personnel selection, discharge, or promotion.

Who Is Affected by Employment Discrimination Law?

As indicated, the law only applies to employers who have over 15 employees for a certain period of time each calendar year. Other exceptions include religious organizations or corporations, employment of family members, and labor firms or associations participating in a state hometown plan approved by the U.S. Department of Labor.[3] Finally, the law does not apply to elected officials who serve in public office, staff of an elected official, appointees

1. 42 U.S.C. § 2000e (1982); Tex. Rev. Civ. Stat. Ann. art. 5221k (Vernon Supp. 1987).
2. Tex. Rev. Civ. Stat. Ann. art. 5221k § 2.01(5) (Vernon Supp. 1987).
3. Tex. Rev. Civ. Stat. Ann. art. 5221k § 5.06 (Vernon Supp. 1987).

on a policymaking level of government, or legal advisers of a public official.[4]

Unlawful Employment Practices

An employer may not:[5]

1. "fail or refuse to hire or discharge an individual or otherwise discriminate against an individual with respect to compensation or the terms, conditions, or privileges of employment because of race, color, handicap, religion, sex, national origin, or age;"
2. segregate or classify employees in any manner that may deprive the employees of employment opportunities or adversely affect the employees' status;
3. discriminate or retaliate against an employee who opposed a discriminatory practice or who files charges, testifies, or assists another employee in pursuing a discrimination case;
4. assist, coerce, or cause another person to employ a discriminatory practice;
5. intentionally interfere with the Texas Commission on Human Rights, the agency that investigates and hears discrimination claims, during an investigation; or
6. print or publish any notice or advertisement relating to employment which indicates "preference, limitation specification, or discrimination."

Additionally, employment agencies may not discriminate against an individual when referring the individual for employment. Labor unions and organizations also are prohibited from discriminating against an individual regarding membership or benefits.

Employers may, however, refuse to hire or discharge an individual based on any "bona fide occupational qualification," which is a job qualification that reasonably relates to performance of a particular job and "for which there is a factual basis for believing that a person of the excluded group would be unable to perform satisfactorily . . . with safety or efficiency."[6] Employers may also establish different standards for compensation or employment benefits based on a bona fide seniority or merit system or apply different standards of compensation to employees who work at

---

4. Tex. Rev. Civ. Stat. Ann. art. 5221k § 2.01(4) (Vernon Supp. 1987).
5. Tex. Rev. Civ. Stat. Ann. art. 5221k §§ 5.01-5.05 (Vernon Supp. 1987).
6. Tex. Rev. Civ. Stat. Ann. art. 5221k §§ 2.01(1), 5.07 (Vernon Supp. 1987).

different jobs. Finally, employers may impose reasonable minimum or maximum age requirements for fire fighters or peace officers.

Section 5

Practice Related to the Law

Section 5C

Civil/Criminal Matters

5C.1

Jury Selection

The selection of a jury is viewed by attorneys as one of the most critical phases of a trial. The selection process permits an attorney to influence the jury panel by excluding jurors both as a matter of right for legal disqualification from service (a challenge "for cause") and as a matter of discretion to exclude a limited number of jurors (a "peremptory challenge") for any reason the attorney chooses. In addition, the selection of the jury is the first opportunity to begin the attorney's presentation of the case to the jury and to evaluate the jury's response to various aspects of the case. MHPs are increasingly playing a role in this process through pretrial community surveys, assistance in the formulation of questions to prospective jurors, evaluation of potential jurors, and mock jury panels.

Juror Qualifications

Potential jurors are randomly selected from a jury wheel prepared annually in each county containing the names of all currently registered voters in the county.[1] Qualifications for service as a juror include the attainment of 18 years of age, citizenship in the state and county in which service as a juror is to occur, "sound mind and good moral character," the ability to read and write, the absence of a felony conviction or present indictment,[2] and the ability to understand the English language.[3] In addition, any per-

1. Tex. Gov't Code Ann. § 62.001 (Vernon Supp. 1988).
2. Tex. Gov't Code Ann. § 62.102 (Vernon Supp. 1988).
3. Tex. Gov't Code Ann. § 62.109 (Vernon Supp. 1988).

son having an interest in a case, related to a party in a case, harboring a bias for or prejudice against a party, or having previously served as a juror in a former trial of that action is disqualified ("for cause") from service as a juror.[4] Individuals may be exempted from jury service if they are over 65 years old, have custody of a child under 10 who would be left without adequate supervision, are a student in secondary school or an institution of higher learning, or are employed by the legislature.[5]

Criminal Trials

When a Jury Is Allowed

A right to trial by jury exists in felony and nonfelony criminal trials in Texas. In noncapital cases, the defendant may waive the right to trial by jury. In capital cases (i.e., those for which the death penalty may be assessed) the right to trial by jury is not waivable if the defendant chooses not to plead guilty and proceed to trial.[6]

Jury Size

In criminal cases tried in district court, the jury consists of 12 jurors. In criminal cases tried in county court, the jury consists of 6 jurors.[7]

Unanimity Requirement

Jury verdicts in felony and misdemeanor cases must be unanimous.[8]

Change of Venue

The venue of a criminal proceeding, i.e., the place of trial, may be changed when local prejudice against the defendant would prevent a "fair and impartial trial."[9] One use of MHPs in the pretrial process may be to evaluate community attitudes about the defendant and, where appropriate, to present them to the court in support of, or in opposition to, a motion for change of venue.

Voir Dire

From the jurors presented, the attorneys are permitted during the voir dire portion of the proceeding to question jurors both as a

---

4. Tex. Gov't Code Ann. § 62.105 (Vernon Supp. 1988).
5. Tex. Gov't Code Ann. § 62.106 (Vernon Supp. 1988).
6. Tex. Code Crim. Proc. Ann. arts. 1.13, 1.14 (Vernon 1977).
7. Tex. Code Crim. Proc. Ann. art. 33.01 (Vernon 1966).
8. Tex. Code Crim. Proc. Ann. art. 36.29 (Vernon Supp. 1988).
9. Tex. Code Crim. Proc. Ann. art. 31.03 (Vernon Supp. 1988).

panel and individually, subject to the discretion of the court, to determine the basis for exercising challenges for cause and peremptory challenges.

An unlimited number of challenges of potential jurors for cause may be made. A juror is required to be excluded for cause if the juror has ever been convicted of a theft or felony, is currently under indictment, is currently insane, has a perceptual defect resulting in unfitness for service, is a witness in the case, has served on a jury which previously heard the case, is biased for or prejudiced against the defendant, has already reached a conclusion about the outcome of the case, is related to the defendant or a person injured by the crime, or in a capital case, is unwilling under any circumstances to impose the death penalty.[10]

In a capital case, the state and the defendant are each entitled to 15 peremptory challenges. If there is more than one defendant, the state and each defendant are entitled to 8 peremptory challenges. In noncapital felony cases the state and the defendant are each entitled to 10 peremptory challenges. If there is more than one defendant, the state and each defendant are entitled to 6 peremptory challenges. In misdemeanor cases tried in district court, the state and the defendant are each entitled to 5 peremptory challenges. If the trial is in county court each is entitled to 3 peremptory challenges. And, if there is more than one defendant, the state and each defendant are entitled to 3 peremptory challenges in misdemeanor cases tried in either court.[11]

Civil Trials

When a Jury Is Allowed

The right to trial by jury in Texas state courts is more expansive than in most other jurisdictions. Under the Texas Constitution, most cases tried in the district court, the court of general jurisdiction, are triable by jury.[12] Included are, for example, personal injury actions and divorce actions. In addition, by statute, the right to jury trial has been added in many other proceedings, such as a suit affecting the parent–child relationship (excluding adoption).[13]

10. Tex. Code Crim. Proc. Ann. art. 35.16 (Vernon Supp. 1988).
11. Tex. Code Crim. Proc. Ann. art. 35.15 (Vernon Supp. 1988).
12. Tex. Const. Art. 5 § 10.
13. Tex. Fam. Code Ann. § 11.13 (Vernon 1986).

Jury Size

In trials in state district court, the jury must consist of 12 jurors unless the parties agree to a smaller number.[14] In state county court, the jury consists of 6 jurors.[15]

Unanimity Requirement

In civil cases tried to a jury of 12, a verdict may be rendered upon the concurrence of 10 jurors. In civil cases tried to a jury of 6, a verdict may be rendered upon the concurrence of 5 jurors.[16]

Change of Venue

The place of trial of a civil proceeding may be changed when a party can show that "there exists in the county where the suit is pending so great a prejudice against him that he cannot obtain a fair and impartial trial."[17] As noted above in the context of a criminal change-of-venue motion, MHPs may be useful in gauging and presenting evidence of these community attitudes.

Voir Dire

Attorneys in civil cases, as in criminal cases, are permitted to question jurors during voir dire, individually and as a panel, subject to the discretion of the court, with the goal of intelligently exercising challenges for cause and peremptory challenges.

An unlimited number of challenges for cause may be made. Exclusion for cause will be granted when a juror has a pecuniary interest in the case,[18] is related to a party, may be a witness in the case, is biased for or prejudiced against a party,[19] or has served as a juror in a prior trial of the case.

After the challenges for cause have been exercised and 24 jurors remain in district court or 12 in county court, counsel may exercise peremptory challenges.[20] In an action tried in the district court with two parties, each is entitled to six peremptory challenges.[21] In a two-party action in the county court, each party is entitled to three peremptory challenges. When more than two parties are involved, the trial judge is required to equalize the challenges with regard to the positions of the parties relative to each other.[22] Thus, for example, if there are three defendants, all

14. Tex. Gov't Code Ann. § 62.201 (Vernon Supp. 1988).
15. Tex. Gov't Code Ann. § 62.301 (Vernon Supp. 1988).
16. Tex. R. Civ. Proc. 292.
17. Tex. R. Civ. Proc. 257.
18. Green v. Ligon, 190 S.W.2d 742 (Tex. Civ. App.-Ft. Worth 1945).
19. Compton v. Henrie, 364 S.W.2d 179 (Tex. 1963).
20. Tex. R. Civ. Proc. 232.
21. Tex. R. Civ Proc. 233.
22. Patterson Dental Co. v. Dunn, 592 S.W.2d 914 (Tex. 1979).

of whom are opposed to the plaintiff and essentially not antagonistic to each other, they should not be given in total three times as many peremptory challenges as the plaintiff.

5C.2

Expert Witnesses

MHPs may be able to assist the judge or jury in resolving issues or understanding evidence that would not otherwise be fully understood by them. Thus MHPs are frequently called as expert witnesses in civil and criminal proceedings. Merely because an MHP has some specialized knowledge not possessed by the judge or jury does not, however, require that the court recognize the MHP as an expert on a particular issue or permit the MHP to testify in a particular fashion or rely on particular information to form an opinion.

Qualifying as an Expert Witness

Before an MHP may be qualified as an expert, the judge must first conclude that the witness has some specialized knowledge to provide the judge or jury to assist them in their determinations. Second, the judge must conclude that this information is based on a body of knowledge or information that has been appropriately validated. Satisfaction of the first requirement, that the witness is "qualified as an expert by knowledge, skill, experience, training, or education,"[1] does not require that the would-be expert have graduated from college,[2] be board certified, if such certification exists in the field, or be the leading person in the field. Rather, all that is required is that the individual be able to assist the judge or jury in understanding the evidence or resolving the issues in the proceed-

1. Tex. R. Civ. Evid. 702; Tex. R. Crim. Evid. 702.
2. Petrolia Ins. Co. v. Everett, 719 S.W.2d 639 (Tex. Civ. App.-El Paso 1986).

ing. The cases have generally granted the trial judge substantial discretion in these determinations; thus the likelihood of appellate court reversal on expert witness qualifications is not great.[3]

The second related aspect of the qualification of the expert involves scrutiny of the body of information upon which the expert's theories or fund of knowledge is based. Thus, for example, in a suit for injuries arising out of an automobile accident, a court is unlikely to permit even the top astrologist in the world to offer an opinion on the likelihood that the defendant would have been careless on the date of the accident. It is on this basis that evidence from polygraph examinations has been excluded.[4] This same principle should require an MHP testifying about a new psychological syndrome, for example, to be prepared to present references from the research literature validating the syndrome's existence and the appropriateness of its use in this context.

When an Expert Witness May Be Called to Testify

The guiding principle underlying the use of expert witnesses is that they may be called to testify when their testimony may help the judge or jury "to understand the evidence or to determine a fact in issue."[5] Conversely, if the subject is one on which the court concludes that the judge or jury would not benefit from the assistance of an expert witness, expert testimony is not permitted. By way of example, it has been held that a psychological autopsy of the state of mind of the beneficiary of a will, who later committed suicide and was claimed to have wrongly caused the death of the author of the will, would not be helpful in assisting the jury to determine the beneficiary's state of mind at the time of the death of the drafter of the will.[6] In most professional malpractice cases,[7] however, expert testimony is not only permitted but is required of the plaintiff if the case is to reach the jury.[8]

---

3. Burlington Northern R.R. Co. v. Harvey, 717 S.W.2d 371 (Tex. Civ. App.-Houston 1986, writ ref'd n.r.e.).
4. Romero v. State, 493 S.W.2d 206 (Tex. Crim. App. 1973). See Chapter 5C.5 for a discussion of psychological autopsy.
5. Tex. R. Civ. Evid. 702; Tex. R. Crim. Evid. 702.
6. Thompson v. Mayes, 707 S.W.2d 951 (Tex. Civ App.- Eastland 1986, writ ref'd n.r.e.).
7. See Section 6 for a discussion of professional liability.
8. Hood v. Phillips, 554 S.W.2d 160 (Tex. 1977).

Form and Content of Testimony

Because the function of an expert witness is generally to explain facts to the judge or jury, rather than to relate them to the judge or jury in the first instance, the expert may testify in the form of an opinion or inference.[9] The information upon which the expert may base this opinion includes personal knowledge of the expert such as that gained from an MHP's examination of a patient; information admitted at trial and conveyed to the expert through a hypothetical question; or, if reasonably relied upon by experts in that field, the expert may rely on other out of court information that need not be admissible in evidence.[10]

The information upon which the expert bases an opinion need not, unless the court otherwise orders, be disclosed prior to presenting the opinion.[11] On cross-examination, however, an opposing party may require an expert to disclose this information and attempt to impeach the resulting opinion by questioning the accuracy of the facts upon which the opinion is based. In addition, it is permissible to attempt to impeach an expert witness based on inconsistent professional literature relied upon by the expert or admitted to be reliable by the expert or by another expert.[12]

One ongoing issue in the treatment of expert testimony has been opinion testimony couched in the language of the ultimate question posed to the judge or jury in the case, i.e., "Doctor, in your opinion, did the defendant, as the result of a mental disorder, know that her conduct was wrong?" Although the Texas rules do not require the exclusion of expert testimony solely "because it embraces an ultimate issue to be decided by the trier of fact,"[13] the first requirement for the admissibility of expert testimony is that it assist the judge or jury. Thus, testimony that only informs the judge or jury about the expert's opinion on the ultimate issue in the case and nothing more should be excluded as unhelpful to the judge or jury in their analysis of the evidence and issues in the case.

---

9. Tex. R. Civ. Evid. 702; Tex. R. Crim. Evid. 702.
10. Tex. R. Civ. Evid. 703; Tex. R. Crim. Evid. 703.
11. Tex. R. Civ. Evid. 705; Tex. R. Crim. Evid. 705.
12. Tex. R. Civ. Evid. 803(18); Tex. R. Crim. Evid. 803(18).
13. Tex. R. Civ. Evid. 704; Tex. R. Crim. Evid. 704.

5C.3

Polygraph Evidence

Polygraph Examinations

The regulations promulgated by the Polygraph Examiners Board define a polygraph examination to include:[1]

> The employment of any instrument to graphically record simultaneously the physiological changes in human respiration, cardiovascular activity, and any other physiological changes that can be recorded for the purpose of verifying truth or deception, and includes the reading and interpretation of polygraph records and results.

The use of polygraph examinations both within and without the courts has been a hotly debated topic. Outside the courtroom, one focus of the appropriateness of the polygraph examination has been on the employment relationship. In the context of the state as an employer requiring its employees in the Department of Mental Health and Mental Retardation to take a polygraph examination during an investigation of patient abuse or other illegal activity, one court held that the examination violates the employees' constitutional rights to privacy.[2] Specifically left open in the opinion is the issue of required examinations for police and fire personnel. In addition, the court's decision does not address the issue of private employers requiring employees to take polygraph examinations.

---

1. Tex. Admin. Code tit. 22, § 393.7 (1987).
2. Texas State Employees Union v. Texas Dep't. of Mental Health and Retardation, 746 S.W.2d 203 (Tex. 1988).

Licensure of Polygraph Examiners

An individual must be licensed to administer a polygraph examination or hold himself out as a polygraph examiner.[3] Nothing in the licensing law exempts individuals otherwise licensed as MHPs from these requirements.

Admissibility of Polygraph Examinations

The results of a polygraph examination are not admissible in criminal trials in the Texas state courts even if the parties agree to their admission.[4] Similarly, in civil cases, at least in the absence of an agreement, the results of a polygraph examination are not admissible in Texas.[5]

3. Tex. Rev. Civ. Stat. Ann. art. 4413 (29cc) (Vernon Supp. 1988).
4. Castillo v. State, 739 S.W.2d 280 (Tex. Crim. App. 1987).
5. Texas Farm Bureau Mut. Ins. Co. v. Baker, 596 S.W.2d 639 (Tex. Civ. App.-Tyler 1980, writ ref'd n.r.e.); Pierson v McClanahan, 531 S.W.2d 672 (Tex. Civ. App.-Austin 1975, writ ref'd n.r.e.).

5C.4

Competency to Testify

The competency of a witness to testify, although a question ultimately decided by the judge, is one on which an MHP may be able to provide valuable input. This issue may arise in cases in which a witness is thought to be too young, mentally ill, or mentally retarded to provide credible testimony in the case. Often the same issues that are raised with respect to competency to testify before the judge are raised on the issue of credibility.

Legal Test of Competency to Testify

Competency to testify raises two types of concerns. At early common law, many witness were not considered competent to testify because they had a sufficient interest in the case that gave rise to a perceived risk of perjury. Thus, the parties themselves were not permitted to give evidence. With the exception of certain individuals suing an estate who are not permitted to testify as to oral statements with the decedent[1] (commonly called the Dead Man's Statute), Texas has done away with disqualification of a witness based on an interest in the controversy. This interest may, however, be brought to the attention of the judge or jury as a factor to

1. Tex. R. Civ. Evid. 601: (b) In actions by or against executors, administrators, or guardians, in which judgment may be rendered for or against them as such, neither party shall be allowed to testify against the others as to any oral statement by the testator, intestate or ward, unless that testimony to the oral statement is corroborated or unless the witness is called at the trial to testify thereto by the opposite party: and, the provision of this article shall extend to and include all actions by or against the heirs or legal representatives of a decedent based in whole or in part on such statement . . . .

consider regarding the weight to be given the testimony. The judge presiding in the case[2] and jurors sitting to hear the case[3] are also disqualified from testifying in the case.

The second concern with disqualification has to do with limitations on the capacity of a witness to perceive, remember, or narrate the event sincerely. Two specific categories of disqualifications are set out in the rules of evidence on this issue, one relating to insane persons and the other to children. If the court concludes that a witness is insane when offered as a witness or at the time of the event to which the witness is to testify, the witness is incompetent to testify. No definition of insanity is provided in the rules. However, the sense of the rule is that insanity at the time of trial need be such as to prevent the witness from understanding and complying with the oath or affirmation to testify truthfully administered to all witnesses.[4] Insanity at the time of the event to which the witness is to testify need be such as to prevent the witness from having perceived relevant information about the event or remembering it at the time of trial.

The other limitation in the rules of evidence on the competency of witnesses permits the court to exclude the testimony of "children or other persons who, after being examined by the court, appear not to possess sufficient intellect to relate transactions with respect to which they are being interrogated."[5] In practice, the judge will examine the child, often in chambers, to determine the child's ability to understand the obligations of the oath. Children 10 years of age and older are routinely found qualified, with children under 10 generally subject to the judge's determination. Children as young as 3 years of age have been found competent to testify.

Determination of Witness Competency

The competency of a witness to testify is a decision the judge must make. Often the judge will make this determination based on an informal examination of the witness. The judge may, however, request the assistance of an MHP to determine this issue.

When the witness is determined to be competent or even when the witness' competence is not challenged, MHPs are often presented to testify about various considerations that may bear on

2. Tex. R. Civ. Evid. 605; Tex. R. Crim. Evid. 605.
3. Tex. R. Civ. Evid. 606; Tex. R. Crim. Evid. 606. In certain limited instances, a juror may testify to matters that may have improperly influenced the jurors' deliberations.
4. Tex. R. Civ. Evid. 603; Tex. R. Crim. Evid. 603.
5. Tex. R. Civ. Evid. 601(a)(1); Tex. R. Crim. Evid. 601(a)(1).

the weight that should be given that testimony. One such subject of testimony, the various factors that are relevant in evaluating eyewitness testimony, is discussed in Chapter 5D.12.

Competency of Rape Victims to Testify

Frequently, defense attorneys challenge the competence of the victim of sexual assault to testify when the victim is a child, mentally ill, or mentally retarded. If the alleged victim and the defendant are the only witnesses to the event and the victim is disqualified from testifying, the defendant is not likely to be convicted whether or not the defendant performed the act. Conversely, if the alleged victim is unable to distinguish fantasy from reality or appreciate the obligation to testify truthfully, the defendant may be convicted regardless of the performance of the act. To assist in their effort to have the victim's competence determined, defense attorneys may seek to have the victim examined by an MHP. Although most courts in other jurisdictions recognize the power of the court to order an examination if corroboration is lacking and there is reason to question the capacity of the victim,[6] no reported cases in Texas address that issue.

Beyond the competency of a rape or sexual abuse victim to testify is the issue of the weight to be given to the victim's testimony. This issue arises with some frequency in the case of alleged sexual assault victims who are children and whose behavior appears inconsistent with the complaint of abuse. Although experts have been permitted to describe in general terms the behavior of child victims of sexual abuse,[7] an opinion relating directly to the credibility of a particular child is not permitted.[8]

---

6. D. Shuman, Psychiatric and Psychological Evidence § 13.10 at 317 n.84 (1986).
7. Rose v. State, 716 S.W.2d 162 (Tex. Civ. App.-Dallas 1986, no writ).
8. Kirkpatrick v. State, 747 S.W.2d 833 (Tex. Civ. App.-Dallas 1987); Garcia v. State, 712 S.W.2d 249 (Tex. Civ. App.-El Paso 1986).

5C.5

Psychological Autopsy

The behavior and accompanying mental state of a person who is now deceased are frequently of legal consequence. They may be relevant in determining whether the cause of death was an accident or suicide, where the issue is the right to collect on a life insurance policy that excludes recovery for death resulting from suicide.[1] Or, the behavior and mental state of the decedent shortly before death may be relevant in determining whether the cause of death was a reasonable use of force within the realm of self-defense or an unreasonable use of force outside the realm of self-defense and thereby constituting murder.[2]

The techniques for the psychological autopsy developed from the efforts of Dr. Edwin Schneidman and his colleagues at the Los Angeles Suicide Prevention Center in the early 1950s, who were investigating deaths from equivocal causes.[3] The resulting technique for a psychological autopsy entails a thorough investigation and reconstruction of a psychological profile of the decedent.[4]

---

1. Widman, *The Use of a Suicidologist in Accidental Death Litigation,* 47 INS. COUNSEL J. 219 (1980).
2. Bendheim, *The Psychiatric Autopsy: Its Legal Implications,* 7 BULL. AM. ACAD. PSYCHIATRY & L. 400 (1979).
3. N. Faberow & E. Schneidman, THE CRY FOR HELP 12 (1961).
4. See, e.g., Ebert, *Guide to Conducting a Psychological Autopsy,* 18 PROF. PSYCHOLOGY 52 (1987); Shafi, Carrigan, Whittinghill, & Derrick, *Psychological Autopsy of Completed Suicide in Children and Adolescents,* 142 AM. J. PSYCHIATRY 1061 (1985). With the addition of medical data from toxicology, pharmacology, and anatomical pathology, the technique is sometimes referred to as a psychiatric autopsy.

Admissibility of Psychological Autopsies

Although the admissibility of the psychological autopsy has been frequently addressed by courts in other states, thus far it has arisen in only one reported case in Texas. In that case,[5] a challenge was made to the distribution of property under a will based on the claim that one of the beneficiaries under the will, a son, had wrongfully caused the death of his father, the author of the will by which he would have inherited. The trial court, affirmed by the court of appeals, ruled that a psychological autopsy bearing on the state of mind of the son (who had later committed suicide) at the time of his father's disappearance was not an issue on which the jury needed assistance in determining whether the son had wrongfully caused the death of his father. Relevant to the trial court and court of appeals' decisions was the failure of the psychologist to relate other instances in which psychological autopsies had been used in this fashion and, implicitly, the literature supporting its validity and reliability in this context. Thus, any witness preparing to testify about a psychological autopsy should be prepared to refer the court to the research on psychological autopsies of the type being sought in that case and references to other judicial proceedings in which they have been accepted.

5. Thompson v. Mayes, 707 S.W.2d 961 (Tex. Civ. App.-Eastland 1986, writ ref'd n.r.e.).

Section 5

Practice Related to the Law

Section 5D

Criminal Matters

5D.1

Screening of Police Officers

Prior to appointment as a peace officer or a county jailer, the candidate must be examined by a licensed psychologist or psychiatrist. The psychologist or psychiatrist is required to state in writing, as a condition of appointment, that the candidate is in satisfactory psychological and emotional health to perform the tasks required of that office.[1]

1. Tex. Gov't Code Ann. § 415.057 (Vernon Supp. 1988).

5D.2

Competency to Waive the Rights to Silence, Counsel, and a Jury

The right not to respond to questions by the police, the right to an attorney, and the right to a trial by jury are some of the various rights enjoyed under the Constitution of the United States by suspects in a criminal proceeding. Because these are typically rights of the accused and not absolute limitations, the accused may, if competent, waive these rights. MHPs may be called upon by the court to assist in determining whether an accused is now, or was at some time in the past, competent to waive these or other rights.

Right to Silence

A suspect in a criminal investigation has the constitutional right not to assist the police by providing them with incriminating evidence. This right has, in everyday police practice, become encapsulated in the *Miranda* warnings that the police are required to give and the suspect is required to waive as a precondition to the custodial interrogation of a suspect. These warnings include the accused's right to silence; the accused's right to the presence of an attorney, appointed if the accused is indigent; and that any statements given may be used against the accused at trial.[1]

The test for waiver of the rights articulated in *Miranda* is that it must be voluntary, knowing, and intelligent. Although the presence of a mental illness may obviously be relevant to the capacity of the accused to waive these rights according to this test, the

1. Miranda v. Arizona, 384 U.S. 436 (1966).

existence of a mental illness alone, in the absence of police coercion, may not invalidate a waiver of these rights.[2]

Right to Counsel

Defendants in criminal cases have the right to be represented by counsel or to represent themselves. The right to be represented by counsel includes the right to court-appointed counsel for indigent defendants in both felony and misdemeanor cases when imprisonment is a possible outcome of a conviction.[3]

The accused may waive the right to counsel. The applicable test is whether the waiver is knowing, intelligent, and voluntary.[4] When the accused has chosen self-representation, the court is obliged to caution the defendant about its advantages and disadvantages so that the accused "knows what he is doing and his choice is made with eyes open."[5]

Right to Waive a Jury Trial

The right to trial by jury in criminal proceedings in Texas is discussed in Chapter 5C.1. As noted there, the defendant enjoys the right to trial by jury in felony and nonfelony criminal proceedings in Texas. That right may not be waived by the defendant in capital cases. In other criminal proceedings, the defendant may, if competent, waive the right to trial by jury.

The test applied in Texas to evaluate a defendant's waiver of the right to trial by jury asks whether the waiver was express, knowing, and intelligent.[6] It is the latter two elements of this test that MHPs may be called upon to address.

---

2. Colorado v. Connelly, 107 S. Ct. 515 (1986); Crawford v. State, 703 S.W.2d 655 (Tex. Crim. App. 1986).
3. Argersinger v. Hamlin, 407 U.S. 25 (1972).
4. Faretta v. California, 422 U.S. 806 (1975).
5. *Id.* at 835.
6. Guillett v. State, 677 S.W.2d 46 (Tex. Crim. App. 1984).

5D.3

Precharging and Pretrial Evaluations

Some states have a provision for a court-ordered mental health evaluation to assist the prosecutor in determining whether to charge a suspect or divert that person to the mental health system or other alternative program. No such formal diversion program exists in Texas.

5D.4

Bail Determinations

As a general rule, all prisoners in Texas have a right to be released from confinement on bail prior to conviction. The principle consideration in setting the conditions of bail is to secure the attendance of the accused at trial.

The exceptions to the general rule that all prisoners are bailable prior to conviction include a person charged with a capital murder where the proof is strong,[1] a person charged with a felony who has twice previously been convicted of a felony, a person charged with committing a felony while on bail for another felony, and a person charged with a felony involving a deadly weapon who has a prior felony conviction.[2] In addition, a person confined in a state institution as insane is not eligible for bail until release from that institution and delivery to the sheriff for trial.[3]

The conditions of bail include its amount and other nonfinancial conditions. The amount may not be excessive,[4] nor should it be used to oppress the defendant. It should be high enough to provide an incentive for compliance, taking into account the offense charged and the defendant's ability to make bail.[5] In addition, a recent statutory amendment requires that consideration of the future safety of the victim be taken into account in the setting of bail.

This issue is one on which MHPs may be able to offer assistance to the court, as well as on other factors that may bear on the likelihood of the defendant's attendance at trial if released on bail.

1. Tex. Const. art. I, § 11 (Vernon 1984).
2. Tex. Const. art. I, § 11a (Vernon 1984).
3. Ex parte Frailey, 177 S.W.2d 72 (Tex. 1944).
4. Tex. Const. art. I, § 13 (Vernon 1984).
5. Tex. Code Crim. Proc. Ann. art. 17.15 (Vernon Supp. 1988)

Another recent statutory amendment permits the judge in a case in which the defendant is charged with a sexual offense against a child under 12 years of age to condition the bail upon the defendant's not communicating with or going near the alleged victim.[6]

6. Tex. Code Crim. Proc. Ann. art. 17.41 (Vernon Supp 1988).

5D.5

Competency to Stand Trial

The requirement that a defendant be competent to stand trial is intended to permit the defendant a meaningful opportunity to participate in the preparation and presentation of a defense. Because the concern is with the trial, the focus of competence to stand trial is on the defendant's mental condition at the time of trial.

Legal Determination of Competency to Stand Trial

Test of Competency

A defendant is incompetent to stand trial in Texas if not possessed of:[1]

1. sufficient present ability to consult with his lawyer with a reasonable degree of rational understanding, or
2. a rational as well as factual understanding of the proceedings against him.

This test is a functional one that does specifically mention the existence of a mental illness. A defendant with a mental illness who could nonetheless understandingly consult with counsel and understand the proceedings would be competent to stand trial.[2] A defendant may, of course, be incompetent to stand trial and yet not be legally "insane" at the time of the offense or vice versa.

1. Tex. Code Crim. Proc. Ann. art. 46.02 (Vernon Supp. 1979).
2. Levya v. State, 552 S.W.2d 158 (Tex. Crim. App. 1977).

Unless there is evidence proving that the defendant is incompetent, the court is required to proceed on the assumption that the defendant is competent.

Raising the Competency Issue

The issue of the defendant's competence to stand trial may be raised by the judge or the defense attorney.[3] Although not specifically provided for by statute, in practice the prosecutor may also present the question to the court to avoid the possibility of a conviction ultimately being reversed for failure to consider this issue. Competence to stand trial may be raised before the start of the trial or at trial if made known then.

Once the issue of competence to stand trial is raised by written motion of the defendant, the defendant's attorney, or the judge, the court may, if a sufficient doubt is raised as to the defendant's competence, appoint qualified experts to examine the defendant. If the defendant is free on bail, the court may order the defendant to submit to an examination or order the defendant confined for up to 21 days.

Competency Hearing

If the trial judge concludes, based upon the written reports of the evaluators and other available evidence, that there is sufficient evidence to support the conclusion that the defendant is incompetent to stand trial, the judge must set the issue for hearing before a jury other than the jury that will determine guilt. At that hearing the jury will be asked whether the defendant is incompetent and, if so, whether there is a reasonable probability of the defendant becoming competent in the near future. If at the conclusion of this hearing the defendant is found incompetent to stand trial, a further proceeding may be instituted to determine whether the defendant requires commitment to a mental health or mental retardation facility. If the defendant is found competent to stand trial, the case proceeds to the trial on the merits.

Competency Evaluation

The court is required to inform the expert appointed for the examination of the specifics of the crime charged and to explain the question of incompetence to stand trial. Within 30 days after the examination, the examiner is required to submit a written report to the court, which the court will in turn provide to the defense counsel and the prosecutor.

3. Tex. Code Crim. Proc. Ann. art. 46.02 (Vernon 1979).

The report should include, at minimum, "a description of the procedures used in the examination, the examiner's observations and findings pertaining to the defendant's competency to stand trial, and recommended treatment."[4] If the report concludes that the defendant is incompetent to stand trial, it should then address the likelihood of the defendant's becoming competent in the foreseeable future and the defendant's committability as a mentally ill or mentally retarded person (see Chapter 5E.4). When the examiner is a physician and the physician concludes that the above requirement is met, submission of a Certificate of Medical Examination for mental illness or an affidavit reciting conclusions regarding the defendant's mental retardation is required.

Confidentiality and Privileged Communications

Formal privilege rules are not operative in competence-to-stand-trial evaluations. In light of this and in an apparent effort to encourage candor by the defendant in these evaluations, the criminal rules provide specifically that "no statement made by the defendant during the examination or hearing on his competency to stand trial may be admitted in evidence against the defendant on the issue of guilt in any criminal proceeding."[5]

Disposition of Defendants Found Incompetent to Stand Trial

If the defendant is found incompetent to stand trial and likely to attain competence in the foreseeable future, the criminal charges are not dismissed. The defendant is then typically criminally committed to a maximum security mental hospital for treatment to attain competence to stand trial for a period of not less than 90 days or more than 18 months. The facility to which the defendant is committed is required to submit progress reports to the court at least every 90 days. It is within the court's power to order the defendant to be treated on an outpatient basis when that is appropriate.[6] The head of the facility to which the defendant is committed is required to inform the court promptly if the defen-

4. Tex. Code Crim. Proc. Ann. art. 46.02 § 3(d) (Vernon 1979).
5. Tex. Code Crim. Proc. Ann. art. 46.02 § 3(g) (Vernon 1979).
6. Tex. Code Crim. Proc. Ann. art 46.02 § 5(a) (Vernon 1979).

dant becomes competent or if it is unlikely that the defendant will become competent in the foreseeable future.

If the defendant is found incompetent to stand trial and not likely to attain competence in the foreseeable future, the court is required to determine whether the defendant is subject to civil commitment. If the defendant is found to meet the requirements for civil commitment, the defendant should be committed under the Mental Health Code or the Mentally Retarded Person Act (see Chapter 5E.4). The Mental Health Code has special provisions for commitment when the criminal charges have not been dismissed.

5D.6

Provocation

The law addresses provocation both as a defense and as a limitation on a defense. As to the latter, in Texas if the defendant provoked the difficulty with the victim, provocation in this context operates as a limitation on the defendant's right of self-defense.[1] In this application of provocation, the test is whether the defendant actually or apparently intended to provoke the victim.

The use of provocation as a defense based upon the conduct of the accused is not recognized as a defense under Texas law.[2] The conduct of a homicide victim may, however, be relevant to determine the intent of the defendant to sustain a charge of murder. If the defendant committed a murder "under the immediate influence of sudden passion arising from an adequate cause,"[3] the act constitutes voluntary manslaughter rather than murder. In determining whether the cause is adequate to reduce the act to manslaughter, the test is not whether this defendant was in fact reasonably provoked, but whether it is a "cause that would commonly produce a degree of anger, rage, resentment, or terror in a person of ordinary temper sufficient to render the mind incapable of cool reflection."[4] Expert testimony is admissible in support of this issue.[5]

---

1. Gasset v. State, 587 S.W.2d 695 (Tex. Crim. App. 1979).
2. Hawkins v. State, 32 S.W.2d 202 (Tex. Crim. App. 1930).
3. Tex. Penal Code Ann. § 19.04 (Vernon 1974).
4. Tex. Penal Code Ann. § 19.04 (c) (Vernon 1974).
5. McClure v. State, 575 S.W.2d 564 (Tex. Crim. App. 1978).

5D.7

Mens Rea

Conviction of a crime requires that the defendant have done some proscribed act or failed to do some lawfully required act and that the defendant have had the requisite mental state accompanying this act. Failure to have this mental state may preclude a conviction for most offenses, as in the case of an act performed under a mistake or while in an unconscious state.

Culpable Mental State

Each specific offense carries its own required state of mind. The four mental states from which this selection is made are:

1. Intentional conduct is conduct performed with the object or desire to cause the result that occurred.
2. Knowing conduct occurs when the actor is or should be aware that the conduct is likely to cause the result that occurred.
3. Reckless conduct exists when the actor has consciously disregarded a risk when it is or should be known that the conduct may cause the result that occurred.
4. Criminally negligent conduct involves the failure to become aware of or perceive a risk that a reasonable person would realize would create a substantial risk of the result that occurred.

5D.8

Diminished Capacity

A defense of diminished capacity is recognized in some jurisdictions, but not Texas. The thrust of this defense, when recognized, is that although the defendant satisfies the mens rea requirement (see Chapter 5D.7), the defendant's reduced or diminished capacity resulting from a mental illness should operate to reduce the degree of the offense.

5D.9

Criminal Responsibility

Legal Determination of Insanity

The Texas Penal Code states that:[1]

> (a) It is an affirmative defense to prosecution that, at the time of the conduct charged, the actor, as a result of a severe mental disease or defect, did not know that his conduct was wrong.
> (b) The term "mental disease or defect" does not include an abnormality manifested only by repeated criminal or otherwise antisocial conduct.

This test is based on the M'Naghten decision, which Texas once followed, then rejected, and to which it has now returned. The test focuses on the cognitive, but not volitional, capacity of the defendant at the time of the offense. Thus, the essential question is whether the defendant did not know at the time of the offense, based upon a mental disorder, that his conduct was wrong. If the defendant knew his conduct was wrong, but was incapable of conforming his conduct to the requirements of the law as the result of a mental disorder, the test is not satisfied.

The cognitive incapacity required by this test must result from a mental disease or defect as defined by the law, which does not necessarily correspond with conclusions about mental disorder reached by MHPs in other contexts. The definition specifically excludes disorders manifested by repeated criminal or antisocial conduct, intending to exclude character or personality disorders.

Texas law specifically rejects voluntary intoxication as a defense. Evidence of intoxication can be admitted during the penalty

1. Tex. Penal Code Ann. § 8.01 (Vernon Supp. 1988).

phase of the trial as mitigating evidence, but only if the state of intoxication has reached the level of insanity.[2]

Burden of Proof

The burden of proof on the insanity defense rests with the defendant. The defendant must show by a preponderance of the evidence that the test has been satisfied for the trier of fact to return a verdict of not guilty by reason of insanity.[3] The application of this test by the trier only comes into operation, however, if the trier first determines beyond a reasonable doubt that the alleged conduct occurred.

Mental Examination

After a defendant gives notice of intent to raise the insanity defense, the court is empowered on its own motion or motion of the prosecutor or defense counsel to appoint qualified and disinterested experts to examine the defendant. This examination may take place on an outpatient basis if the defendant is free on bail, or the court may order the defendant confined for a period not to exceed 21 days.[4]

The court is required to inform the appointed expert of the specifics of the crime charged and the elements of the test for the insanity defense. Within 30 days after the order for examination, the expert is required to submit a written report to the court which will then furnish copies to counsel. The report is required to include, at minimum, "a description of the procedures used in the examination and the examiner's observations and findings pertaining to the insanity defense."[5] In addition, the report should address the defendant's committability as a mentally ill or mentally retarded person.

Confidentiality and Privileged Information

The fifth amendment privilege against self-incrimination requires that the defendant be informed of the risk that his statements may

2. Tex. Penal Code Ann. § 8.04 (Vernon 1974).
3. Tex. Code Crim. Proc. Ann. art. 46.03 § 1(c) (Vernon Supp. 1988).
4. Tex. Code Crim. Proc. Ann. art. 46.03 § 3 (Vernon 1978).
5. Tex. Code Crim. Proc. Ann. art. 46.03 § 3(d) (Vernon 1978).

be used against him at the trial on the merits. However, Texas courts have ruled that the defendant's raising of and introducing expert testimony on the insanity defense waives the privilege against self-incrimination as to court-appointed experts.[6] Furthermore, the sixth amendment right to counsel includes the right for the defendant's lawyer to be informed in advance of the mental status examination. Thus, the defendant's lawyer may advise the defendant not to cooperate in the examination.

The attorney–client privilege protects communications between the attorney's clients and individuals employed by the attorney to assist in the provision of legal services. Thus, if the defense attorney retains an MHP to evaluate a client, but does not call that MHP as a witness or present written evidence from that MHP, the attorney–client privilege prevents the prosecutor from calling the MHP as a witness without the defendant's consent.[7]

Commitment of Defendants Found Not Guilty by Reason of Insanity

Following a finding of not guilty by reason of insanity, the trial judge is required to determine if the defendant's conduct involved "an act, attempt, or threat of serious bodily injury to another person."[8] If serious bodily harm was not involved in the defendant's conduct and the defendant is mentally ill or retarded, the court is required to transfer the defendant to the appropriate court for civil commitment proceedings within 30 days of the acquittal by reason of insanity. If the defendant is found committable, commitment may occur under the Mental Health Code or Mentally Retarded Persons Act to an appropriate facility for inpatient care or, if appropriate, for supervised outpatient care (see Chapter 5E.4). If the defendant is not presently mentally ill or retarded, the defendant is required to be discharged.

If the court concludes that the offense involved serious bodily harm, the trial court retains jurisdiction and is required to commit the defendant to a maximum security mental health or retardation facility. Under this procedure or the procedure described above, the person acquitted by reason of insanity may only be released upon an order of the committing court. Thus, any proposal to release or discharge the person absolutely or for outpatient care requires judicial approval.

---

6. Heflin v. State, 640 S.W.2d 58 (Tex. Civ. App. 1982).
7. Ballew v. State, 640 S.W.2d 237 (Tex. Crim. App. 1982).
8. Tex. Code Crim. Proc. Ann. art. 46.03 § 4(a) (Vernon Supp. 1988).

5D.10

Battered Wives Syndrome

In some states, expert testimony about the battered wives syndrome, a post-traumatic stress disorder explaining behavior thought typical of women who have been regularly battered over an extended period of time, has been admitted to support either an insanity defense or a plea of self-defense by a woman who killed her husband at a time when she was not in apparent danger.[1] In the one reported appellate court opinion on this question in Texas to date, expert testimony about this syndrome was rejected because, among other reasons, the expert had not examined the defendant in that case.[2] Whether expert testimony would have been admitted if the expert had examined the defendant is subject to some doubt. The court construed the self-defense statute upon which the defendant relied to require an objective evaluation of the reasonableness of the defendant's conduct, whereas the thrust of the expert's testimony in explaining the syndrome would have been the subjective reasonableness, from the defendant's point of view, of her conduct.

1. D. Shuman, Psychiatric and Psychological Evidence § 12.01 at 275 (1986).
2. Fielder v. State, 683 S.W.2d 565 (Tex. Civ. App.-Ft. Worth 1985).

5D.11

Rape Trauma Syndrome

Rape trauma syndrome is another post-traumatic stress disorder thought to describe typical post-assault behavior of victims of sexual abuse. It has been the subject of much judicial decision making in other jurisdictions. A frequent attempted use of expert testimony about this syndrome is in response to a charge of rape or sexual assault when the sexual act is admitted but the defense of consent is raised. In these instances, the prosecution often offers an expert to testify that the victim's behavior following the event is similar to the behavior of individuals who are known to have been raped or sexually assaulted, so that the defense of consent is less likely to be accepted.

To date only one reported appellate decision in Texas has addressed the admissibility of evidence of this syndrome. In that case, the court ruled that the testimony should not have been admitted over a proper objection because the defense presented was an alibi rather than consent.[1] In those jurisdictions that have addressed this issue, a slight majority have permitted its admission where the defense of consent was raised.[2] Those states that have rejected this evidence have questioned its scientific validity in general or, at minimum, the ability to distinguish it from other post-traumatic stress disorders. Even in those jurisdictions in which the testimony is admissible, a properly qualified expert is not permitted to offer an opinion that the alleged victim was raped or is telling the truth. Rather, the expert is only permitted to demonstrate the similar, or dissimilar, behavior between the alleged victim and known rape victims.

---

1. Brown v. State, 757 S.W.2d 739 (Tex. Crim. App. 1988).
2. D. Shuman, Psychiatric and Psychological Evidence § 17.02 at 385 (1986).

5D.12

Hypnosis of Witnesses

The United States Supreme Court has ruled that a blanket exclusion of hypnotically induced testimony by the defendant violates the defendant's right to testify in her own behalf.[1] Following that decision, Texas adopted a pragmatic approach to the admissibility of hypnotically induced testimony in criminal cases from the defendant or the prosecution.[2] The proponent of such testimony must convince the court, by clear and convincing evidence, that the testimony is trustworthy. This determination should take into account the dangers of hypnosis (hypersuggestibility, loss of critical judgment, confabulation, and memory cementing); the qualifications of the hypnotist; the relation of the hypnotist to those interested in the case, i.e., law enforcement agencies or the defense; the presence of a record of all contacts between the hypnotist and the subject; the location and presence of third persons during the hypnosis; the techniques used and their appropriateness in these circumstances; and corroboration of the hypnotically induced testimony.

---

1. Rock v. Arkansas, 107 S. Ct. 2704 (1987).
2. Zani v. State, 1988 Tex. Crim. App. LEXIS 137.

5D.13

Eyewitness Identification

Eyewitness testimony is often very critical in trials. Because there is a body of research that suggests that eyewitness testimony may often be unreliable in ways not commonly realized by judges or jurors, attorneys have frequently sought to present MHPs to testify about what the various research has revealed to encourage closer scrutiny in evaluating eyewitness testimony.[1] The Texas courts that have addressed the admissibility of expert testimony about factors influencing the reliability of eyewitness testimony have rejected that evidence as a mode of attacking the credibility of a witness that impermissibly intrudes upon the province of the jury.[2]

1. E. Loftus, Eyewitness Testimony (1979).
2. Thomas v. State, 748 S.W.2d 539 (Tex. Civ. App.-Houston 1988); Welch v. State, 677 S.W.2d 562 (Tex. Civ. App. - Eastland 1984). In a related vein, the testimony that a defendant does not conform to the psychological profile of a child abuser has also been rejected based upon similar reasoning. Dorsett v. State, 1988 Tex. App. LEXIS 2661.

5D.14

Competency to Be Sentenced

If, at the time of sentencing, a defendant meets the standards for incompetence to stand trial, sentence may not be pronounced and the court must proceed under the procedures set forth in Chapter 5D.5.[1]

1. Tex. Code Crim. Proc. Ann. art. 42.07 (Vernon Supp. 1988).

5D.15

Sentencing

Following a determination of guilt, the court or jury is required to reach a determination of the sentence to be imposed. This process generally involves a second hearing following the determination of guilt.[1] At this hearing, evidence not admissible on the determination of guilt may be admissible. Thus, for example, although the testimony of an MHP about a defendant's remorse following the event should not be admissible on the question of guilt, that testimony should be admissible on mitigation of punishment at the sentencing hearing.

The judge may, but is not required, to order a presentence report by the probation office. No specific provision is made for a presentence mental examination in Texas law. In addition to the presentence report, the defendant and the prosecution may introduce evidence of the defendant's criminal record and evidence relevant to mitigation of the sentence, and the sentencer may consider evidence introduced on the issue of guilt.

If a jury is used to assess punishment, it may, in the case of certain offenses, recommend probation if requested by the defendant.

1. Tex. Code Crim. Proc. Ann. art. 36.07 (Vernon Supp. 1988).

5D.16

Probation

The options available to the court in sentencing a convicted person may include probation. When this option is exercised, the convicted defendant is subject to certain conditions for a specified period of time and the sentence of confinement is suspended conditional upon the defendant's complying with those conditions. If the defendant fails to comply with those conditions, the sentence of confinement may be reinstated and the defendant sent to prison for the remainder of the sentence.

A defendant is only eligible for probation when the maximum punishment assessed is 10 years or less and the defendant has not previously been convicted of a felony.[1] The maximum term of probation is 10 years. The terms of probation, which include obeying all laws, remaining in a specified area, maintaining employment, and avoiding persons, places, and things that are harmful, also include conditions related to the activities of MHPs. The court may order participation in various community-based programs, participation in psychological counseling, or participation in a substance abuse control program. MHPs may be able to assist the court in determining the defendant's suitability for these programs or other related activities. An MHP supervising such a program or activity may be required to make periodic reports to the court or probation office of the defendant's progress. Similarly, if the defendant is not participating in a program or activity in good faith as ordered by the court, an MHP operating or participating in that program may be obliged to inform the court of the failure to meet the conditions of probation.

1. Tex. Code Crim. Proc. Ann. art. 42.12 (Vernon Supp. 1988).

5D.17

Dangerous Offenders

The law in Texas provides for taking the dangerousness of the defendant into account in the sentencing process in both capital and noncapital crimes. In the case of capital crimes, the sentencing determination following a conviction for capital murder requires the jury to determine whether to sentence the defendant to be executed or imprisoned for life.[1] The questions to be answered by the jury in this determination include the deliberateness of the defendant's conduct, whether there was provocation, and "whether there is a probability that the defendant would commit criminal acts of violence that would constitute a continuing threat to society."[2] It is this latter issue that has prompted much debate and litigation over the ability of MHPs to predict violence.[3] Currently, MHPs determined to be qualified as experts on this issue by the court have been permitted to offer opinions on the risk the defendant would pose if not executed.[4]

In noncapital cases, a defendant's sentence may be increased based upon the existence of prior convictions.[5]

---

1. Tex. Code Crim. Proc. Ann. art. 37.071 (Vernon Supp. 1988).
2. Tex. Code Crim. Proc. Ann. art. 37.01(b)(2) (Vernon Supp. 1988).
3. *See* J. Monohan, The Clinical Prediction of Violent Behavior (NIMH 1981).
4. Barefoot v. Estelle, 463 U.S. 880 (1983).
5. Tex. Penal Code Ann. § 12.42 (Vernon 1974).

5D.18

Habitual Offenders

As discussed in Chapter 5D.17, defendants who have previously been convicted may, based upon those convictions, be subject to enhanced punishment. The determination that enhanced punishment for a habitual offender is appropriate under this statutory scheme depends on the nature of the prior offenses rather than on an individualized judgment of the personality traits of the particular defendant. Thus, the role of MHPs in this process is limited.

5D.19

Competency to Serve a Sentence

Although some states require that a defendant be competent to serve a sentence, no general requirement to that effect exists in Texas. As discussed in Chapters 5D.20 and 5D.21, mentally ill prisoners may be treated within the Department of Corrections facilities for their illnesses. And, as discussed in Chapter 5D.23, prisoners sentenced to be executed who are insane may not, while insane, be executed.

5D.20

Mental Health Services in Jails and Prisons

The provision of mental health services in Texas jails and prisons has been a hotly litigated issue. Therefore, much of the legally mandated provision of these services has been decided in decrees issues by courts, sometimes upon the consent of the parties and other times upon adversary proceedings. These decrees have been subject to reinterpretation and modification by the courts. There are, however, some statutes that define governmental obligations a little more concretely.

Mental Health Services in Texas Jails

Persons confined to a county jail who are mentally ill may be hospitalized for treatment following the same procedures as for any other person (see Chapter 5E.4). Additionally the court may order a prisoner transferred to a state mental hospital if the county health officer or prison physician certifies that the prisoner is eligible and space is available. After the head of the facility determines that the prisoner no longer requires hospitalization, the prisoner is required to be returned to jail. Otherwise, the prisoner may remain until the sentence is completed. The obligation of city and county jails to provide mental health services to prisoners has been the subject of numerous cases that require screening of prisoners for serious mental health problems and, where appropriate, transfer to an appropriate facility.[1]

---

1. *See, e.g.*, Partridge v. Two Unknown Police Officers of Houston, 791 F.2d 1182 (5th Cir. 1986: Alberti v. Sheriff of Harris County, 406 F.Supp. 649 (S.D.Tex. 1975).

Mental Health Services in Texas Prisons

Texas law requires the Department of Corrections, the Board of Pardons and Paroles, the Texas Department of Mental Health and Mental Retardation, the Texas Adult Probation Commission, and representatives of community mental health centers to establish a memorandum of understanding to provide for continuity of care for mentally ill and mentally retarded inmates.[2]

In addition, as discussed below, the Department of Corrections operates three maximum security mental hospitals for the care of mentally ill inmates.

2. Tex. Rev. Civ. Stat. Ann. art. 6203c-11 (Vernon Supp. 1988).

5D.21

Transfer From Penal to Mental Health Facilities

Prisoners confined in facilities operated by the Texas Department of Corrections who require inpatient psychiatric hospitalization may be transferred to one of the three maximum security mental hospitals operated by the Department of Corrections. If a prisoner nearing release is thought to meet the criteria for civil commitment,[1] that prisoner may be committed to a maximum security hospital pending the expiration of the criminal sentence and thereafter transferred to a facility operated by the Department of Mental Health and Mental Retardation.[2]

---

1. See Chapter 5E.4.
2. Tex. Rev. Civ. Stat. Ann. art. 6203c-8 (Vernon Supp. 1988); Tex. Code Crim. Proc. Ann. art. 46.01 § 7 (Vernon 1978).

5D.22

Parole Determinations

Parole of an inmate is a decision to release that person from physical confinement prior to the expiration of the sentence. Probation, as contrasted with parole, is a decision not to sentence a convicted person to a period of confinement. The decision to grant parole is made by the Board of Pardons and Paroles (Board). MHPs employed by the Department of Corrections and other MHPs may be able to assist the Board on this decision.

Eligibility for Parole

To be eligible for parole, an inmate must not be under a sentence of death and must have served one quarter of the sentence or 15 years, whichever is less.[1] If the conviction is for capital murder, aggravated kidnapping, aggravated sexual assault, or aggravated robbery; is for a crime involving a deadly weapon; or the judgment of conviction contains a specific finding that the prisoner is not eligible for parole until the actual "calender time" is served, the prisoner must serve at least 2 years before being eligible for parole, and good conduct credit may not be taken into account in the computation.

Board of Pardons and Paroles

The Board consists of six members appointed by the governor with the advice and consent of the Senate. Board members are required

1. Tex. Code Crim. Proc. Ann. art. 42.18 § 8(b) (Vernon Supp. 1988).

to be representative of the general public and are disqualified from service if in a position of conflict such as owning a business that transacts business with the Department of Corrections.

To assist the Board in making these decisions, it is empowered to appoint up to six parole commissioners, and their votes on parole have the same legal effect as a vote by the Board. These commissioners may sit in three-member panels.

Parole Criteria

In crimes involving specific victims, the Board is required to notify, among others, the victim, or where appropriate, a close relative of the victim to give that person an opportunity to make a written presentation to the Board. This statement should be considered by the Board in making its decision. The Board may require the presence of the prisoner for an interview.

The criteria by which the Board is required to make parole determinations is the "best interest of society."[2] The Board should only authorize parole when it concludes that satisfactory arrangements for the employment or maintenance of the prisoner exist and when there is reason to conclude that the prisoner is likely to be a law abiding citizen.

---

2. Tex. Code Crim. Proc. Ann. art. 42.18 § 8(f)(1) (Vernon Supp. 1988).

5D.23

Competency to Be Executed

The United States Supreme Court has ruled that execution of a prisoner who is insane at the time of the execution violates the ban on cruel and unusual punishment found in the eighth amendment to the United States Constitution.[1] The reasons supporting this conclusion include the notion that it is inhumane, that it adds nothing to the deterrent effect of capital punishment, and that the retributive effect of the punishment is not effectuated. Thus, MHPs may be asked to evaluate the mental condition of a prisoner who has been sentenced to death prior to the scheduled execution. The questions to be addressed are the prisoner's capacity to comprehend the "nature, pendency, and purpose of his execution."[2]

1. Ford v. Wainwright, 106 S. Ct. 2595 (1986).
2. Ex parte Jordon, 1988 Tex. Crim. App. LEXIS 167.

5D.24

Pornography

Texas law prohibits the promotion, production, or distribution of obscene materials or devices. Obscene material is defined as that which, according to contemporary standards, when taken as a whole "appeals to the prurient interest in sex," contains a depiction or description of patently offensive sexual acts or devices, and when considered in its entirety is lacking in serious "literary, artistic, political, and scientific value."[1] Expert testimony is not necessary to convict someone under this law.[2] However, MHPs who have expertise in this area may be called upon to assist in identifying materials as falling within or without these boundaries, such as the literary, artistic, political, or scientific value of the material, or in mounting or defending a challenge to these prohibitions.

1. Tex. Pen. Code Ann. § 43.21 (Vernon Supp. 1988).
2. Goodwin v. State, 514 S.W.2d 942 (Tex. Crim. App. 1974).

5D.25

Services for Sex Offenders

Texas does not have a specialized sex offender commitment program that seeks to identify and provide specialized treatment as an aspect of the sentencing process. Instead, services to sex offenders who are confined by the Department of Corrections may be provided at the discretion of the department.

5D.26

Services for Victims of Crimes

Texas has established by statute certain rights for victims of crimes.[1] One of those rights, set forth in a separate statute, is compensation for "medical, hospital, nursing, or psychiatric care or counseling, and physical therapy"[2] or direct or contractual provision of counseling services. In addition, MHPs may be asked to examine the mental or emotional condition of the victim of a crime to assist in verifying the validity of the victim's claim for compensation.

1. Tex. Code Crim. Proc. Ann. art. 56.01 - 56.05 (Vernon Supp. 1988).
2. Tex. Rev. Civ. Stat. Ann. art. 8308-1 (Vernon Supp. 1988).

Section 5

Practice Related to the Law

Section 5E

Voluntary or Involuntary Receipt of State Services

5E.1

Medicaid

Certain categories of people are eligible for Medicaid, a federally supported program in which the states make direct payments for medical care to service providers. Eligible persons include those persons who are 65 years of age or older and who receive supplemental security income, blind or disabled adults or children, families with dependent children who meet certain income criteria, children and pregnant women who meet income criteria, and foster children for certain expenses.[1] Thus, the benefits primarily go to elderly adults or children whose parents receive welfare. In Texas, the Texas Department of Human Services administers this program (see Chapter 5E.2).[2]

1. *See* Tex. Hum. Res. Code Ann. §§ 31.001-31.010 (Vernon 1980).
2. *See* Tex. Admin. Code tit. 40, §§ 15.5002-15.5105 (1988)(application procedures and requirements).

5E.2

Medical Assistance Program

Indigents in Texas are entitled to receive medical services through the Texas Department of Human Services under the Indigent Health Care and Treatment Act or Medical Assistance Program.[1] Under this law, an indigent may receive laboratory and X-ray tests, nursing services, physician services, social services, family planning services, prescription drugs, and inpatient or outpatient care through a local health department, public hospital, or private provider who contracts with a county to provide for these services. The law, however, expressly mentions only these specific professionals and services. Therefore, the law probably does not apply to nonlisted MHPs.

Inpatient Treatment

Under the indigent health care system, eligible persons must obtain the services from a designated provider except in emergencies.[2] The person is free to choose, however, from among the designated providers. After the person establishes eligibility under the federal income and resources requirements, the health care provider renders services that are reimbursed by the county and state. Persons are eligible if they meet the standards established by the Medicaid program, which include having an income of 150% or less of the established federal poverty level.[3] The county may,

1. Tex. Rev. Civ. Stat. Ann. art. 4438f (Vernon Supp. 1988); Tex. Hum. Res. Code Ann. § 32.037 (Vernon 1980).
2. Tex. Rev. Civ. Stat. Ann. art. 4438f § 3.03 (Vernon Supp. 1988).
3. Tex. Admin. Code tit. 25, § 39.8 (1988).

however, request that a person reimburse the system if the person's income exceeds the eligibility requirements to the extent that the person is able to pay for part of the expenses. If the person is unable to contribute toward the expenses, the county and health care provider may not refuse to treat the person or reduce the assistance that the person would otherwise receive.[4] Additionally, after qualifying, the person has a duty to inform the provider and county within 30 days of any changes in income or resources that could disqualify the person.

Each applicant must provide, at a minimum, the following: name and address; social security number, if applicable; number of persons in the applicant's household; county of residence; insurance coverage, if any; annual income; and value of real property and/or other assets, if any.[5] After receiving an application, the provider must determine the person's eligibility within 14 days. If the provider fails to do so, the applicant is automatically deemed eligible.[6]

The county is eligible for reimbursement from the state if the person receiving the services met all eligibility requirements. Counties may provide additional services, although these services are not reimbursable.[7]

Under the medical assistance program, persons must also obtain the services from a designated provider following application and certification of eligibility.[8] Both eligibility and services available are determined under the Social Security Act. Also, a person must be recertified monthly for eligibility and must carry a card indicating this to present to a health care provider. Under the medical assistance program, limited mental health coverage exists if the person is a patient in a nursing home and needs services for rehabilitation, dealing with terminal illness, or mental retardation.[9] Other people who may qualify include single pregnant women, foster children, and abandoned children.[10]

4. Tex. Rev. Civ. Stat. Ann. art. 4438f § 1.05 (Vernon Supp. 1988).
5. Tex. Rev. Civ. Stat. Ann. art. 4438f § 1.06 (Vernon Supp. 1988).
6. Tex. Rev. Civ. Stat. Ann. art. 4438f § 2.04 (Vernon Supp. 1988).
7. Tex. Rev. Civ. Stat. Ann. art. 4438f § 3.01 (Vernon Supp. 1988).
8. Tex. Hum. Res. Code Ann. §§ 32.025-32.027 (Vernon Supp. 1988).
9. Tex. Admin. Code tit. 40, § 45.604 (1988).
10. Tex. Admin. Code tit. 40, § 2.1004 (1988).

5E.3

Voluntary Civil Admission of Mentally Ill Adults

Mentally ill adults and minors who are at least 16 years of age may seek voluntary admission to a state-operated or private mental health facility for treatment.[1] MHPs may become involved either by evaluating the individual for admission or by providing treatment.

Differences Between Voluntary and Involuntary Admission

Several differences between voluntary admission and involuntary commitment exist. Voluntary admission applies only to persons 16 years of age or older. Additionally, if a person meets the criteria for involuntary commitment, the state must treat the person, whereas under voluntary admission, the state may treat the person if the criteria are met. Finally, voluntary admission covers a broader range of disorders and conditions, compared with involuntary commitment, which is limited to more severe disorders resulting in dangerousness or serious deterioration. The law generally favors voluntary treatment over involuntary commitment.

Voluntary Admission

Any person 16 years of age or older may make a written application to a state mental health facility, including community health

1. Tex. Rev. Civ. Stat. Ann. art. 5547 §§ 22-25 (Vernon Supp. 1988).

centers, for voluntary admission. The head of the facility may admit the person following a request if the head of the facility finds, after a preliminary examination, that the prospective patient has "symptoms of mental illness and will benefit from the services."[2] A mental illness is defined as "an illness, disease, or condition which either: substantially impairs the person's thought, perception of reality, emotional process, or judgment, or grossly impairs behavior as manifested by recent disturbed behavior."[3] The law expressly excludes admission based solely on senility, alcoholism, or mental deficiency. It provides, however, that persons who suffer from one of these conditions may be admitted if they also suffer from mental illness. Prior to admission, the head of the facility must also inform the prospective patient of the patient's rights.

If the person is admitted, the facility must release the person within 96 hours after the person makes a written request for discharge to the head of the facility. However, if the head of the facility determines that the person meets the criteria for court-ordered involuntary commitment, the head of the facility may file a petition with a court requesting involuntary commitment (see Chapter 5E.4). The head of the facility must also determine that the patient is unable to consent to the necessary treatment to file for involuntary commitment. If the head of the facility files this petition, the facility may detain the person beyond the 96-hour limit. Additionally, the person may be discharged if diagnosis and treatment are complete.[4]

---

2. Tex. Rev. Civ. Stat. Ann. art. 5547 § 22 (Vernon Supp. 1988). Minors who are 16 or older may be admitted without the consent of parents, guardians, or conservators. *Id.*
3. Tex. Rev. Civ. Stat. Ann. art. 5547 § 4(8) (Vernon Supp. 1988).
4. Tex. Rev. Civ. Stat. Ann. art. 5547 § 23 (Vernon Supp. 1988).

5E.4

Involuntary Civil Commitment of Mentally Ill Adults

Mentally ill adults may be subject to involuntary civil commitment. MHPs may become involved in the evaluation process prior to admission, as witnesses at a hearing, or by providing treatment after admission. While the statutes require physicians' input in the process, other MHPs may also assist.

Terms and Definitions

To understand fully the law concerning involuntary commitment, MHPs should be familiar with the following terms and their legal meanings:[1]

1. *Mental illness* means a disease or condition that either grossly impairs a person's behavior or substantially impairs the person's "thought, perception of reality, emotional process, or judgment."[2] The law expressly excludes alcoholism, drug addiction, and senility from the definition unless the person is also mentally ill.
2. *Physician* means a person licensed to practice medicine in Texas.
3. *Nonphysician mental health professional* means a licensed psychologist, a registered nurse with a master's or doctoral degree in psychiatric nursing, or a certified social worker with a master's or doctoral degree and advanced clinical practitioner recognition.

---

1. Tex. Rev. Civ. Stat. Ann. art. 5547 § 4 (Vernon Supp. 1988).
2. Tex. Rev. Civ. Stat. Ann. art. 5547 § 4 (Vernon Supp. 1988).

4. *Court* means a county probate court.
5. *Temporary mental health services* means court-ordered services for a period of 90 days, applicable if the person is mentally ill, likely to injure someone, or likely to continue to deteriorate without help and is unable to consent to the necessary treatment.[3]
6. *Extended mental health services* means court-ordered treatment and detention for a period of not more than 1 year, which may only be ordered if the court determines that the person has received at least 60 consecutive days of inpatient treatment in the preceding 12 months, and that the person is mentally ill, is likely to injure self or others, is unable to consent to the necessary treatment, and will continue to deteriorate without the treatment.
7. *Application for court-ordered mental health services* means a written application filed by any adult or district attorney with the court stating the name and address of the proposed patient and whether the proposed patient is charged with a crime, is mentally ill, and meets the appropriate criteria for either temporary or extended mental health services.
8. *Outpatient mental health services* means court-ordered services that require the person to report to a mental health facility as an outpatient for mental health treatment.

Admission

The process for involuntarily commitment may be commenced two ways. First, any adult or district attorney may petition a court for involuntary commitment, after which the court may determine whether the patient should be confined prior to a hearing. Second, on an emergency basis, a peace officer may apprehend and transport a person to a mental health facility if the officer has reason to believe that the person is mentally ill and poses a substantial risk of serious harm to someone.

Regular Admission

Any adult or district attorney may make a sworn written application to a court in the county where the proposed patient resides.[4] The petition must indicate whether temporary or extended treatment is sought and contain the necessary information for the type of treatment sought. All petitions are filed using the proposed

3. Tex. Rev. Civ. Stat. Ann. art. 5547 § 50 (Vernon Supp. 1988).
4. Tex. Rev. Civ. Stat. Ann. art. 5547 § 32 (Vernon Supp. 1988).

patient's initials, rather than the person's full name. If the proposed patient has been charged with a crime, the petition must also indicate that the criminal court ordered a transfer for mental health reasons and dismissed the charges.[5]

After the court receives a petition, the court may order an examination by a physician. The physician is required to file a sworn certificate of medical examination with the court, stating:[6]

1. the names and addresses of the physician and person examined;
2. the date and place of examination;
3. the diagnosis of the person's physical and mental health;
4. the person's previous history if the physician has been treating the person;
5. the proposed mental health treatment; and
6. the opinions, and detailed basis for the opinions, indicating whether the patient meets the following three criteria:
    a. the person is likely to harm himself seriously;
    b. the person is likely to harm another person seriously;
    c. the person will, if not treated, continue to suffer severe and abnormal mental, emotional, or physical distress; will continue to experience deterioration of the ability to function independently; and is unable to make a rational and informed decision whether or not to submit to treatment.

If the petition requests extended mental health services, the physician must also state whether the proposed patient's condition will probably continue for at least 90 days.

Following the examination, the head of a state facility is required to file with the court a recommendation on the proposed involuntary commitment. The recommendation should indicate whether the person should be involuntarily committed, as well as the "most appropriate treatment alternative."[7] During the examination and recommendation period, the proposed patient may remain at liberty unless there is an application and hearing for emergency detention and protective custody.[8] In practice, however, it is exceptional for proposed patients to remain at liberty during this process.

After a petition for involuntary commitment is filed with a court, either the court or the district attorney may make a motion for protective custody. The motion must state that the petitioning

5. Tex. Rev. Civ. Stat. Ann. art. 5547 § 32 (Vernon Supp. 1988).
6. Tex. Rev. Civ. Stat. Ann. art. 5547 § 33 (Vernon Supp. 1988).
7. Tex. Rev. Civ. Stat. Ann. art. 5547 § 34 (Vernon Supp. 1988).
8. Tex. Rev. Civ. Stat. Ann. art. 5547 § 35 (Vernon Supp. 1988).

party has reason to believe, based on the proposed patient's acts or the representations of a credible person, that the proposed patient "presents a substantial risk of serious harm" to someone and the proposed patient is mentally ill.[9] A certificate of medical examination is also necessary for a protective order. If the court issues a protective order, a peace officer may apprehend and transport the person to a mental health facility. The mental health facility, however, must first consent to custody.

Simultaneously with signing a protective order, the court must appoint counsel to represent the proposed patient and give notice of the probable-cause hearing regarding protective custody.[10] The probable-cause hearing must occur within 72 hours after the person is taken into protective custody. At the hearing, the person has a right to be present and to present evidence challenging the determination that the proposed patient poses a substantial risk to someone. If the court determines that there is probable cause to believe that the person is a risk, however, the person must remain in custody pending the commitment hearing. If the court determines that the person is not a risk, the person is required to be released pending the commitment hearing.[11]

The commitment hearing must occur within 14 days after the court receives a petition for involuntary commitment.[12] After the court sets the date for the hearing, the proposed patient is required to be given written notice of the time and place of the hearing.[13] Additionally, the proposed patient and the person's counsel must receive, as an indication of the evidence that the state may use at the hearing, a statement indicating whether temporary or extended services are sought, the names and addresses of witnesses, the acts upon which the petition is based, and why the treatment is required. The court may, however, allow other evidence not disclosed at this time at the commitment hearing if the court determines that the admission will not deprive the proposed patient of a full and fair opportunity to contest the case. The proposed patient and counsel must also receive access to all relevant records and papers, including hospital and physician records, prior to the commitment hearing.[14]

Also prior to the commitment hearing, two physicians, at least one of whom is a psychiatrist, if available, must examine the patient.[15] When the examination is performed pursuant to a court

9. Tex. Rev. Civ. Stat. Ann. art. 5547 § 36 (Vernon Supp. 1988).
10. Tex. Rev. Civ. Stat. Ann. art. 5547 § 37 (Vernon Supp. 1988).
11. Tex. Rev. Civ. Stat. Ann. art. 5547 § 38 (Vernon Supp. 1988).
12. Tex. Rev. Civ. Stat. Ann. art. 5547 § 42 (Vernon Supp. 1988).
13. Tex. Rev. Civ. Stat. Ann. art. 5547 § 43 (Vernon Supp. 1988).
14. Tex. Rev. Civ. Stat. Ann. art. 5547 § 44 (Vernon Supp. 1988).
15. Tex. Rev. Civ. Stat. Ann. art. 5547 § 46 (Vernon Supp. 1988).

order and the patient is informed prior to the examination that it is not privileged, the rules of privilege are excepted to the resulting examination.[16] In addition, one appellate court has also required that the individual being examined be informed of a right to consult with counsel prior to the examination.[17] Further, the court may issue a warrant to take the proposed patient into custody for the examinations if the person refuses to consent. As noted earlier, although the statutes contemplate outpatient examinations as the rule, in practice they are the exception. After the examinations, the physicians must file with the court certificates of medical examination, which should contain the information described above.

At the commitment hearing, the proposed patient and patient's counsel have a right to be present and to present evidence. Additionally, the proposed patient may cross-examine witnesses.[18] If the proposed patient chooses to waive the right to cross-examine, the court may admit the certificates of medical examination as evidence in lieu of live medical testimony. If the petition seeks extended mental health services, however, the court must hear additional evidence about the proposed patient's condition. This additional evidence must include expert medical or psychiatric testimony and may include testimony from nonphysician MHPs. The evidence must also include proof of recent acts or patterns of behavior indicating that the person is likely to injure someone seriously. The hearing is public unless good cause is shown for closing the hearing. The hearing is also before a judge unless the proposed patient requests a jury trial.[19] A hearing for extended mental health services, however, must be before a jury unless the proposed patient formally, in writing, waives the right to a jury trial.

If, after the hearing, the court determines that there is not clear and convincing evidence showing that the proposed patient meets the criteria for either temporary or extended mental health services, the proposed patient should be released immediately.[20] If the court determines that the criteria are met by clear and convincing evidence, the court may order temporary or extended mental health services, or require the person to participate in outpatient treatment at a community mental health facility. It is not common, however, for the court to order outpatient services following a contested hearing.[21]

---

16. Tex. R. Civ. Evid. 510(d)(4).
17. Lanett v. State, 750 S.W.2d 302, Tex. Civ. App.-Dallas (1988).
18. Tex. Rev. Civ. Stat. Ann. art. 5547 § 47 (Vernon Supp. 1988).
19. Tex. Rev. Civ. Stat. Ann. art. 5547 § 49 (Vernon Supp. 1988).
20. Tex. Rev. Civ. Stat. Ann. art. 5547 §§ 48-51 (Vernon Supp. 1988).
21. Shuman & Hawkins, *The Use of Alternatives to Institutionalization and the Mentally Ill*, 33 Sw. L. Rev. 1181 (1980).

If the court orders outpatient treatment, the court must also appoint a person at the mental health facility to be responsible for providing and overseeing the treatment.[22] The responsible person must then submit to the court, within 2 weeks, a program for treatment. If the patient fails to participate in outpatient treatment, the responsible person must inform the court. Failure to comply may result in a modification hearing at which the court may order temporary or extended mental health services. The court may also modify the outpatient order on its own motion or the request of any interested party.

The court may modify an order requiring inpatient temporary or extended mental health treatment if the head of the facility at which the person is committed petitions the court requesting outpatient care.[23] The petition must state why the modification is sought and have a certificate of medical examination attached. The examination must have been performed within the preceding 7 days. At the hearing, the patient and patient's counsel may be present and may present evidence. The state must prove that modification is necessary and desirable by clear and convincing evidence.[24]

A court may also renew an order for extended mental health treatment upon application by any adult or the district attorney.[25] The petition for renewal must contain two certificates of medical examination, and the examinations must have been done in the 30 days prior to the application. The application should state the basis for renewal and what type of commitment is sought. After the court receives a renewal application, the court is required to appoint counsel to represent the patient and sets a date for a hearing. At the hearing, the state must prove the need for renewal by clear and convincing evidence, based on the criteria for the type of services sought.

Finally, at any time, a court may order a new hearing and reexamination if it finds good cause, such as changed circumstances, for this action.[26] The rehearing process begins after any adult or the patient asks the court for a new hearing. If the person does not meet the criteria for protective custody, the person should be released until the new trial. Following the filing of the application, the judge is required to set a time and place for the hearing and appoint a physician, who must be a psychiatrist if one is available, and who is not affiliated with the facility at which the

22. Tex. Rev. Civ. Stat. Ann. art. 5547 § 52 (Vernon Supp. 1988).
23. Tex. Rev. Civ. Stat. Ann. art. 5547 § 54 (Vernon Supp. 1988).
24. Tex. Rev. Civ. Stat. Ann. art. 5547 § 48 (Vernon Supp. 1988).
25. Tex. Rev. Civ. Stat. Ann. art. 5547 § 55 (Vernon Supp. 1988).
26. Tex. Rev. Civ. Stat. Ann. art. 5547 § 56 (Vernon Supp. 1988).

patient is detained, to examine the patient.[27] The patient may also obtain a physician of the patient's choice for an examination at the patient's own expense. The physician must then file a certificate of medical examination with the court within 10 days. If the court finds that the patient still meets commitment criteria, by clear and convincing evidence, the original order remains in place. If the court determines that the person does not meet the standards by clear and convincing evidence, the patient must be released. One important qualification, however, is that a court has no duty to conduct a rehearing and reexamination if the request is filed before 6 months of court-ordered extended mental health services has expired.

A person may appeal any order, whether for a rehearing or mental health services, in the court of appeals in the county in which the original action occurred.[28] The party must appeal the decision within 10 days by filing the request with the appropriate court's clerk. The trial judge may, at his discretion, release the person pending the appeal unless the person meets the criteria for protective custody.

Emergency Detention

Any peace officer may apprehend a person for emergency detention if the officer has reason to believe, based either on the statement of a credible person or the conduct of the person in question, that the person is mentally ill and poses a substantial risk of harm to self or others unless immediately restrained.[29] The officer must also believe that there is not time to obtain a warrant prior to apprehension. Following apprehension, the officer must transport the person to the nearest mental health facility or another place designated by a mental health authority to be sufficient for such detention. However, the person may not be taken to a jail or other nonmedical facility except in extreme emergencies. If the person is taken to a jail or nonmedical facility, the person must remain separate from the prisoners or other persons present.

After transporting the patient, the officer must immediately file with the facility an application stating the following:

1. the officer believes that the person is mentally ill;
2. the officer believes that the person poses a substantial risk of harm to someone, including a specific description of the harm;
3. the officer believes that the risk of harm is imminent;
4. the specific recent behavior or acts supporting the officer's be-

27. Tex. Rev. Civ. Stat. Ann. art. 5547 § 56 (Vernon Supp. 1988).
28. Tex. Rev. Civ. Stat. Ann. art. 5547 § 57 (Vernon Supp. 1988).
29. Tex. Rev. Civ. Stat. Ann. art. 5547 § 26 (Vernon Supp. 1988).

liefs or the statements made to the officer from another credible person describing the behavior or acts in detail; and

5. the names and relationships of the person or persons reporting the acts or behavior, if any.

Next the facility must conduct an examination of the person, with a physician, within 24 hours (sooner if possible). The physician must then file a report with the head of the facility.[30] The physician's statement must state the following for the facility to detain the person further: that the person is mentally ill; the probable nature of the illness; the physician's opinion that the person poses a substantial risk of serious harm to someone; the acts or behavior supporting the beliefs; the probable harm that may occur; the physician's belief that the harm is imminent; and the physician's opinion that emergency detention is the least restrictive means of necessary restraint to prevent the harm. The facility must release the person unless, in the physician's opinion, the person meets these criteria for emergency detention.

Additionally, any adult may file an application for emergency detention of another person. The application must be written and must state the applicant's belief that the person is mentally ill and the supporting reasons; that the person poses a substantial risk of seriously harming someone; the belief that the risk of harm is imminent; the specific acts or behavior demonstrating the illness and potential harm; and the applicant's relationship, if any, to the proposed patient.[31] The applicant must present the application personally to a judge, who may question and interview the applicant. The court must deny the petition unless it finds that there is reasonable cause to believe the person meets the stated criteria. If the court determines that the person meets the criteria, the court is required to issue a warrant for the person's apprehension. After the officer apprehends the person, the procedures are the same as when an officer detains a person based on the officer's own beliefs. Detention may not exceed 24 hours in either case. During detention, however, an adult or the state may request protective custody or other mental health services by filing the appropriate application with the court.

Finally, if during emergency detention the head of a facility determines that the person does not meet the criteria for emergency detention, the head of the facility must release the person. The facility may not release the person, however, if the person committed a crime or objects to release.

---

30. Tex. Rev. Civ. Stat. Ann. art. 5547 § 26 (Vernon Supp. 1988).
31. Tex. Rev. Civ. Stat. Ann. art. 5547 § 28 (Vernon Supp. 1988).

Civil Liability

Any person who acts in good faith, without negligence, "in connection with the examination, certification, apprehension, custody, transportation, detention, treatment, or discharge" of another person concerning involuntary commitment may not be held liable, either civilly or criminally, for the acts.[32] Additionally, physicians who perform medical examinations are not liable for the examinations or their testimony unless they acted with malice. Other MHPs are not specifically included within the latter group of limited immunity.

32. Tex. Rev. Civ. Stat. Ann. art. 5547 § 18 (Vernon Supp. 1988).

5E.5

Voluntary Admission and Involuntary Commitment of Alcoholics

In Texas, the law provides for both voluntary and involuntary treatment of persons who are seriously affected by alcohol, focusing on treatment rather than separation from society. MHPs may become involved either by evaluating or treating the person.

Terms and Definitions

To understand fully the law concerning alcoholism, an MHP should be familiar with the following terms:[1]

1. *treatment facility:* a private or public detoxification facility, intensive care facility, primary care facility, long-term care facility, outpatient center, community health center, or any other facility licensed by the state and approved by the Texas Commission on Alcohol and Drug Abuse;
2. *treatment:* a program "designed to initiate and promote a person's chemical-free status, or to maintain the person free of alcohol;"[2]
3. *alcohol abuse:* "the excessive use of alcohol in a manner that interferes with one or more of the following to a less than chronic extent: physical or psychological functioning, social adaption, educational performance, or occupational functioning;"[3]
4. *alcoholism:* "the loss of self-control with respect to the use of

1. Tex. Rev. Civ. Stat. Ann. art. 5561cc (Vernon Supp. 1988).
2. *Id.*
3. *Id.*

alcohol, or the pathological use of alcohol that chronically impairs social or occupational functioning, or physiological dependence on alcohol as evidenced by tolerance or withdrawal symptoms;"[4]

5. *prevention:* programs or treatment aimed at reducing a person's risk of abusing or becoming addicted to alcohol;
6. *intervention:* programs or treatment aimed at interrupting "the onset or progression" of abuse or dependency on alcohol;[5]
7. *rehabilitation:* "a planned and organized program designed to reestablish the social and vocational life of a substance-free person;"[6]
8. *evaluation:* evaluation of the person's health and social and emotional state, including a history of drinking, family relationships, education, social and economic status, legal history, cultural background, and vocational training and background, to prepare a treatment plan;[7] and
9. *detoxification:* "a process of safe and medically supervised withdrawal from alcohol."[8]

Voluntary Admissions

Any adult person who suffers from alcoholism and is a resident of Texas is eligible for admission on a space-available basis to a state hospital if a licensed physician determines that the person is an alcoholic.

Involuntary Commitment and Emergency Detention

Any adult may make an application for emergency detention of another adult by submitting a written application to a probate court that states that the applicant has reasonable grounds to believe that the other person is an alcoholic and that there is a substantial risk the other will seriously harm someone; that the risk of harm is imminent; the relationship of the applicant to the other person, if any; and the recent and specific behavior or acts

4. *Id.*
5. *Id.*
6. *Id.*
7. Tex. Admin. Code tit. 40, § 151.101 (1988).
8. Tex. Admin. Code tit. 40, § 151.21 (1988).

that support the applicant's beliefs.[9] The court may not grant an application unless it finds reasonable grounds to believe that the person is an alcoholic and meets the stated criteria. If the court approves the application, it is required to issue a warrant for the immediate apprehension of the person to be taken to an approved treatment facility. Within 24 hours after admission, a physician is required to examine the person and file a written report with the court verifying the detention criteria. If the court denies the application or the examining physician determines that the person does not meet the emergency detention criteria, the person is required to be released.

If a person is taken into custody under an emergency detention order, the person has a right to know the reasons for detention; to know where the detention will occur; to contact an attorney or have an attorney appointed; and to know that all communication with the treatment professionals may be used against the person in further detention proceedings.[10]

Additionally, any adult may submit an application for involuntary commitment to a probate court if the person believes another person suffers from alcoholism. The application must state that the other person is an alcoholic; may harm someone; "will suffer abnormal mental, emotional, or physical distress, and will continue to deteriorate in ability to function independently if not treated;" "is unable to make a rational and informed choice as to whether or not to submit to treatment;" and is not charged with a crime.[11]

After receiving an application, the court is required to give notice to the alleged alcoholic and conduct a hearing within 5 to 14 days. The alleged alcoholic has a right to appear at the hearing with counsel and present opposing evidence. If the person does not have an attorney, the court is required to appoint one to represent the person.[12] Further, the court must inform the person's relatives and other interested persons of the hearing and provide them with an opportunity to present evidence at the hearing. The court may also order that the person submit to a physical examination prior to the hearing, the results of which may be used as evidence. If the court determines that the person meets the stated criteria alleged in the application, the court may order involuntary commitment.

The alleged alcoholic may appeal a court decision by filing a written request for an appeal within 10 days after the court signs

9. Tex. Rev. Civ. Stat. Ann. art. 5561c-2 (Vernon Supp. 1988).
10. Tex. Rev. Civ. Stat. Ann. art. 5561c-2 §2.03 (Vernon Supp. 1988).
11. Tex. Rev. Civ. Stat. Ann. art. 5561c-2 § 3.02 (Vernon Supp. 1988).
12. *Id.*

the order for involuntary commitment.[13] Pending the appeal hearing, however, the court may order that the person be detained at a state facility unless the court determines that the person may be safely released. The person is required to be discharged from treatment at the end of the court-ordered period or any time before that date if the administrator of the facility determines that the person no longer meets the criteria for court-ordered commitment and treatment.

Finally, a criminal court may transfer a proceeding to a probate court if the person who committed the offense abuses alcohol and the offense committed was a misdemeanor.[14] The court may order treatment as described above, which may not exceed 90 days, to take the place of the usual incarceration or fine. Similarly, a juvenile court may transfer a case to the probate court if the juvenile in question abuses alcohol.

13. Tex. Rev. Civ. Stat. Ann. art. 5561c-2 § 3.03 (Vernon Supp. 1988).
14. Tex. Rev. Civ. Stat. Ann. art. 5561c-2 § 3.07 (Vernon Supp. 1988).

5E.6

Voluntary Admission and Involuntary Commitment of Drug Addicts

In Texas, drug-dependent persons may be committed to a mental health facility for treatment. MHPs may become involved either in the evaluation process or the treatment program.[1]

Terms and Definitions

The following terms are helpful in understanding the law regarding commitment and treatment of drug-dependent persons:[2]

1. *drug-dependent person:* "a person who is using a controlled substance and who is in a state of psychic or physical dependence or both arising from administration of a controlled substance"[3] and whose behavior is characterized by "a strong compulsion to take a controlled substance in order to experience its psychic effects or to avoid the discomfort of its absence;"[4]
2. *controlled substance:* any drug or toxic inhalant designated by Texas law as a controlled substance;[5]
3. *toxic inhalant:* any gaseous substance inhaled to create a physical or psychological effect which may also cause personal injury to the inhaler;
4. *mental health facility:* any inpatient or outpatient mental health

1. Tex. Rev. Civ. Stat. Ann. art. 5561c-1 (Vernon Supp. 1988).
2. *Id.*
3. *Id.*
4. *Id.*
5. *See* Tex. Rev. Civ. Stat. Ann. art. 4476-15 (Vernon Supp. 1988).

facility of the Texas Department of Mental Health and Mental Retardation; community mental health center; or specific part of a general hospital specializing in the diagnosis and treatment of mentally ill or drug-dependent persons.

Procedure and Application

A district attorney or any adult may file a sworn written application for extended commitment of a drug-dependent person with a court. The application must use only the alleged drug-dependent person's initials rather than full name and must state the following:

1. the proposed patient's initials, address, and county of residence;
2. that the proposed patient is a drug-dependent person who needs hospitalization "for his own welfare and protection or the protection of others;"[6] and
3. whether the proposed patient is charged with a crime.

The application must also have at least one certificate of medical examination from a physician stating the physician's and proposed patient's names (initials only for the proposed patient) and addresses; the date of examination; any previous history, if the physician has been treating the proposed patient; and the physician's opinion as to whether the proposed patient is a drug-dependent person who requires hospitalization. If there is not a certificate of examination, the court is required to appoint at least one physician to perform the examination. The court may also issue a warrant and require the proposed patient to submit to the examination.

Following the application, a commitment hearing must occur within 14 days, before which the court is required to appoint counsel to represent the person if the person does not already have counsel. The attorney is required to be given access to all records, including the physician's report, prior to the hearing. Additionally, prior to the hearing, the court must have two certificates of medical examination, at least one of which was done by a psychiatrist if one was available in the county. The examinations must have been done within 30 days prior to the hearing. The hearing is required to be held before a jury unless the proposed patient files a written waiver of the right to a jury trial with the court. Pending and during the hearing, the proposed patient may remain at lib-

6. *Id.*

erty unless legally detained under protective custody. If the state proves by clear and convincing evidence that the person is drug-dependent and requires hospitalization, the court may order commitment for up to 6 months at a mental health facility or treatment on an outpatient basis for a period not to exceed 6 months.

A person may appeal the order by filing a request for an appeal with the court within 10 days after the court's order for commitment. Pending the appeal, if the judge determines that the patient does not require protective custody, the patient may be released.

Emergency Detention

If, during the pendency of an appeal, the district attorney files a petition for protective custody with the court, the person may be detained. Additionally, the district attorney may request protective custody pending a commitment hearing. The protective custody petition must state that the district attorney has reason to believe, based either on the proposed patient's conduct or the representations of credible persons, that the person is drug-dependent and poses a substantial risk of seriously harming someone. The application must be accompanied by at least one certificate of medical examination confirming this belief. If the court determines that the person meets these criteria, the court is required to issue a warrant ordering a peace officer to take the person into custody and transport the person to a mental health facility. Simultaneously with signing the order for protective custody, the court must appoint counsel to represent the person and set a date for a probable-cause hearing.

The probable-cause hearing must occur within 72 hours after protective custody detention begins. The patient and patient's counsel have a right to be present at the hearing and to present evidence challenging the fact that the person either is drug dependent or poses a substantial risk of harm to someone. If the court determines that the evidence does not support the protective custody criteria, the person is required to be released pending the commitment hearing. Otherwise, the person may be detained at the facility until the commitment hearing or appeal occurs, providing the hearing occurs within 14 days after protective custody begins.

Civil Liability

Any person who acts in good faith and without malice in the "examination, certification, apprehension, custody, transportation, detention, treatment or discharge" of a person regarding drug dependency is not civilly or criminally liable for these acts. Also, any physician who performs a medical examination for certification or testifies at a hearing is not liable unless the physician acts with malice. Nonphysicians are not included within this latter grant of limited immunity.

5E.7

Services for Developmentally Disabled Persons

Mentally retarded persons in Texas are entitled to various treatments and services at state expense. The Texas Department of Mental Health and Mental Retardation oversees the programs, which may include screening and referral services, crisis stabilization, psychosocial rehabilitation, vocational training, residential services, entitlement assistance, support for the family, and medical services.[1] MHPs may provide either evaluation or treatment under these programs.[2]

Texas does not have a separate program at the present time for individuals who are developmentally disabled but do not meet the statutory criteria for receiving benefits for the mentally retarded or mentally ill. The Texas legislature has, however, authorized a pilot program, modeled after the mental retardation program, that is currently under development.[3] Under the pilot program, a developmental disability is defined as a "severe, chronic disability that is attributable to a physical impairment or a combination of mental and physical impairments; is manifested before the person reaches 22 years of age; is likely to continue indefinitely; results in substantial functional limitation in three or more of the following areas of life activity: self-care, receptive and expressive language, learning, mobility, self-direction, capacity for independent living, work skills or work tolerance, and economic self-sufficiency; and reflects the person's need for a combination and sequence of special, interdisciplinary, or generic care, treat-

1. Tex. Admin. Code tit. 25, § 405.753; Tex. Rev. Civ. Stat. Ann. art. 5547-300 (Vernon Supp. 1988).
2. Tex. Rev. Civ. Stat. Ann. art. 5547 §§ 201, 300 (Vernon Supp. 1988).
3. Tex. Rev. Civ. Stat. Ann. art. 5561l (Vernon Supp. 1988).

ment, vocational rehabilitation, or other services that are of lifelong or extended duration and that are individually planned and coordinated."[4]

Terms and Definitions

To understand fully the law regarding mental retardation services, the following terms should be understood:[5]

1. *mental retardation:* "significantly subaverage general intellectual functioning existing concurrently with deficits in adaptive behavior and originating during the developmental period;"[6]
2. *subaverage general intellectual functioning:* measured intelligence, according to a standard psychometric test, of two or more standard deviations below the mean for the same age group;
3. *mental retardation services:* "programs and assistance for mentally retarded persons which may include, but shall not be limited to, diagnosis and evaluation, education, special training, supervision, care, treatment, rehabilitation, residential care, and counseling"[7] for mentally retarded persons;
4. *habilitation:* the processes of assisting a person to acquire life skills so that the person may cope within a community and increasing the person's physical, mental and social efficiency;
5. *legally adequate consent:* consent, given by a person who is at least 18 years of age and who has not been judged incompetent to manage his or her own affairs, after the person has been informed and comprehends the consequences, alternatives, and nature of the consent and treatment;
6. *comprehensive diagnosis and evaluation:* "a study, including a sequence of observations and examination of a person leading to conclusions and recommendations formulated jointly, with dissenting opinions, if any, by a diagnosis and evaluation team,"[8] including if necessary social and medical history and neurological, audiological, visual, educational, psychological, or sociological tests or adaptive behavior examinations; and
7. *diagnosis and evaluation team:* "a group of persons with special training and experience in the diagnosis, management, and

---

4. *Id.*
5. Tex. Rev. Civ. Stat. Ann. art. 5547-300 § 3 (Vernon Supp. 1988).
6. Tex. Admin. Code tit. 25, § 115.15 (1988).
7. *Id.*
8. *Id.*

needs of mentally retarded persons"[9] composed of certified and/or licensed professionals.

Procedure and Application

Upon a petition by any adult on behalf of another or the person in question, any person has a right to a prompt, comprehensive diagnosis and evaluation. The process begins by filing an application either for evaluation or specific services. The evaluation should be adapted to a person's background, language, and ethnic origin.

Following the comprehensive evaluation, the diagnosis and evaluation team is required to make a written recommendation as to whether the person is eligible for services and what the best treatment for the person should be. If the person disagrees with the findings of the evaluation team, the person has a right to an administrative hearing, as well as the right to obtain an independent diagnosis and evaluation from another physician or other licensed professional. Moreover, even if a person can give legally adequate consent, a comprehensive diagnosis and evaluation must be done prior to admission to any mental retardation services program.

If the diagnosis and evaluation team determines that a person qualifies for mental retardation services, the person may then apply for the specific service desired or determined necessary by the evaluation team. The person is entitled to be admitted to a program as soon as a position becomes available. If the team determines that a person requires long-term placement at a residential care facility, the court, agency, person, or a community center may then petition the court for the appropriate court order. Following admission to a residential care center on a voluntary or court-ordered basis, the person must be released within 96 hours after making a written request for discharge with the facility. However, if the head of the facility determines that the patient poses a substantial danger to self or others if released and files a request for judicial commitment, the person may be detained for a longer period.

A court may order commitment after the filing of a petition by a facility if the court determines that the person is (a) mentally retarded and (b) poses a substantial risk of harm to someone or is unable to properly provide for basic living needs. Additionally, the court must determine that the person cannot be adequately rehabilitated in a less restrictive setting and that the particular center in

9. *Id.*

question may adequately provide the necessary services. If an adult makes an application for commitment, the application must state the proposed resident's name, sex, address, and birthday; the name and address of the person's guardian, if any; the facts supporting the necessity of residential commitment; and the reasons why other means of care are inappropriate. The application must also contain a copy of the recommendation of the diagnosis and evaluation team, if complete. A hearing must then occur within 10 days after the application is filed. At the hearing, the person has a right to be present and to present evidence.

5E.8

Hospice Care

Patients who are terminally ill may receive hospice care, which usually consists of psychological and/or physical support in the patient's home. The purpose of hospice care is to increase the quality of life during the final days or months of the patient's life through family contact and participation in the treatment and to assist the family and patient in dealing with death. The program of care may include medication to control pain or other symptoms, nursing services or medical social services, or other medical support. Some programs have three phases: home care with nursing, emotional, and religious support; inpatient care coordination; and bereavement services for the family.[1] MHPs may become involved in any or all of the three phases.

In Texas, hospices must be licensed[2] and may offer the following: nursing services; speech, occupational, physical, or respiratory therapy; medical social services; medical supplies such as drugs or medical equipment; and nutritional counseling.[3] Besides treating the patient in the patient's home, hospice employees may also treat patients in nursing or convalescent homes and coordinate home care with necessary periodical inpatient treatment.

The Texas Department of Health oversees hospices and other home health agencies and sets the licensing requirements and the qualification criteria for both professional and nonprofessional employees of these agencies. Certain businesses and persons are exempt from the licensing requirement, however. These include physicians, dentists, registered nurses, and physical therapists

1. Tex. Admin. Code tit. 25, §§ 115.1-115.17 (1988).
2. Tex. Rev. Civ. Stat. Ann. art. 4447u (Vernon Supp. 1988).
3. *Id.*

who are licensed by the state; registered nurses, licensed vocational nurses, physical therapists, occupational therapists, speech therapists, medical social workers, or other health care professionals who provide home services solely as sole practitioners; nonprofit national or state associations that merely act as a clearinghouse to refer patients to licensed care providers; persons whose permanent residence is with the patient; employees of a home health agency who meet employment criteria; licensed nursing or convalescent homes; medical supply companies; pharmacies; hospitals or other licensed facilities providing inpatient care; and visiting nurses who provide services in conjunction with any "well-recognized church or religious denomination" and who provide treatment only by prayer or spiritual means.[4]

After a person requests hospice care, a team or member of a team is required to do an initial assessment of the patient's and family's needs within 72 hours.[5] A team consists of a physician, registered nurse, social worker, and minister or other religious counselor. Following the assessment, the team should prepare a written treatment plan, to be revised every 90 days if necessary. The team should also conduct a conference with the patient and family every 2 weeks.

Hospice licenses must be renewed annually. Additionally, hospices are subject to investigation and inspection by the Texas Department of Health, and the department may revoke or suspend a license if it determines that the health and safety of patients are threatened. Failure to obtain a license may result in a fine of not less than $100 but not more than $500 for each day of operation without the license.[6] Hospices must also provide patients and their families with information on how to file a complaint against the hospice and the address of the Texas Department of Health.[7]

---

4. *Id.*
5. Tex. Admin. Code tit. 25, § 115.10 (1988).
6. *Id.*
7. Tex. Admin. Code tit. 25, § 115.15 (1988).

Section 6

Limitations on and Liability for Practice

6.1

Informed Consent for Services

The relationship between an MHP and a client is based upon an agreement between them or the MHP and someone legally constituted to act for the client. The MHP enjoys no unilateral right or obligation to render services to the client. Thus, the informed consent of the client is necessary before the rendition of services, disclosure of client information to third parties, or any other action that may have an impact upon the client.

The concept of informed consent, as contrasted with consent, is designed to emphasize the distinction between the process of discussions leading to an informed choice by the client and a mere perfunctory signature on a document labeled a consent form. In general, informed consent requires that the client be informed of all relevant information about the current problem, including the treatment proposed, the risks and benefits of that treatment, and the alternative treatments.

In Texas, two systems for evaluating these requirements exist. If the procedure is one that has been addressed by the Texas Medical Disclosure Panel, its risks, established by the panel, are adequately disclosed if given in writing on the consent form signed by the client and a witness.[1] At present, the only procedure listed under the category of Psychotherapeutic Procedures is electroconvulsive therapy. The risks required to be disclosed by the panel in conjunction with this procedure include memory changes, bone fractures or dislocations, and temporary confusion. Failure to disclose these risks creates a rebuttable presumption of negligence. If the panel has determined that a procedure is one for which disclosure of risks is not required, no disclosure need be

1. Tex. Rev. Civ. Stat. Ann. art. 4590i § 6.01 et seq. (Vernon Supp. 1988).

made. At present, no procedures are assigned to the list requiring no disclosure under the category Psychotherapeutic Procedures.

If the panel has not addressed the procedure, then the disclosure that must be given is "the risks and hazards that could have influenced a reasonable person in making a decision to give or withhold treatment."[2] This approach is not focused on what the average MHP would disclose under the circumstances, but instead on what material risks the average client would want disclosed. Thus, for example, in one case in which a patient brought suit against a physician for failing to disclose the risks of tardive dyskinesia in conjunction with a neuroleptic medication, treatment with this drug had not been addressed by the panel and the physician's duty to disclose was therefore addressed under the reasonable patient standard.[3] The physician was found negligent for failing to disclose this risk, even though evidence was introduced that a reasonable practitioner would not have disclosed these risks to a patient in this plaintiff's condition.

There is no requirement that the disclosure of the risks for procedures not addressed by the panel or the evidence of consent to these procedures be in writing. However, the existence of a written or other type of record of this process may, at some later date, prevent or reduce the controversy surrounding the process.

2. Tex. Rev. Civ. Stat. Ann. art. 4590i (Vernon Supp. 1988).
3. Barclay v. Campbell, 704 S.W.2d 8 (Tex. 1986).

6.2

Right to Refuse Treatment

Individuals who seek voluntary treatment may also, by implication, refuse that treatment. In the case of involuntary patients, however, that right to refuse treatment is less subject to agreement. In many jurisdictions, it is now recognized that competent involuntary patients retain the right to refuse nonemergency care. This issue has not specifically been addressed in Texas. The Mental Health Code does, however, recognize the rights of patients to the least restrictive treatment, to avoid unnecessary or excessive medication, and to refuse to participate in research programs.[1] In addition, the code specifically provides that an order for involuntary mental health treatment does not constitute a finding of incompetence.[2]

---

1. Tex. Rev. Civ. Stat. Ann. art. 5547-80 (Vernon Supp. 1988).
2. Tex. Rev. Civ. Stat. Ann. art. 5547-83 (Vernon Supp. 1988).

6.3

Regulation of Aversive and Avoidance Conditioning

Although some jurisdictions specifically limit the use of behavioral therapies involving aversive stimuli, no such specific limitations exist in Texas. Other general statements of patients' rights, however, including those recognizing the rights of involuntary patients to refuse to participate in a research program and to a humane treatment environment,[1] may bear on the conduct of aversive conditioning.

1. Tex. Rev. Civ. Stat. Ann. art. 5547-80 (Vernon Supp. 1988).

6.4

Quality Assurance for Hospital Care

Although medical staff and peer review committees that address professional practice and the quality of patient care within the hospital are not expressly required by state law, their existence is effectively mandated through the accreditation standards of the Joint Commission on Accreditation of Healthcare Organizations[1] and federal law,[2] thus virtually assuring their existence in all Texas hospitals.

The records and proceedings of such committees created specifically for this type of investigation or review are confidential and may not be subpoenaed by a court.[3] This limitation on the subpoena power of a court does not, however, apply to patient and other hospital records normally prepared in the ordinary course of business not specifically by or at the direction of such a committee.[4]

State law provides immunity for committee members from an action for damages for actions taken within the scope of the committee's function if these actions were taken without malice and based upon a reasonable belief that the facts justified the action taken.[5] Similarly, persons providing records or other data concerning the treatment or examination of a patient to such committees may not be held liable for damages.

---

1. Joint Commission on Accreditation of Healthcare Organizations, Accreditation Manual for Hospitals (1989 ed.).
2. 5 U.S.C. §§ 11101 et seq.
3. Tex. Rev. Civ. Stat. Ann. art. 4447d § 3 (Vernon Supp 1988).
4. Barnes v. Whittington, 751 S.W.2d 493 (Tex. 1988).
5. Tex. Rev. Civ. Stat. Ann. art. 4447d § 3 (Vernon Supp. 1988).

6.5

Malpractice Liability

A professional malpractice action against an MHP is a claim that the MHP failed to act as society expects an MHP to act under the circumstances and that as a direct and proximate result injury occurred. In general, the law setting forth the standards governing these duties and society's expectations has evolved from the judicially created common law and is thus not legislative in origin. In recent years, however, attempts to respond to a perceived crisis in malpractice litigation in health care have resulted in numerous legislative inroads into this body of law.

In many jurisdictions, the liability of MHPs for malpractice is divided into two categories: negligence and battery. In this division, "negligence" is the failure to perform according to the standards of a reasonable professional and "battery" is the failure to obtain the client's informed consent. Texas has merged these categories and treats informed consent under a negligence approach but utilizes the expectations of a reasonable patient rather than the practice of a reasonable MHP to gauge the sufficiency of disclosure in those situations not addressed by the Medical Disclosure Panel.[1]

A claim for professional malpractice requires proof of a deviation from the professional's standard of care and a sufficient causal link between this conduct and the injuries sustained. The criterion by which professional negligence is judged in Texas is whether the professional has acted according to the standards of a reasonable practitioner of the same school and the same or a

1. Tex. Rev. Civ. Stat. Ann. art. 4590i § 6.02 (Vernon Supp. 1988). See Section 6.1 for a discussion of informed consent.

similar community under like circumstances.[2] At minimum, the licensing statutes and regulations, which incorporate professional codes of ethics, provide minimum standards of professional conduct for purposes of assessing tort liability. Generally, unless the manner in which a professional should act under the circumstances is obvious even to the lay public, expert testimony is required to establish this standard. To be properly qualified, the expert must be familiar with the professional practice of the particular school (e.g., child psychology or psychoanalytic treatment) and the practice in the same or a similar community.

The causal link between the professional's conduct and the injury must be sufficiently established before recovery by the plaintiff is permitted. For example, if an MHP has erred in treating a patient but it cannot be shown that the patient's condition would likely have been different even if proper treatment was given, the claim will not be successful. Because of these problems of proof in linking professional conduct and injury in cases of mental disorders for which effective treatments may not be the subject of a professional consensus, the malpractice claims by patients that have been successful have tended to be in other areas such as drug prescriptions[3] and sexual misconduct with patients[4] rather than the conduct of psychotherapy alone.

Statute of Limitations

The time within which a claim must be brought or abandoned, called the "statute of limitations," is for most malpractice claims 2 years from the date of the injury-producing event or, in the case of minors under 12 years old, at least until their 14th birthday.[5] When the injury or the nature of its cause is not learned until after this 2-year period, courts will, in many instances, apply an exception to this rule called the "discovery rule." Under the discovery rule, the 2 years begins to run from the date that the patient did or should have discovered the injury.[6]

---

2. Roark v. Allen, 633 S.W.2d 804 (Tex. 1982).
3. Barclay v. Campbell, 704 S.W.2d 8 (Tex. 1986).
4. Dennis v. Allison, 698 S.W.2d 94 (Tex. 1985).
5. Tex. Rev. Civ. Stat. Ann. art. 4590i § 10.01 (Vernon Supp. 1988). In a decision under a previous law, the Supreme Court of Texas held unconstitutional a statute of limitations that ran against a minor during the period of her minority. Sax v. Votteler, 648 S.W.2d 661 (Tex. 1983). Therefore there is reason to doubt the likelihood that the current provision will survive constitutional scrutiny.
6. Weaver v. Witt, 561 S.W.2d 792 (Tex. 1977).

6.6

Other Forms of Professional Liability

Although it is common to think of MHP civil liability to patients exclusively in terms of malpractice liability for negligence in rendering professional services, other legal rules govern the relationship between an MHP and client and may provide the basis for professional liability. It is these other rules to which this chapter is addressed.

Intentional Torts

Negligence, the basis for much malpractice liability described in Chapter 6.5, involves conduct that is not as safe as society expects of the actor under the circumstances. It involves action or inaction in the face of an unreasonable risk; it does not involve proof that the actor desired to obtain the result that occurred. Intentional torts, as distinguished from negligent torts, require that the actor desire the result obtained or be substantially certain that it will occur.

Criminal-Related Acts

When an MHP has violated a criminal law (see Chapter 6.7), that same violation will generally serve as the basis for civil liability if a client has been injured by that act. Thus, for example, a violation of the criminal laws on assault will serve as the basis for a finding of civil liability to the victim for the same act. The criminal proceeding is brought in the name of the state and prosecuted by the county or district attorney, whereas the civil suit is brought by the victim and its prosecution is controlled by the victim. Although a victim compensation system does exist in Texas (see Chapter 5D.26), that system is not structured to permit a victim-initiated request to the court to order a convicted defendant to make restitution to a victim. Thus, a civil action is generally the only vehicle for a victim to compel compensation by a criminal defendant.

Defamation of Character

Defamation is an intentional tort designed to protect a person's reputation from injurious oral or written statements to some third person.[1] When the defamatory statement is oral the tort is slander, and when written it is libel. A defendant who is alleged to have defamed another may defend not only by denying the making of the defamatory statement, but also by showing that it was true or that the defendant was legally entitled to make the statement (in legal parlance, that it was "privileged"). Thus, for example, an MHP who testifies in a child custody dispute that the defendant is not an adequate parent or in an involuntary hospitalization proceeding that a patient is committable, will be entitled to immunity for that testimony, even if it is clearly not true. This is because statements made while testifying in judicial proceedings are privileged, to encourage witnesses to testify truthfully without fear of repercussion.[2] This privilege is absolute and not conditioned upon the reasonableness of the declarant's actions. Other privileges, for example, involving the actions of peer review committees, are qualified and turn on an evaluation of the reasonableness of the declarant's conduct (see Chapter 6.4).

Invasion of Privacy

The tort of invasion of privacy involves several different possible torts, including the public revelation of information legally recognized as being entitled to privacy. In the case of an MHP, professional and legal norms for confidentiality (see Chapters 4.2 and 4.3) will largely define the scope of the professional's obligation and the standards by which a breach of that obligation will be judged.

Malicious Prosecution, False Imprisonment, and Abuse of Process

The tort of malicious prosecution provides for liability when civil or criminal proceedings are instituted without a reasonable basis in fact or law. The tort of false imprisonment occurs when someone

---

1. Putter v. Anderson, 601 S.W.2d 73 (Tex. Civ. App. - Dallas 1980, writ ref'd n.r.e.).
2. James v. Brown, 629 S.W.2d 781 (Tex. Civ. App.-Dallas 1981), aff'd in part, rev'd on other grounds, 637 S.W.2d 914 (Tex. 1982); Russell v. Clark, 620 S.W.2d 865 (Tex. Civ. App.-Dallas 1981).

physically restrains, although not necessarily through physical force, another's freedom of movement. The tort of abuse of process involves the misuse of the judicial process, otherwise justified for some proper end, for an improper purpose. MHPs are not by virtue of their professional status immune from liability for these torts. In the context of civil commitment, however, where MHPs are frequently involved in the institution of legal proceedings and the confinement of individuals, a specific provision of the Mental Health Code provides a limited grant of immunity:[3]

> All persons acting in good faith, reasonably, and without negligence in connection with examination, certification, apprehension, custody, transportation, detention, treatment, or discharge of any person or in the performance of any other act required or authorized by this code shall be free from all liability, civil or criminal, by reason of such action. Provided, however, that physicians performing medical evaluations and providing information to the courts in any court proceeding held pursuant to the code shall be considered an officer of the court and shall not be held liable for such examination or testimony when acting without malice.

MHPs other than psychiatrists are not specifically included within the latter grant of immunity.

Other Types of Civil Liability

Breach of Contract

An MHP, like any other person in society, who enters into a contract requiring the performance of some act, is liable for failure to perform that act barring some legally sufficient excuse. Contracts between MHPs and nonclients, for example, to pay rent on office space or to pay a message service may, if breached by the MHP without sufficient justification, result in an action for damages to put the injured party in the same position as if the contract had not been breached.

An MHP may also enter into a contract with a client, whether oral or written, and may be held liable for failure to live up to that contract. At the extreme, an MHP who promises to cure a patient provided that the patient participates in some therapy and who fails to provide that cure may be liable for breach of contract regardless of the quality of care provided.

The relationship between an MHP and a private client is defined in large measure by the contractual agreement between the two. One of the principal consequences of this arrangement is

3. Tex. Rev. Civ. Stat. Ann. art. 5547-18 (Vernon Supp. 1988).

that an MHP is not obliged to take on any person as a client. Once the relationship is undertaken, however, principles of tort law superimposed upon this contractual relationship limit the circumstances under which the relationship may be terminated. In general, an MHP who has undertaken to treat a client still in need of mental health services and who desires to terminate that relationship must provide the client with sufficient notice to permit the client to obtain the services of another MHP without any consequential gap in services. The MHP may be required to assist the client in identifying and contacting other MHPs. And in no event may the MHP terminate the relationship in a manner that leaves the client without necessary mental health care in an emergency situation. A violation of these requirements constitutes the tort of abandonment.[4]

4. Lee v. Dewbre, 362 S.W.2d 900 (Tex. Civ. App.-Amarillo 1962).

6.7

Criminal Liability

Although Texas criminal laws do not make certain conduct of MHPs criminal, certain criminal laws may be of particular relevance to MHPs.

Sexual Offenses

Texas law specifically defines a crime of sexual assault, which subsumes the crime of rape, as the intentional or knowing and nonconsensual penetration of the anus, mouth, or female sexual organ of another not the spouse of the actor.[1] The statute defines the absence of consent to include conduct compelled by the use or the threat to use violence, instances in which another is unconscious or physically incapable of resisting, instances in which another is incapable of resisting because of a mental disease or defect, and instances in which another is incapable of controlling his or her conduct because the actor has, without the subject's knowledge, administered any substance which impairs the ability to control or appraise conduct. Therefore, an MHP who has sexual relations with a person, not his or her spouse, who is mentally disordered or is a person to whom the MHP has administered any medication, risks conviction for sexual assault.

Assault

The crime of assault is defined as intentionally causing physical injury to another or threatening to do so or intentionally causing

1. Tex. Penal Code Ann. § 22.011 (Vernon Supp. 1988).

physical contact with another person knowing or reasonably believing that the contact will be regarded as offensive or provocative.[2] This prohibition of the criminal law should be considered by MHPs before even casually touching a patient in the absence of prior consent by the patient. When this offense is committed by an owner or employee of a medical or psychiatric institution upon a resident of that facility, the severity of the offense is increased.

The criminal law does permit the use of reasonable force resulting in physical injury to another in certain limited circumstances. These circumstances include the use of reasonable force to avoid imminent harm to the actor (i.e., self-defense) or to protect a third person in circumstances in which that third person would be justified in using force to protect himself.[3] In addition, a specific provision of the penal code permits the use of reasonable force to prevent another from "committing suicide or inflicting serious bodily injury to himself."[4] Thus, when an MHP believes that a client is about to commit suicide or inflict serious bodily harm upon himself or herself and that physical force is immediately necessary to prevent that from occurring, the MHP may use reasonable force to prevent that act from occurring. The magnitude of force permitted is the minimal amount necessary to avert the suicide or serious bodily harm. In no event may it involve the use of force that itself kills or seriously injures.

Negligent Homicide

Criminally negligent homicide is defined in Texas as causing the death of another through criminal negligence.[5] Criminal negligence is intended to be more limited in scope than negligence as it is contemplated in a civil tort action. Instead, by reference to the civil tort law, criminal negligence would more closely correspond with the civil tort law's concept of gross negligence. Thus criminal negligence requires more than unreasonable conduct in the face of a risk. It requires a failure to respond reasonably to a substantial and unjustified risk of death. Whether this definition might apply to an MHP's treatment decisions that resulted in the death of a patient and were grossly outside the standard of care exercised in the profession is a question that has not been addressed in Texas.

2. Tex. Penal Code Ann. § 22.01 (Vernon Supp. 1988).
3. Tex. Penal Code Ann. §§ 9.31, 9.33 (Vernon Supp. 1988).
4. Tex. Penal Code Ann. § 9.34 (Vernon 1974).
5. Tex. Penal Code Ann. § 19.07 (Vernon 1974).

6.8

Liability of Credentialing Boards

Because MHPs may be members of or affected by the actions of credentialing boards that regulate professional practice, the liability of these boards to persons affected by their actions is a subject of no small interest to MHPs. In Texas, the doctrine of sovereign immunity restricts suits against governmental units, which include state agencies, boards, and commissions.

A number of exceptions to this doctrine exist. The Texas Tort Claims Act waives this immunity. This waiver is, however, limited largely to cases arising out of the operation or use of a motor vehicle.[1] In addition, certain actions under federal civil rights laws[2] are not limited by sovereign immunity. Thus, in general, it can be said that members of credentialing boards may not be held liable in an action for damages for their performance or failure to perform acts within the scope of their duties as members of these boards.

1. Tex. Civ. Prac. & Rem. Code Ann. § 101.021 (Vernon 1986).
2. See, e.g., 42 U.S.C. § 1983.

6.9

Antitrust Limitations to Practice

The antitrust laws exist to limit restraints on competition, whether in the form of agreements to restrain price or market competition. Increasingly, aspects of the delivery of health care services, from hospital staff privileges to fee schedules, have been subject to scrutiny under the antitrust laws. Although much of that scrutiny has been under federal antitrust law, there is a separate body of state antitrust law that is the subject of this chapter.

The Texas law, entitled the Texas Free Enterprise and Antitrust Act of 1983,[1] is designed to foster economic competition in the state for the benefit of consumers. It outlaws:[2]

1. agreements in restraint of trade or competition;
2. monopolies or attempts to monopolize trade or commerce;
3. sales, leases, or contracts conditioned upon a refusal to utilize the goods of a competitor where the effect of that agreement is to restrain trade or commerce;
4. acquisition of another's stock or assets where the effect would be to reduce competition; and
5. agreements between management and labor to condition employment upon union membership or nonmembership.

Any person injured by any of the above acts may bring a civil action to recover damages, tripled in the case of willful or flagrant violations, plus reasonable attorney's fees. In addition, any injured person may seek an injunction to halt these practices. An action to recover damages must be brought within 4 years of the date of the

1. Tex. Bus. & Com. Code Ann. §§ 15.01 et seq (Vernon 1987).
2. Tex. Bus. & Com. Code Ann. § 15.05 (Vernon 1987).

injury.[3] These same prohibited acts also constitute a felony and are punishable under the criminal laws in an action brought by the district attorney. The maximum term of imprisonment is 3 years for each violation and a fine of $5,000.

One of the subjects involving health care providers that has been litigated under this law involves noncompetition agreements. The enforceability of these agreements turns on their reasonableness, both in time and space, and their necessity to protect legitimate interests of the employer. For example, one Texas case involved an agreement between a hospital and a hospital consulting corporation to provide physicians for an emergency room service on a 24-hour basis and limiting for 3 years after the termination of the contract the employment of any physician providing these emergency room services under the plan. This agreement was found to be unreasonable and not necessary to protect the interests of the hospital.[4]

3. Tex. Bus. & Com. Code Ann. § 15.25 (Vernon 1987).
4. Hospital Consultants, Inc. v. Potyka, 531 S.W.2d 657 (Tex. Civ. App.-San Antonio 1975).

Appendix

Table of Cases

Table of Statutes

Table of Rules of Court

Table of Administrative Rules and Regulations

Table of Cases

References are to page numbers in this book

A

B

C

D

F

G

H

J

K

L

M

N

O

P

R

S

T

W

Z

Table of Statutes

Page numbers represent pages in this book

Texas Revised Civil Statutes Annotated

Texas Revised Civil Statutes Annotated

Texas Revised Civil Statutes Annotated

Texas Business & Commerce Code

Texas Civil Practice & Remedies Code

Texas Code of Criminal Procedure

Texas Family Code

Texas Government Code

Texas Human Resources Code

Texas Insurance Code

Texas Penal Code

Texas Penal Code

Section	Page
9.34	311
12.22	56, 131
12.34	21
12.42	252
19.04	239
19.07	311
22.01	311
22.011	310
37.02, 37.10	20
43.21	261

Texas Probate Code

Section	Page
57	192
109	114, 139
110	114
110	139
111	113
111	138
118	139
119	139
130	187
130F	115
130G	115
130H	116, 187
130J	116
131	112
229	140
230	114, 140
234	114, 140
416	114
426	115

Texas Constitution

Article	Page
3 § 51(a)	179
5 § 10	211
16 § 6	179
I, § 11	233
I, § 11a	233
I, § 13	233

United States Code

Title	Page
5 U.S.C. §§ 11101 *et seq.*	303
26 U.S.C. § 162	83
26 U.S.C. § 213(a)	82
26 U.S.C. § 231(d)	82
42 U.S.C. § 2000e	201

Table of Rules of Court

Page numbers represent pages in this book

Rules of Civil Evidence

Rules of Civil Procedure

Rules of Criminal Evidence

Rules of Evidence

Table of Administrative Rules and Regulations

Page numbers represent pages in this book

Texas Administrative Code

Title	Page
19, § 141.181	49
19, § 141.2	50
19, § 141.241	48
19, § 141.3	48
19, § 149.42	49
22, § 163.3(b)(2),(3)	15
22, §§ 163.6, 171.4	14
22, § 163.6(a)	15
22, § 179.2	91
22, § 217.13	27
22, § 218.10(1)–(5)	26
22, § 221.1	23
22, § 393.7	217
22, § 461.3	94
22, § 463.1	35
22, § 463.14	32
22, § 463.16(b)	30
22, § 463.17	30
22, § 463.18	30, 33
22, § 463.19	31
22, § 463.23	32
22, § 463.8	35
22, § 465.19(d)	33
22, § 465.2	94
22, § 465.20(a)–(b)	34
22, § 465.22	87
22, § 465.23	31
22, § 465.7	35
22, § 681.125	44
22, § 681.201(f)	45
22, § 681.244(1)–(10)	45
22, § 681.253	44
22, § 681.45	46
22, § 681.50	44
22, §§ 681.75, 681.94	47
25, §§ 115.1–115.17	295
25, § 115.15	292, 293, 296
25, § 119.7	69
25, § 39.8	270
25, § 405.366	126
25, § 405.753	291
28, § 3.3005	79
28, § 3.3006	79
28, § 3.3016	79, 80
28, § 3.3074	79
28, § 3.3304	80
28, § 3.3305	80
40, § 101.11	180
40, § 101.2	179
40, § 101.4	179
40 § 103.1	179
40, § 103.13	181
40, § 103.15	180
40, § 103.16	180
40, §§ 103.2, 103.41	179
40, § 103.21	181
40, § 103.4	180
40, § 103.44	180
40, § 103.5	180, 181
40, § 103.6–14	181
40, § 151.101	284
40, § 151.21	284
40, §§ 15.5002–15.5105	269
40, § 2.1004	271
40, § 45.604	271
40, § 49.1502	144
40, § 83.236	142
40, § 85.6003(b)	39
40, § 85.6003(c)	39
40, § 85.6009	40

Index

References are to chapters

A

B

C

D

E

F

G

H

I

S

T

U

V

W

Z